JON L. DYBDAHL, PH.D.

THE ABUNDANT LIFE
BIBLE
AMPLIFIER

EXODUS

God Creates a People

GEORGE R. KNIGHT
General Editor

Pacific Press Publishing Association
Boise, Idaho
Oshawa, Ontario, Canada

Edited by Marvin Moore
Designed by Tim Larson
Typeset in 11/14 Janson Text

Copyright © 1994 by
Pacific Press Publishing Association
Printed in the United States of America
All Rights Reserved

Unless otherwise noted, all Bible quotations in this book are from
the New International Version.

Library of Congress Cataloging-in-Publication Data:

Dybdahl, Jon.
   Exodus: God creates a people / by Jon Dybdahl.
       p.   cm.
   Includes bibliographical references.
   ISBN 0-8163-1202-8 (hard cover). — ISBN 0-8163-1199-4
(pbk.)
   1. Bible. O. T. Exodus—Criticism, interpretation, etc.
I. Title.
BS1245.2.D934   1994
222'.1206—dc20   93-40867
                                            CIP

94 95 96 97 98 • 5 4 3 2 1

CONTENTS

In memory of my mother,
Erma Olivia Glantz Dybdahl.
Her example of love and service
continues to inspire.

PREFACE

The Abundant Life Bible Amplifier series is aimed at helping readers understand the Bible better. Rather than merely offering comments on or about the Bible, each volume seeks to enable people to study their Bibles with fuller understanding.

To accomplish that task, scholars who are also proven communicators have been selected to author each volume. The basic idea underlying this combination is that scholarship and the ability to communicate on a popular level are compatible skills.

While the Bible Amplifier is written with the needs and abilities of laypeople in mind, it will also prove helpful to pastors and teachers. Beyond individual readers, the series will be useful in church study groups and as guides to enrich participation in the weekly prayer meeting.

Rather than focusing on the details of each verse, the Bible Amplifier series seeks to give readers an understanding of the themes and patterns of each biblical book as a whole and how each passage fits into that context. As a result, the series does not seek to solve all the problems or answer all the questions that may be related to a given text. In the process of accomplishing the goal for the series, both inductive and explanatory methodologies are used.

Each volume in this series presents its author's understanding of the biblical book being studied. As such, it does not necessarily represent the "official" position of the Seventh-day Adventist Church.

It should be noted that the Bible Amplifier series utilizes the New International Version of the Bible as its basic text. *Every reader should read the "How to Use This Book" section to get the fullest benefit from the Bible Amplifier volumes.*

Dr. Jon Dybdahl, director of the Seventh-day Adventist Institute of World Mission, completed a doctoral degree on the Pentateuch at Fuller Theological Seminary. Prior to taking his current assignment, Dr. Dybdahl served as a pastor, a Bible teacher at Walla Walla College, and a missionary to Southeast Asia. Thus he brings a wealth of both scholarship and experience to his treatment of the book of Exodus.

George R. Knight

AUTHOR'S PREFACE

Living with the book of Exodus this past year has convinced me that the writer of a book about the Bible always gains more than the readers. The task of putting into words what you understand and feel about a Bible book is like declaring devotion to your beloved spouse. The relationship and time that lie behind the declaration make the bond of love and understanding deeper.

My serious interest in Exodus goes back to the time a Walla Walla College colleague's leave sent his Pentateuch class my way. Teaching college undergraduates demands a teacher's best. Students don't settle for pat answers, and they want to know why Exodus is important *now*. My academic training taught me to ask what Exodus *meant*. My students showed me I needed to also ask seriously what it *means*. I've tried to make both of these questions central in this book. As readers become participants in the process of finding answers to these two questions, I'm convinced change and new understanding will come.

Special thanks to George R. Knight, my colleague and friend, for entrusting this assignment to me. His wise nurturing has been most helpful. Commendation to Pacific Press for the vision and courage needed to embark on such a major project as this Bible-study series entails.

My teaching colleagues in the Institute of World Mission and the department of World Mission at Andrews University have been very supportive. I trust they can tell that my interest in mission and cross-cultural communication affects even the way I view Exodus. Thanks also to our former administrative assistant, Pam Swanson, who did special work in preparing the first several chapters.

My wife Kathy's continuing patience with the time I spend writing and her constant encouragement and support have made this

9

whole project possible. Special thanks to our daughter, Krista Croft, for her work in turning my pencil scribblings into a typed manuscript. Each passing year brings growing appreciation for the blessing of a united, supportive family.

As I write this, the sound of fireworks breaks the silence of a warm summer night. The celebration of American political independence is a good time to remember that the only lasting freedom is the one God graciously bestows on those who choose to be part of His people. This book is meant to light up a part of the world's sky with fireworks celebrating the mighty God of Israel's independence—and ours too!

Jon Dybdahl
Berrien Springs, Michigan

How to Use This Book

The Abundant Life Bible Amplifier series treats each major portion of each Bible book in five main sections.

The first section is called "Getting Into the Word." The purpose of this section is to encourage readers to study their own Bibles. For that reason, the text of the Bible has not been printed in the volumes in this series.

You will get the most out of your study if you work through the exercises in each of the "Getting Into the Word" sections. This will not only aid you in learning more about the Bible but will also increase your skill in using Bible tools and in asking (and answering) meaningful questions about the Bible.

It will be helpful if you write out the answers and keep them in a notebook or file folder for each biblical book. Writing out your thoughts will enhance your understanding. The benefit derived from such study, of course, will be proportionate to the amount of effort expended.

The "Getting Into the Word" sections assume that the reader has certain minimal tools available. Among these are a concordance and a Bible with maps and marginal cross-references. If you don't have a New International Version of the Bible, we recommend that you obtain one for use with this series, since all the Bible Amplifier authors are using the NIV as their basic text. For the same reason, your best choice of a concordance is the *NIV*

Exhaustive Concordance, edited by E. W. Goodrick and J. R. Kohlenberger. *Strong's Exhaustive Concordance of the Bible* and Young's *Analytical Concordance to the Bible* are also useful. However, even if all you have is Cruden's Concordance, you will be able to do all of the "Getting Into the Word" exercises and most of the "Researching the Word" exercises.

The "Getting Into the Word" sections also assume that the reader has a Bible dictionary. The *Seventh-day Adventist Bible Dictionary* is quite helpful, but those interested in greater depth may want to acquire the four-volume *International Standard Bible Encyclopedia* (1974-1988 edition) or the six-volume *Anchor Bible Dictionary*.

The second section in the treatment of the biblical passages is called "Exploring the Word." The purpose of this section is to discuss the major themes in each biblical book. Thus the comments will typically deal with fairly large portions of Scripture (often an entire chapter) rather than providing a verse-by-verse treatment, such as is found in the *Seventh-day Adventist Bible Commentary*. In fact, many verses and perhaps whole passages in some biblical books may be treated minimally or passed over altogether.

Another thing that should be noted is that the purpose of the "Exploring the Word" sections is not to respond to all the problems or answer all the questions that might arise in each passage. Rather, as stated above, the "Exploring the Word" sections are to develop the Bible writers' major themes. In the process, the author of each volume will bring the best of modern scholarship into the discussion and thus enrich the reader's understanding of the biblical passage at hand. The "Exploring the Word" sections will also develop and provide insight into many of the issues first raised in the "Getting Into the Word" exercises.

The third section in the treatment of the biblical passages is "Applying the Word." This section is aimed at bringing the lessons of each passage into daily life. Once again, you may want to write out a response to these questions and keep them in your notebook or file folder on the biblical book being studied.

The fourth section, "Researching the Word," is for those students who want to delve more deeply into the Bible passage under study or into the history behind it. It is recognized that not everyone will have the research tools for this section. Those expecting to use the research sections should have an exhaustive Bible concordance, the *Seventh-day Adventist Bible Commentary*, a good Bible dictionary, and a Bible atlas. It also will be helpful to have several versions of the Bible.

The final component in each chapter of this book will be a list of recommendations for "Further Study of the Word." While most readers will not have all of these works, many of them may be available in local libraries. Others can be purchased through your local book dealer. It is assumed that many users of this series will already own the seven-volume *Seventh-day Adventist Bible Commentary* and the one-volume *Seventh-day Adventist Bible Dictionary*.

In closing, it should be noted that while a reader will learn much about the Bible from a *reading* of the books in the Bible Amplifier series, he or she will gain infinitely more by *studying* the Bible in connection with that reading.

The Book of Exodus

One of the best ways to begin the study of a Bible book is to read the entire book through in one or two sittings. Such reading enables one to begin grasping the broad sweep of the book. The following suggestions are meant to help you do this in a profitable way.

1. **As you read Exodus, notice the main headings in your Bible, and compare what you are reading with the outline you find in this book. Do the headings and the outline fit with what you are reading? If not, it would be helpful to make your own outline.**
2. **As you read, write down in your own words what you think the main idea of each chapter or group of chapters is. How do these ideas fit with the main theme and message of the book?**
3. **Try to enter into the story of Exodus. What do you think the people who are experiencing Exodus feel and think? Do your best to identify with the Israelites as they interact with God.**

Theme and Name

In the book of Genesis, God creates a world. In the book of Exodus, He creates a people. He does this creating by acting to deliver Abraham's descendants from Egyptian oppression. This mighty deliverance becomes the divine pattern for all of God's subsequent saving actions. For this reason, Exodus and its story are central not only to the Old Testament, but to the New Testament as well. In a very real sense, Exodus is, as John Durham calls it, the "first book of the Bible" (Durham, *Exodus*, xix).

The name *Exodus*, meaning "exit" or "departure," is appropriate because the book details the Israelite exit from Egypt. That name, however, is not original but comes from the Latin version of Scripture. Hebrews called the book "These Are the Names," following the pattern of naming the books of the Bible by their opening words.

Exodus and the Pentateuch or Torah

Strictly speaking, Exodus was not a separate book to the Hebrews. They viewed what we call the first five books of the Bible as one book. This book they called *torah*, meaning "law," or better yet, "instruction." Most Christians today call it the Pentateuch, meaning "five-part work/book." Exodus is part two of this five-part book of the law.

The Torah is the most important part of the Hebrew Scriptures for Jews. They consider it the earliest, holiest, and most authoritative part of God's Word to them. This foundational document of Judaism records not only the key events that led to the founding of the nation and religion, but also contains the laws and statutes that guide and govern all parts of life.

The Pentateuch is crucial to Christians as well. Many Christians forget that the first generation of Jesus' followers had no New Testament. Their only Scripture was the Hebrew Bible, of which the Pentateuch was the central part. Christians preached the gospel of Jesus using Exodus.

Muslims believe that God sent a variety of holy books through several prophets before He revealed the Koran to the prophet Mohammed. The first of these books is the book of the law, which came through the prophet Moses. The Koran mentions Moses no less than 196 times and portrays him as the only prophet God conversed with face to face.

The book of Exodus is at the heart of the Torah and is thus crucial in the lives of more than 19 million Jews, 2.1 billion Christians, and 1.2 billion Muslims. This amounts to over 53 percent of the world's population! No other sacred book can claim such wide reverence.

Exodus and the Rest of the Bible

Another mark of a book's importance is the number of times it is quoted or alluded to in later biblical books. Exodus is almost unparalleled in the amount of usage it receives by later biblical writers. Old Testament prophets continually refer back to Israel's deliverance from Egypt.[1] There are at least 149 quotations from or allusions to the book of Exodus in the New Testament. The only Old Testament books with a higher number are Psalms and Isaiah, which are also much longer books. Not only does the New Testament quote Exodus extensively, but themes and vocabulary from Exodus are widely used.

Strictly speaking, Exodus and the Pentateuch are anonymous in that neither names an author. A long tradition, however, links Exodus to Moses. Certain sections of the book are specifically said to stem from Moses (17:14; 24:4; 34:27). The New Testament also connects Moses to the Pentateuch, and he is certainly the major human character standing behind the book of Exodus.

Structure of Exodus

The material in the book of Exodus, like the rest of the Pentateuch, is mainly composed of two types of literature—narrative (story) and legal writings. The basic framework is clearly the story. However, embedded in this framework are various legal texts and laws. What is important for understanding the book

---

[1] See, for example, Amos 2:10; 3:1; 9:7; Mic. 6:4; 7:15; Hos. 2:15; 11:1; 12:9, 13; 13:4; Isa. 11:16; Jer. 2:6; 7:22-25; 11:4, 7; 16:14; 23:7; 32:21; 34:13. At least eighteen psalms reflect the Exodus motif: 18, 44, 60, 68, 74, 75, 78, 80, 81, 83, 89, 95, 100, 106, 114, 135, 136.

is that the laws cannot be properly understood apart from their narrative context.

This means more than simply understanding the historical and cultural background of the various commands and statues. The laws must be understood as a whole in the context of Israel's experience with God. Major misunderstandings develop if the laws are interpreted outside the story of how God delivered and dealt with Israel.

What, then, is the main point of the story? It is how God creates His people, Israel. God starts with a group of oppressed slaves in Egypt, and by the end of the book they are a free people with their own leadership and system of worship. God's creation of His people moves through five steps.

1. God takes notice of the problems of the people.
2. God acts in a powerful and decisive way to deliver the Israelites from bondage.
3. God makes a deal with the people in a formal covenant.
4. God gives His people laws or instruction on how to live.
5. God sets up a system of worship so His presence may be constantly experienced.

The order in this case is crucial. The laws are only given to people who recognize that God has graciously delivered them. Grace always comes before law. Valid calls to keep the law can only be made to people who know about their deliverance and are willing to covenant with God.

The same order is present and valid in all parts of Scripture. It remains the way God works with people even now. If Christians call on unbelievers to follow Jesus, the same process should be followed. When evangelists or missionaries proclaim the good news and start churches, they are creating a new segment of the people of God, and the Exodus order should be followed. The Exodus story remains the story of every person today who cries out to God from his or her own place of slavery and is brought to freedom by a powerful and merciful God.

Themes in Exodus

In telling the story of the Exodus, certain themes or recurring ideas are used. Understanding these themes gives us a key to clearly perceiving the messages of the book.

Promise and fulfillment. The promises of God are a theme, not only for the book of Exodus, but for the whole Pentateuch. The story begins in Genesis 12:1-4, where God gives a series of promises to Abram. The passage pledges that God will: (a) give Abram many descendants; (b) establish a special relationship with him and his posterity; (c) bestow the land of Canaan, and (d) bless all other nations through him.

These promises are repeated in full or in part over and over again in the Pentateuch. They are made not only to Abraham, but to his offspring Isaac, Jacob, and Joseph as well. Exodus specifically states that God responded to Israel's distress and delivered them because of the covenant and promises He had made with Abraham, Isaac, and Jacob (2:23-25; 6:2-6).

Each promise unfolds in the following sequence: God makes or repeats the promise, but all kinds of obstacles arise that hinder fulfillment of the promise. God, however, does not give up, but persists and uses His faithfulness and power to fulfill His pledge. God triumphs in spite of opposition, both from within Abraham's family and from without by enemies.

Further, each section of the Pentateuch tends to emphasize a particular element in God's fourfold pledge. Genesis emphasizes the first element and shows Abram becoming a great nation in spite of infertility and family problems. Exodus, along with Leviticus, stresses the second element of promise—Israel's special relationship with God. In spite of Israelite lack of faith and Pharaoh and his army, God establishes His covenant at Mt. Sinai. Numbers and Deuteronomy trace events leading to the occupation of Canaan.

The covenant. Closely linked to the theme of promise and fulfillment is the idea of covenant. The word *covenant* describes a formal agreement between two parties. This agreement is often quite extensive, with many parts or steps that detail the obligations and privileges of the parties involved. Broken covenants can often be renewed, as is the case in Exodus 34 after Israel had sinned and worshiped the golden calf.

In Exodus, some passages seem to equate the covenant and the promises (2:23-25; 6:2-8). Probably the best way to understand this is to see the promises as part of the covenant agreement. A detailed explanation of covenant will be made in later pages when the covenant passages are examined.

The power of Yahweh. Exodus delights in showing the power and might of Israel's God. The supreme evidence of this power is, of course, the deliverance of helpless Israel from the mighty Egyptians. Moses sings:

> Thy right hand, O Lord, glorious in power, thy right hand, O Lord, shatters the enemy.
> In the greatness of thy majesty thou overthrowest thy adversaries (15:6, 7, RSV).

The Lord's power is active in all kinds of less majestic circumstances. Yahweh blesses the faithful midwives (1:20, 21) and performs wonders to lead Moses to commitment in his (Moses') mission (chaps. 3, 4). He strikes Egypt with ten plagues and provides manna in the wilderness.

Not only does God perform powerful deeds; He promises to continue exercising that power. He vows to drive out before the Israelites the Amorites, Canaanites, Hittites, Perizzites, and Hivites and enlarge Israel's borders (see, for example, 34:11, 24).

While many in Western cultures are deeply concerned about the justice of God, a helpless and weak Israel needed to be convinced of the power of her Lord to save. In Exodus, Yahweh graciously provided ample evidence.

The presence of Yahweh. Israel's God is not an absent, uninterested Lord. He actually draws near to His people to be present with them. That nearness forms the basis for His acts of love and power.

Yahweh is near the midwives and blesses them (1:20, 21). He

sees and knows about Israel's oppression (2:24, 25). He appears to Moses in Midian (chap. 3). He reveals His name to Moses as a sign of intimacy (3:13-16). The list goes on. Yahweh "meets" His people at Mt. Sinai and answers Moses in thunder (19:17-20). Time and again, the Lord meets Moses on the top of the mountain to talk.

The climax comes at the conclusion of the book in chapter 40, especially verses 34 to 38. The sanctuary is completed, and the cloud covers the tent while glory fills the place. God thus visibly comes to live in the midst of Israel's camp. Whenever the cloud of the presence moves, the people follow. Wherever the cloud rests, there they pitch camp. The crowning event in the creation of Yahweh's people is the establishment of His presence as a visible, permanent fixture so that communion can be a reality.

Israel's flawed response. Exodus constantly reminds us of the contrast between the faithful action of Yahweh and the unfaithful response of the people. God provides food—the people complain. God is powerfully present at Sinai—the people are so frightened they don't want a repeat performance. God meets all of their needs, but as soon as Moses leaves, the people build a golden idol. Yet a weak, murmuring, failing Israel does *not* stop God's faithfulness but provides the backdrop for a clear understanding of His mercy.

Understanding Exodus

The spread of Western education around the world has made prevalent a certain understanding of history. Since Exodus is history, we read it through the glasses of what we define history to be. However, if those glasses happen to be our typical modern view of history, we will probably miss the real power of Exodus, which its Israelite and early Christian readers felt.

For many modern readers, history happened back then to other people. For Israel, the Exodus story happened *to them.* Years later, when most of the actual people alive at Sinai are dead, Moses says to Israel that the covenant at the mountain was made "with us":

> Not with our fathers did the Lord
> make this covenant, but with us,
> we who are all of us here alive this day
> (Deut. 5:3, RSV).

All descendants of Abraham in a very real sense *participate* in the Exodus. Using modern psychological terms, we might say they "identify" with the events, although the word does not adequately express the depth of feeling involved.

For most of us, history may at times repeat itself, usually in a general sense. For Israel, the mighty event of the Exodus was repeatable in many ways. Later deliverances, like the return from Babylonian exile, are new exoduses. For early Christians, the redemption wrought by Jesus was a new exodus deliverance (1 Cor. 10:1-4). In a very real sense, African slaves in the American South, who in their oppression sang "Go Down Moses," understood Exodus better than many who have spent their time arguing over the date of the original Exodus.

The Exodus story was also repeatable on a regular basis through the ritual of yearly feasts. This took place most clearly in the Passover but was to some extent a fact in all the festivals of Israel.

In a biblical sense, anyone who now sees Exodus with the eye of faith sees and hears his or her own story. Egyptian oppression may be the slavery of sin, the restrictions of political tyranny, the yoke of poverty, psychological or addictive bondage, or whatever causes one to cry out to God in distress. The Lord of the Exodus is still able to deliver and bring freedom and establish His presence.

Outline of Exodus

I. God sees oppression (1:1–2:25)
  a. Israel oppressed (1:1-22)
  b. Moses and oppression (2:1-22)
  c. God reacts to oppression (2:23-25)
II. God acts to deliver (3:1–18:27)

a. God calls a leader (3:1–4:31)
b. God deals with Pharaoh (5:1–7:7)
c. God sends ten plagues (7:8–11:10)
d. God leads out of Egypt (12:1–13:16)
e. God vanquishes the Egyptian army (13:17–15:21)
f. God provides in the desert (15:22–18:27)

III. God makes a covenant (19:1–24:18)
a. God prepares a meeting at Mt. Sinai (19:1-25)
b. God speaks the Ten Commandments (20:1-26)
c. God instructs about servants, property, social responsibility (21:1–22:31)
d. God teaches about Sabbath and justice (23:1-13)
e. God teaches about festivals and angelic guidance (23:14-33).
f. God instructs Moses on the mountain (24:1-18)

IV. God dwells with His people (25:1–40:38)
a. God's presence in tabernacle and priesthood (25:1–31:18 and 35:1–39:31)
b. God's presence interrupted and restored (32:1–34:35)
c. God's glory fills the tabernacle (39:32–40:38)

For Further Reading

1. Dunnam, Maxie D. *Exodus.*
2. Durham, John I. *Understanding the Basis Theme of Exodus.*
3. _____. *Exodus.* Word Biblical Commentary. Vol. 3.
4. Fretheim, Terence E. *Interpretation: A Bible Commentary for Teaching and Preaching: Exodus.*
5. LaSor, William S. et. al. *Old Testament Survey.*
6. Nichol, Francis D., ed. *Seventh-day Adventist Bible Commentary.* Vol. 1. s.v. "Exodus."
7. Ramm, Bernard L. *His Way Out.*
8. Sarna, Nahum M. *Exploring Exodus.*
9. Williams, Mark E., ed. *The Storyteller's Companion to the Bible.* Vol. 2, *Exodus-Joshua.*
10. Wittenberg, Gunther H. *I Have Heard the Cry of My People.*

LIST OF WORKS CITED

Achtemeier, Paul J., ed. *Harper's Bible Dictionary*. San Francisco: Harper & Row, 1985.

Andreason, Niels-Erik. *The Old Testament Sabbath*. Missoula, Mont.: Society of Biblical Literature, 1972.

Balentine, Samuel E. *Prayer in the Hebrew Bible*. Minneapolis: Fortress, 1993.

Botterweck, G. Johannes, and Helmer Ringgren, eds. *Theological Dictionary of the Old Testament*, vol. 4. Grand Rapids, Mich.: Eerdmans, 1980.

Clements, R. E. *Old Testament Theology*. Atlanta: John Knox, 1978.

Douglas, J. D., ed. *The New Bible Dictionary*. Grand Rapids, Mich.: Eerdmans, 1979.

Dunnam, Maxie D. *Exodus*. The Communicator's Commentary. Waco, Tex.: Word, 1987.

Durham, John I. *Understanding the Basic Themes of Exodus*. Dallas: Word, 1990 (abbreviated as *Themes*).

———. *Exodus*. Word Biblical Commentary, vol. 3. Waco, Tex.: Word, 1987 (abbreviated as *Exodus*).

Dybdahl, Jon L. *Old Testament Grace*. Boise, Idaho: Pacific Press, 1990.

Dyrness, William. *Themes in Old Testament Theology*. Downers Grove, Ill.: InterVarsity, 1979.

Foster, Richard. *Prayer*. San Francisco: Harper San Francisco, 1992.

Fretheim, Terence E. *Exodus*. Interpretation: A Bible Commentary for Teaching and Preaching. Louisville, Ky.: John Knox, 1991.

Hasel, Gerhard F. *Covenant in Blood*. Boise, Idaho: Pacific Press, 1982.

———. "Reflections on Alden Thompson's 'Law Pyramid' within

a Casebook/Codebook Dichotomy." In *Issues in Revelation and Inspiration*, edited by Frank Holbrook and Leo Van Dolson. Berrien Springs, Mich.: Adventist Theological Society Publications, 1992.

Holbrook, Frank. "The Israelite Sanctuary." In *The Sanctuary and the Atonement*. Washington, D.C.: General Conference of Seventh-day Adventists, 1981.

Horn, Siegfried H., et. al. *Seventh-day Adventist Bible Dictionary*, rev. ed., edited by Raymond H. Woolsey. Hagerstown, Md.: Review and Herald, 1979.

LaSor, William Sandford, David Allan Hubbard, and Frederic William Bush. *Old Testament Survey*. Grand Rapids, Mich.: Eerdmans, 1982.

Nichol, Francis D., et. al. *Seventh-day Adventist Bible Commentary*, rev. ed., 7 vols. Hagerstown, Md.: Review and Herald, 1976-1980.

Nims, C. F. "Bricks Without Straw." *Biblical Archeologist*. 13:2, (1950).

Pritchard, James B. *Everyday Life in Bible Times*. Washington, D.C.: National Geographic Society, 1967.

Ramm, Bernard L. *His Way Out*. Glendale, Calif.: Regal, 1974.

Sarna, Nahum, M. *Exploring Exodus*. New York: Schocken, 1986.

Thompson, Alden. *Inspiration*. Hagerstown, Md.: Review and Herald, 1991.

White, Ellen G. *Patriarchs and Prophets*. Boise, Idaho: Pacific Press Publishing Association, 1958.

Williams, Michael E., ed. *The Storyteller's Companion to the Bible*. Vol. 2, *Exodus-Joshua*. Nashville: Abingdon, 1992.

Wittenberg, Gunther H. *I Have Heard the Cry of My People*. Pietermaritzburg, South Africa: Institute for the Study of the Bible, 1991.

PART ONE

God Sees
Oppression

Exodus 1, 2

CHAPTER ONE

God Sees Oppression

Exodus 1, 2

The first two chapters of Exodus appropriately introduce the book. First, they clearly tie Exodus to the preceding book of Genesis. The sons of Jacob, or Israel, we meet in the first few verses are the same men who go into Egypt in the last chapters of Genesis. The God we meet is the same God who made a covenant with Abraham, Isaac, and Jacob in earlier days. We can understand Exodus only if we see it as a continuation and sequel of Genesis.

Second, the first two chapters prepare the way for the message of Exodus by presenting the need for deliverance and introducing the human leader of the deliverance. The Israelites, who had started out as honored guests of Pharaoh, end up as a persecuted group of slaves who groan and cry out for help. Moses, who becomes their leader, is an example in suffering from that oppression at the very beginning of his life.

The rest of Exodus contains the answer or solution to the problem of oppression outlined in these first two chapters. That solution begins even here with God hearing the Israelites' groans and remembering His earlier covenant with the patriarchs. God therefore sees the problem and is concerned (2:23-29).

In well-written books like Exodus, the introduction plays a crucial role and deserves special attention. The reader who treats the beginning of Exodus lightly runs the risk of missing the full impact of the message. Listen carefully to the beginning of this powerful saga.

■ Getting Into the Word

Exodus 1

Read Exodus 1 through two times. As you read, think about the following questions:

1. In connection with the names in Exodus 1:1-5, read Genesis 46:8-27 and 49:1-28. What kinds of people are counted and what kinds are not counted in the number 70 (Gen. 46:27 and Exod. 1:5)? Why? What are the ways these lists differ? What do you think are the reasons for the differences? When so much is said about these people in Genesis, why does Exodus repeat the names?

2. Make a list of all the statements in Exodus 1 that point to Israel's growth. What are the reasons that Exodus gives for this growth? How does this growth compare with the problems of Abraham, Isaac, and Jacob in Genesis (Gen. 15:2; 16:1; 25:21; 29:31; 30:1)? What had God promised (Gen. 12:1; 13:16; 15:5; 17:2, 4; 26:4; 28:14; 35:11)? What does this growth lead to, and why is it important?

3. List the progressive steps taken by Pharaoh in the oppression of Israel. Can you find a pattern in what he does? What seems to motivate him? What works against his plan?

4. Who was this Pharaoh of the Exodus, and what was the historical situation? What does a "new king" (vs. 8) mean? Use the *SDA Bible Dictionary* or a similar Bible dictionary, and read the relevant parts of the article "Exodus" to gain some knowledge of the history.

5. Who do you think are the heroes and the heroines in this story? What roles does each play? What can we learn from their stories about how God uses people?

6. Does this chapter present women in a favorable light? Why do you say so?

7. **Think about the midwives' response to Pharaoh. Do you think they did the right thing when they gave their reason for not killing Hebrew male babies? What does this story teach us?**

■ Exploring the Word

The Israelite Population Explosion

Whenever conflict or oppression arises, there must be at least two sides involved. Chapter 1 paints a portrait of the two sides confronting each other in the Exodus story. If we know the two protagonists, we can understand the conflict.

The saga begins with the side of the underdog—the Israelites or sons of Jacob. Israel's (Jacob's) eleven sons are specifically named as accompanying Jacob to Egypt. In Hebrew the first six words in Exodus 1:1 are the exact same six words that we find in Genesis 46:8. The Genesis passage lists the eleven sons (in a different order) as well as their sons, and in some cases, grandsons. The eleven sons have fifty-five sons and grandsons. Joseph is not mentioned because he is already in Egypt. If you count Jacob, Joseph, and his two sons, you arrive at the seventy mentioned in Exodus 1:5.

Clearly, this is not the total number of Israelites who entered Egypt. By ancient Hebrew reckoning, women were not counted (Gen. 46:8-27). If you want to number the entire family, the total should be at least doubled. If you counted the whole party, including slaves and servants, you would have well over two hundred people.

This list of names is vital. The people who are oppressed in Egypt are the very same people we met in Genesis. They reach back in an unbroken line to Abraham, with whom God originally made the covenant. *All* of the descendants of Jacob are there— none are missing.

If you attend your child's graduation, you look at the program to make sure her name is written there. When the class will is read, you want *your* name to be present. In the same way, a Hebrew wanted to know that when God's people were described, his ancestors' names and his tribe's name were listed. All must be a part of the Exodus experience.

The fact is, the number 70 is given to show smallness rather than largeness. Exodus 1 wants to emphasize the phenomenal growth of these descendants of Abraham and Jacob. Over and over again, the growth is referred to. The Israelites were "fruitful and multiplied greatly and became exceedingly numerous so that the land was filled with them" (1:7). Pharaoh recognized the growth (1:9, 10). Oppression didn't hinder the growth (1:12), and the midwives' kindness enabled growth to continue (1:20).

The growth is important for two reasons. First, it is a direct fulfillment of the covenant promises. God's first promise to Abraham (Gen. 12:2) is that He will make him a great and numerous nation. That promise is renewed over and over. It comes to Abraham in Genesis 13:16; 15:5; 17:2, 4; 18:18; 22:17, to Isaac in Genesis 26:4, and to Jacob in Genesis 28:14; 35:11; 46:3.

Although Exodus 1 does not specifically mention God as the One behind the rapid increase, the Israelites could not help but see this as a clear fulfillment of the promises made by God to their ancestors.

All this needs to be considered in light of the fertility problems of the patriarchal wives. An obstetrician who specialized in fertility problems could have made a small fortune as personal physician to the patriarchs' wives! Sarah initially can't have children and then miraculously conceives at age ninety. The next generation is not much better. Isaac's wife, Rebekah, barren for twenty years, only becomes pregnant in response to prayer by Isaac (Gen. 25:19-21) and then bears twins. Jacob's beloved wife Rachel is initially barren and only conceives in answer to prayer (Gen. 29:31; 30:22, 23).

But in Exodus all this is over. God has blessed Abraham's descendants with great fertility. Clearly, if God has so abundantly blessed in keeping the first part of His covenant promise, it is only a matter of time until He delivers on the second part—a land for Israel!

The Progression of Oppression

The second reason why this growth is crucial is that it is a major factor leading to Israel's enslavement. We now meet the other protagonists in the story—Pharaoh, and, by extension, the Egyptian nation.

Pharaoh reasons that a large Israelite community might join forces with one of Egypt's enemies. Thus, Israel is a dangerous threat to internal security. The very growth in population that is an evidence of God's blessing becomes an excuse for oppression to a fearful Pharaoh.

As is often the case in suppression and oppression, what begins as straightforward enslavement becomes progressively more brutal and deadly. The first step is forced labor under slave masters. This doesn't make the Israelites decrease, so the Egyptians begin to dread them even more and thus become more cruel. Not only do they require the Israelites to build, but also to work in the fields and do all kinds of hard labor under Egyptians who "used them ruthlessly" (1:14).

One of the activities the Israelites are required to perform is brickmaking (1:14). The Egyptians were great builders, and their construction projects required vast numbers of bricks. The pyramids of Sesostris III at Dashur needed about 24.5 million bricks for their construction (Sarna, 23)!

The brickmakers are given quotas. A leather scroll from the fifth year of Rameses II tells of a brickmaker team of forty men. Each worker was assigned to make 2,000 bricks a day, but the target was high and rarely reached. Punishment would often follow for those not reaching their quota. Such was the Israelites' lot under Pharaoh's persecution program.

In addition to hard labor, Pharaoh institutes a program of infanticide. Midwives with Hebrew names are commanded to kill all baby boys. They undoubtedly faced punishment from Pharaoh if they were caught not complying with his commands.

The midwives righteously decide not to follow Pharaoh's cruel orders, so, as a last step, the ruler gives all Egyptians license to kill

Israelite baby boys. Jewish commentators on the passage say that Egyptians would take their own babies and wander among the houses of the Israelites. They would cause their own babies to cry, hoping that the wails would induce hidden Israelite babies to also cry and thus be discovered.

The oppression has now moved from simple slavery to genocide. Never is there a reason for genocide, but, as already mentioned, from a human point of view, Pharaoh claimed to have a reason. According to some estimates, as much as a third of the population of Egypt at that time was foreign (Ramm, 8). If that many aliens in your country turned against you, it could be a threat. Nothing, however, is more likely to cause rebellion than the kind of oppression Pharaoh instigated!

Who was the ruler who did all of this? Exodus 1:8 calls him "a new king." Most students of Exodus understand this to mean a new dynasty or ruling family. This ruling group did not personally know Joseph (and his family) and all he had done to save Egypt in earlier times.

We are not sure of the pharaoh's[1] name. Who he is depends on when you believe the Exodus took place. Some scholars date the Exodus in the first half of the thirteenth century B.C., between 1300 and 1250. (For details, see LaSor, Bush, Hubbard, 125-128.) This would make the pharaoh of the oppression Seti I (1305–1290) and the pharaoh of the Exodus Rameses II (1290–1224).

Others date the Exodus at about 1445 B.C. The *SDA Bible Dictionary* has an able defense of this position (331, 332). If this date is correct, the key pharaohs in the oppression and in the Exodus would have been Thutmose III (c. 1492–1450) and Amenhotep (1490–1425?).

However, our uncertainty about which pharaoh or date is involved does not change the fact of the Exodus or the value and meaning of the story. Some have argued that the pharaoh is provi-

---

[1] Pharaoh was the title of Egyptian rulers, just as the word president is the title of the rulers in many countries today. Thus it is appropriate to say "the pharaoh," just as we would say "the president."

dentially left nameless, making him an ideal symbol of all oppressive rulers who fight against God's people. Oppressors tend to operate in certain ways. The Egyptian pharaoh is not as much an isolated evil man as he is a prototype of many who have followed similar paths—from Haman to Herod to Hussein. These men are representatives of oppressive systems.

One hero and two heroines stand out in this story. God is the great hero who fulfills the covenant. Although His name is not often mentioned, He brings about Israel's great multiplication. He is clearly pointed out as the One who inspires the two midwife heroines and their righteous actions and brings a subsequent blessing that gives them families of their own (1:20, 21).

The two midwives (probably along with their assistants) are a prime biblical example of civil disobedience for a righteous cause. The story clearly teaches that they did the right thing in disobeying Pharaoh's murderous command. The midwives are blessed because they "fear God" (vss. 17, 21) more than they fear Pharaoh's power and punishment.

This story raises other questions. The Bible clearly implies that the midwives' cover-up was a lie. Hebrew baby boys lived, not because their mothers were vigorous, but because the midwives chose to disobey Pharaoh. Does the story teach that despotic rulers are not only to be disobeyed but also lied to and deceived? Not necessarily. The blessing comes not because of deception but because of obedience to God. The blessing may even come in spite of deception. The fact that God blesses people who, in a time of crisis and dealing with tyrants, bend the truth does not mean that He condones the lying and other questionable methods used.

The story is ironic because the mighty ruler of Egypt is nameless while two obscure Hebrew midwives are remembered by name. God's standard of judging importance is certainly different from the one usually used by humans.

The stage is set for what follows. Both oppressor and oppressed have been introduced. We know what the problem is—Jacob's family faces genocide. What will God do next?

■ Getting Into the Word

Exodus 2

Read Exodus 2 through twice. As you read, think about the following questions:

1. Using a Bible dictionary and/or concordance, study the names of Moses (vs. 10), Reuel (vs. 18), and Gershom (vs. 22). What language do they come from, and what do they mean? What are the other names given to Reuel? Why so many names? How many people are we dealing with? What does all this teach about Bible names and naming?

2. List the parts of the story about the birth of Moses that would have delighted downtrodden Israelite slaves and seemed ironic. Three clever women are behind the saving of baby Moses. Enumerate the brave things each of them did. What seems to have motivated them?

3. Three stories are told here about Moses—his birth (vss. 1-10), his flight (vss. 11-19), and his life in Midian (vss. 16-22). Why are these three incidents important? What do they teach us?

4. List the four words used to describe God's response to Israel's groaning (2:24, 25). What steps are involved in God's action? What does this say about God's care?

5. Read Genesis 15:12-21 in connection with Exodus 2:24, 25. Could this be a part of what God is thinking of when He mentions His covenant in verse 24? What does this teach us about God and His covenants?

■ Exploring the Word

Meeting Moses

In Exodus 1 we meet the oppressed and the oppressor. Exodus 2 introduces us to the two deliverers—the human agent (Moses) and the divine agent (the God of Abraham, Isaac, and Jacob).

Who is this Moses? While the entire book of Exodus enlarges our picture, this passage tells more about his background and origin than any other single chapter.

In chapter 2:1 we learn that his parents were both Levites. This information is important for what follows in the Pentateuch. Neither parent is named in Exodus 2, but Exodus 6:20 names Amram and Jochebed as parents, or at least progenitors of Moses. Amram was of the Kohathite section of the tribe of Levi. Moses' brother Aaron was, of course, also a Kohathite Levite and progenitor of the Jewish priesthood.

Moses would certainly have been given a Hebrew name by his parents. We have no knowledge today of what that name was. Moses was the name given him by Pharaoh's daughter. The word is Egyptian and in its noun form means "boy-child." Its verb form means "to bear or give birth" (Durham, *Exodus*, 17). The name is a common element in Egyptian male names, occurring as part of such common Egyptian names as Ptahmose, Thutmose, Ahmose, and Harmose.

The name also sounds like the Hebrew word meaning "to draw out." This derived Hebrew meaning can refer either to Moses' providential deliverance from the Nile or Israel's deliverance at the Red Sea.

While we choose names because they sound nice or remind us of a beloved relative or friend, people in Old Testament times chose names because of their meaning. Notice that Moses names his firstborn son Gershom, which in Hebrew means "an alien there." We will return to the significance of this name later.

Sometimes a person can go by more than one name. An example of this is Moses' father-in-law. He is consistently said to be a priest of Midian, but his name varies. In Exodus 2:18 he is called Reuel ("companion of God"). Numbers 10:29 gives the same name to his father as well. Jethro ("his abundance") is his name according to Exodus 3:1; 4:18; and chapter 18. He is called Hobab ("loving, embracing one") in Numbers 10:29 and Judges 4:11.

While many explanations have been given for this, it could well be that the man did, in fact, have different names. Examples of name changes exist in the Pentateuch—like Abram to Abraham and Jacob to Israel—and many societies today allow name changes as well as multiple names. It is also possible that 2:18 does, in fact, refer to Moses' father-in-law's father, since *father* in Hebrew can refer to grandfather or great-grandfather.

Meanwhile, back to this baby named Moses. He himself suffers in the oppression like his people. His life is threatened by Pharaoh's decree calling for death to Hebrew baby boys. His life is marvelously delivered just as his people are going to be miraculously delivered. Moses' own life thus mirrors the experience of his people. As Israel is temporarily in Egyptian exile, so Moses experiences a temporary exile in Midian.

Moses' experience is divided into three parts—his birth (vss. 1-10), his flight (vss. 11:18), and his life in Midian (vss. 16-22). Each story is packed with significance and lays the basis for later parts of the story. First, Moses' birth intimates of deliverance to come. It is clear that parts of the story would have been seen as wonderfully ironic to Jews. The Nile, the river sacred to the Egyptians, was where he should have been drowned. Instead, the river helps to save Moses. The daughter of the persecutor takes pity on Moses and adopts him while his sister arranges for his own mother to get paid for raising him. In a subtle way, Moses' deliverance is a prophecy that, as God delivered Moses from Pharaoh in strange and wonderful ways, so He will deliver the people as a whole.

This story is told with a careful choice of words. When Moses' mother "saw that he was a goodly child" (2:2, RSV), or literally, "that he was good," she hid him. The phrase calls to mind the statement from the Genesis story of creation about God seeing how good His new creation was (Gen. 1:12, 18, 21, 25, 31). As God created a good world, so He is now in the process of another good creation—a deliverer for His people.

The basket Moses is placed in is called an "ark." The only other place the word is used is in the story of Noah. Both arks are vessels of salvation. This ark is placed among the "reeds" (2:5). The same word is used to refer to the sea of reeds when God delivered His people from the pursuing Egyptian army.

All of these things show the deep significance of this event and convey meaning to hearers of the story. Semitic peoples loved this kind of subtle comparison.

Three clever female heroines affect the deliverance of Moses. First, his mother, determined to defy Pharaoh's death decree and save her child, hatches the "basket in the Nile" scheme. Second, his sister comes up with the idea of a Hebrew nurse during her encounter with the Egyptian princess. And third, Pharaoh's daughter dares to adopt and save a Hebrew baby in the face of her father's death decree. One can only wonder what stories she told her family and others about her adopted son.

Rameses had fifty-nine daughters! Assuming that Rameses was the pharaoh at this time, we still are not sure this princess was his daughter. In any case, she probably came from a large family, which may have helped to hide Moses. Egyptian records tell us that non-Egyptians were sometimes part of Pharaoh's household, so Moses may not have been unique.

If we put this trio of women together with the midwives of chapter 1, we have a wonderful series of examples of how God uses women to bring freedom and deliverance to His people. They form an important part of the narrative.

The second story, Moses' flight from Egypt, moves us on to the next issues faced by the chosen leader. He was miraculously delivered as a child, but what will he do as an adult? He is favored as an adopted son of Pharaoh, so the natural question is, Which group will he identify with—the Hebrew slaves or their Egyptian taskmasters? This story answers that question. Moses considers the Hebrews "his own people" (vs. 11). He is not just of Hebrew blood, but he identifies and involves himself with his people. He is willing to kill to defend them. He must have already known something about God's call in his life. The implied accusation of his fellow Hebrew, "Who made you ruler and judge over us?" (vs. 14), is that he had been acting like he was a ruler in killing the Egyptian and trying to mediate in Hebrew squabbles.

This flight story is vital for another reason. It gives us a clear glimpse into the very nature of God-called deliverers and divine deliverance. Moses senses he is called by God to deliver, but he pushes things too fast and tries to do them on his own. God had not told him to bring deliverance and/or start killing Egyptians. Both timing and methodology were Moses' decisions, not God's.

In story after Old Testament story, God's chosen people try both to rush the fulfillment of God's promises and bring them to pass by their own power. Abraham tries to help God give a son of promise by marrying Hagar. Jacob tries to get the birthright by deception and intrigue. Gideon tries to deliver Midian by raising a mighty army. In *all* cases, even though they are God's chosen, they fail. They must wait for God's time and God's way. He, the Lord, must deliver—not they, the human instruments! Moses, clever leader and martial arts killer, must become Moses the meek shepherd. Only then can God act through him to bring about the Exodus. Have God's people today learned the Exodus lesson about deliverers and deliverance?

We come to story number three—Moses' life in Midian. Though Moses has fled and is, according to Pharaoh, a criminal fugitive, he finds a home. He finds that home with a priestly family. He finds a wife. He begets a son. He settles down. The son's name, Gershom ("a stranger there"), becomes a fitting symbol of what has happened to Moses. The interpretation of the name is given in verse 22 as "I have become an alien in a foreign land." The verb in Hebrew actually is in the past tense—literally, "I *was* an alien." The meaning, then, should be a reference to his being a stranger in Egypt—*not Midian*. This is supported by the second part of the name Gershom, which means "there." Moses now realizes he had been an alien *there* in Egypt, not *here* in Midian. He is now in a place where he has a wife and a son, and they are free to worship God. This is the area where he will soon meet God face to face (3:1–4:17). It is to just such a free area that God proposes to deliver His people so they can have a home like Moses.

The stage has been set. The deliverer has been born, he has a home, and he is in the process of preparation. He is waiting for God's call. Where, then, is God in all this? What is He doing? The last few verses of chapter 2 answer these questions.

A God Who Hears and Remembers

Exodus 2:23-25 is a crucial passage. It is a conclusion, intro-duction, transition, and summary all rolled into one. It covers past, present, and future, and it ignites hope. Such a pivotal passage deserves careful attention.

All this oppression of Israel has gone on for "many days," as the Hebrew literally says, or for a "long period" (2:23), as the NIV translates it. The long, hard oppression elicits a natural human response. The passage uses vivid, powerful words to describe the agonized response of Israel. The people "groan" (or "sigh in grief") and "cry out" ("call" or "shout"). The same two ideas are expressed in noun form as well (2:23b, 24).

The people have passed the level of just inner feelings and are so deeply affected that they verbalize their desperation. The sound is loud. The word for *groan* is the cry of starving beasts (Joel 1:18) and occurs most often in the book of Lamentations, which is the agonized death cry of Israel when their beloved city of Jerusalem falls.

The word translated "cry out" can literally mean a call for help. The word is a cry or call for help in a time of affliction. As such, it might best be translated "Help!" When it is addressed to God, it thus becomes a form of prayer (Botterwek and Ringgren, 4:121). The interesting thing in this passage is that though the passage does not explicitly say the cry is addressed to God, He hears any-way and responds.

This description of the desperate situation of Israel forms a summary of and conclusion to their Egyptian bondage. Fortu-nately, the story doesn't end here. As an introduction to the deliv-erance that follows, the passage also outlines God's response to the oppression. While suffering is past and present, God is also past, present, and future as well. Notice how He acts.

God's response, according to these verses, is summarized in four verbs. God *heard* their groaning (vs. 24) and *remembered* His cov-enant with Abraham, Isaac, and Jacob (vs. 24). He also *saw* the Israelites and *knew*. The clear message is that God is personally involved with the situation.

These four responses seem to be organized into two pairs. The first words in each pair—the sensory words *heard* and *seen*—tell us that God is aware of the situation. He senses clearly what is going on with His people in Egypt.

The second words in each pair—*remembered* and *knew*—are the result of this sensing. Because God senses what is going on, He is able to act in response.

The second word or phrase in each pair deserves special attention, especially by people in Western culture, who can remember and know and not do anything. The remembering and knowing can take place only in the mind, and have to do only with abstract facts. For Hebrews, this is impossible.

Truly, remembering means action in the Hebrew mind. Exodus 20:8 says, "Remember the Sabbath day by keeping it holy." Remembering actually includes keeping. In Exodus 2, God's remembering means not just recalling the covenant He made with Abraham, Isaac, and Jacob, but keeping it and acting on it. For God to remember His covenant means in the Hebrew mind to fulfill it.

In the same way, really knowing means experiencing—personal experience. One recent commentary actually translates Exodus 2:25 as "God saw the sons of Israel, and so God knew, by experience" (Durham, *Exodus*, 25). That powerful sense of identification with His people ties Israel closely to Yahweh.

That their God remembers and knows in this way gives a powerful sense of hope to Israel. The future is brighter because in the midst of oppression, God is sensing and remembering and knowing, and the end of all this must be saving.

We should note that this passage sees God's response as based on two things. First is the desperate need of the people. God's response springs from His empathy with the agony of the people. He is active because He has feelings for people.

Second, the response is based on God's covenant. God acts because He has made a covenant with Abraham, Isaac, and Jacob. God has chosen to obligate Himself to His people. This is the legal basis for His response.

Both of these aspects are crucial. If God is only legally bound to His people, the relationship could at times seem cold and formal. The response could seem like a mere contractual obligation.

On the other hand, if God only responded on the basis of need and feelings, one could wonder how much lasting obligation there was—whether His response might be a temporary emotional whim. Exodus portrays God as deliverer of Israel on *both* bases—in a powerful combination of both feeling and binding covenantal principle. Since God is the author of the covenant, He sticks to His word of promise. But that covenant of faithfulness is based on a strong love and care for His people.

These facts about God are what make Him such a great Deliverer. These truths about God bring about the Exodus. This good news about God is what ignited hope in Israelite hearts. It should do the same today for all who suffer under oppression of any kind, for the God of Abraham, Isaac, and Jacob is the same yesterday, today, and forever.

■ Applying the Word

Exodus 1, 2

1. What kinds of discrimination or oppression have you suffered? What do you know about the oppression or persecution of others? What lessons can you learn from Exodus 1 and 2 about how oppression takes place and what a believer's response might be? What have you learned about God's response?

2. Do you know what your name means? Where did it come from? Is it "Israelite" or "Egyptian"? If you were to pick a name for yourself, what would it be? What would you like your name to mean? Which of your character traits would you most like it to describe? What work of God in your life would you like it to refer to? What kind of list or story would you like it to appear in?

3. Which heroine or hero in this story do you most identify with? Why? What personal lessons can you learn
   from such unsung heroines and heroes as the midwives,
   Moses' mother and sister, Pharaoh's daughter, and
   Moses' father-in-law?
4. How is your sense for God's timing? Moses tries to rush
   God's plan. Have you ever done that? What did you learn?
   Israel groaned for a long time before deliverance came.
   Why was God "slow" in responding? Why did Moses
   have to spend so long in Midian? How can Exodus 1 and
   2 help those who wonder about God's timing?
5. What is your personal "Egyptian slavery"? What is it
   that you can't escape from? Do you believe God can deliver you? Or has He already done so? If so, how did He
   deliver you? What can these chapters teach you about
   why and how God's deliverance operates?
6. What kinds of prayers do you think God hears? Have
   you ever felt like just calling, "Help!" to God? What can
   you learn about prayer from God's response to Israel's
   sighs, groans, and cries for help?

■ Researching the Word

1. Do further study on the date of the Exodus by reading
   the *Seventh-day Adventist Bible Dictionary*, pages 331, 332,
   and the *Seventh-day Adventist Bible Commentary*, vol. 1,
   pages 184-196. Notice the various Bible texts that are
   used in the discussion and the other biblical events that
   are impacted by the date of the Exodus. In your mind,
   what are the strongest arguments for the earlier date?
   On the basis of this study, how important do you think
   the dating of Exodus is? Why?
2. Look up other stories in the Bible about the persecution of God's people by heathen governments. Examples
   are the three Hebrews in the fiery furnace and Daniel in
   the lions' den (Dan. 3 and 6), the Jews at the time of

Esther (the book of Esther), and Jesus at His trial and crucifixion (the last few chapters of each of the four Gospels). Make a list of the similarities these stories have to the oppression of the Hebrews by Pharaoh, another list of the differences, and a third list of the spiritual lessons you learn from each story.

3. Do a similar study of the persecution of God's people described in the book Revelation. What do Exodus and Revelation each contribute that can help you to deal with any fear you may have of persecution or oppression?

■ Further Study of the Word

1. For general insight, see Ellen G. White, *Patriarchs and Prophets*, 241-251.

2. For detailed information on the historical background of Exodus, see William Sanford LaSor, et. al., Old Testament Survey, 117-128; Nahum M. Sarna, *Exploring Exodus*, 15-22.

3. For a beautifully illustrated introduction to Egyptian life from the time of Moses, see James B. Pritchard, *Everyday Life in Bible Times*, 106-175.

PART TWO

God Acts
to Deliver

Exodus 3–18

CHAPTER TWO

God Calls
a Leader

Exodus 3, 4

The first two chapters of Exodus tell the story of Israel's oppression and slavery in Egypt. Against this backdrop, we can understand the story of God's deliverance, which is told in the next section of the book. While conditions in Egypt are terrible, a covenant-keeping, loving God has taken notice of Israel's plight and is poised to act.

The first act in this drama of deliverance is the calling and preparing of a leader. When God begins to create a people or start a new community, as He does in Exodus, He uses a key person. We met Moses in chapter 2 of Exodus, and we last saw him as a shepherd in the land of Midian, settling down as a family man with a wife and son.

In Exodus 3 and 4, Moses' life takes a dramatic turn as God calls him to lead his people out of Egypt. By the time the story ends, Moses is back in Egypt with his brother Aaron. Together, they lead God's Israelite freedom movement.

■ Getting Into the Word

Exodus 3

Read Exodus 3 through a couple of times. As you read, think about the following questions. If you are keeping an Exodus notebook, have it nearby as you study so that you can write down your answers and other thoughts that come to you.

1. Where are Midian, the "far side of the desert," and "Mt. Horeb" (3:1)? Do they go by other names? Look up these places in the *SDA Bible Dictionary* and on a Bible map or atlas. Read chapter 3:12, 18. Do these verses refer to the same place as 3:1? Why did God promise that the Israelites would return to the same place? What happened at this place? All through Exodus, the Pentateuch, and the rest of the Bible, you will find this place significant. Using a concordance, look up other places where this site is mentioned.

2. List the steps God took in calling Moses. What does this reveal about how God calls people? Compare Moses' call with other Old Testament calls like that of Gideon (Judg. 6:11-14), Isaiah (Isa. 6:1-13), and Jeremiah (Jer. 1:1-14). How are they the same, and how do they differ?

3. God appeared to Moses in a fiery bush. Using a concordance, find other passages where God came with fire to reveal Himself to people.

4. Enumerate what God said about Himself to Moses in this chapter. How did He restate, then build on, and expand what is said in chapter 2:23-25? Note especially His feelings and actions and the reasons for His actions. Why and how will He rescue Israel?

5. What does verse 14 mean? Is God's name "I am" important? Why? What does it mean? What is new about God's revelation of His name? You will find help by looking in the *SDA Bible Dictionary* or another Bible dictionary, under the words *Yahweh* or *Names of God* (or *God, names of*).

6. Try to put yourself in Moses' place. How would you react to God's presence? What did Moses do in response to the revelation of God (vss. 5, 6)? Notice that this theme of worship recurs in the chapter in verses 12 and 18. Why do you think it is mentioned? Why is it important? What does this teach us?

■ GOD CALLS A LEADER

■ Exploring the Word

Moses' Call

The story of Moses' call opens with a picture of him following his usual pattern of behavior—tending his father-in-law's flock. He seems to have wandered farther than usual—to the far side of the desert, away from Midian. In that section of desert at Horeb (called the Mountain of God—vs. 1), Moses' vision of God, which we call a theophany (appearance of God), takes place. Before looking in detail at *what* happened, it is helpful to consider *where* this all happened.

The place called Horeb or the Mountain of God goes by several terms. Most authorities equate it with Mount Sinai or Sinai. Other terms used are *the mount, the Mount of Horeb,* and *the Mountain of God in Horeb.*

The exact location of this mountain is uncertain, but most authorities believe it is located in south central Sinai and is either the mountain now called Ras Es-Safsafeh (*SDA Bible Dictionary,* 1021) or the one named Jebel Musa (*Harpers Bible Dictionary*).

More important than the exact location of the mountain is its significance. This place *is* the wonderful site where an important divine revelation comes. Not only does Moses receive the message of his call and the revelation of God's name at that place, but the covenant is also made there (Deut. 5:2), and the law is delivered from the mountaintop (Exod. 19:1, 2). Israel is numbered at this location (Num. 1:19), and God's people set out for Canaan from there (Deut. 1:19). The peak has such significance that Paul uses the mountain to represent the covenant made there. The mountain becomes for Paul a symbol of a whole system of religion (Gal. 4:24, 25).

The mount is more than the place par excellence of God's revelation; it is also a "sign" (Exod. 3:12). Moses is unsure of God's call. As a clear signal that God has truly met and called him, the delivered people of Israel will also meet God on the same mountain. God's revelation to His people at the same mountain will prove His initial revelation to the leader Moses. Thus Horeb becomes a sign of God's leading and presence.

For every people or community God creates, there is a Mountain of God—a Sinai desert and a wilderness of revelation—where God has shown Himself, first of all, to His appointed leader and then to His people. Without that revelation, there can be no call, no leader, and no new God-created people. Moses emerged from the desert and his experience at the mountain ready to go on his mission.

Many see parallels between Moses' experience and that of Jesus. Before God can create His renewed people through Jesus, it is necessary for Jesus, the leader, to go into the wilderness for forty days and then emerge ready to go on His mission.

What did God do at this mountain of revelation? He met Moses in a fire and told him who He was and what He wanted him to do. He combined theophany (an appearance of God) and call to ministry.

Fire seems to be an important part of the scene when God shows up on the mountain. In Exodus 19:18 the Lord descends on Mt. Sinai "in fire." Exodus 24:17 says God appeared in the sight of Israel as fire on the top of the mountain. Deuteronomy 4:11, 12 is even more descriptive of the fire that was ablaze on the mountain as God spoke to Israel. Israel must have expected fire on such occasions. Certainly the fire that descended at Pentecost must have called to Jewish minds the earlier fire on Sinai. While many associate fire with judgment, the Old Testament connects it also with the appearance of God.

Out of this fire God called Moses. Many calls in the Old Testament seem to follow the same pattern. The calls of Jeremiah and Gideon have the same basic elements as the call of Moses (Wittenberg, p. 26-28). Notice the following sequence:

1. A theophany or revelation of God takes place.
   Moses: Exodus 3:1-4; Gideon: Judges 6; Jeremiah: Jeremiah 1:4.
2. God makes an introductory statement.

Moses: Exodus 3:4; Gideon: Judges 6:12, 13; Jeremiah: Jeremiah 1:5.

3. God commissions the messenger.
   Moses: Exodus 3:10; Gideon: Judges 6:14; Jeremiah: Jeremiah 1:5.

4. The messenger questions God.
   Moses: Exodus 3:11; Gideon: Judges 6:15; Jeremiah: Jeremiah 1:6.

5. God reassures the messenger.
   Moses: Exodus 3:12; Gideon: Judges 6:16; Jeremiah: Jeremiah 1:7, 8.

6. God gives a sign or signs.
   Moses: Exodus 3:12; Gideon: Judges 6:17; Jeremiah: Jeremiah 1:9, 10.

Isaiah's call in Isaiah 6 has many similarities but a slightly different set of steps. Isaiah feels so inadequate that he is overwhelmed even before God says anything to him. His guilt must be cared for before God can ask him to be a messenger.

Whatever the steps followed, there seem to be certain basic principles inherent in Moses' call and these other call narratives. We can learn from them.

First, God reveals Himself *before* He asks for a specific task to be done. The call arises out of a mighty revelation of God. Second, the one called always feels inadequate and/or overwhelmed by God and the task. Third, God provides answers and help that enable the messenger to fill the call.

The messenger needs a sense of inadequacy as a prerequisite for proper mission. People who feel adequate lack a sense of the awesomeness and responsibility of the mission and the fact that *only* God's presence and power can make the mission a success.

The story in Exodus 3 and 4 is full of Moses' questions and inadequacies (3:11, 13; 4:1, 10, 13, 18). It may be true that Moses pushed his questions and fears too far (4:13, 14). Nevertheless, a universal characteristic of truly called people is a deep sense of personal need. It could be that the same is true today for the people

God asks to work with Him. Such people should realize that God Himself is willing to *act*, to Himself ensure the completion of the mission He has called us to perform.

"I Am"

Exodus 3 is without parallel in the Old Testament as a statement about God—the ways He reveals Himself, what His feelings are, how He wants to act, and the reason He acts the way He does. Because of this, chapter 3 deserves careful thought and prayerful meditation.

Exodus 2:23-25 has already told us that God saw and remembered as well as heard and personally knew Israel's situation. Exodus 3 builds on that. God has "indeed seen" and "heard" and is "concerned" (verse 7), but how He intends to act on the matter is now stated as well.

First, God arrests Moses' attention by appearing in a thorn bush, and then leads him to worship. The significance and use of fire by God was discussed earlier. The fire is referred to no less than five times in verses 2 and 3 alone. The story makes it clear that Moses recognized the fire as strange. That was indeed its purpose. God wanted Moses to come and look so He could speak to him.

Twentieth-century Western scientific minds have problems with this kind of fire and this type of story. Some have tried to dampen the questions by calling this a vision and making it a psychological experience for Moses. First, that doesn't fit the story—Moses went over to see the bush. Second, how does it help? As Bernard Ramm says, "If we escape from the chemist we manage only to bang into another scientist—the psychologist" (Ramm, 23). Making the fire psychological only leads skeptics to think all these experiences only take place inside people's heads.

We may be helped by remembering that only a select group of people (mainly Western civilization) during a short period of history (late nineteenth and twentieth centuries) has questioned this kind of thing. Most people in nearly all periods of history accepted special acts of God in the real world. The story makes it plain that this is also an amazing experience for Moses. He is surprised and awed, and that is the way God planned it.

The God revealed here is *intensely personal*. His interaction with Moses is real. He calls Moses by name and refers to his father and Abraham, Isaac, and Jacob. He knows who real, individual people are. He listens to and then reacts to Moses' questions. He doesn't speak His piece and then leave Moses confused and full of queries.

The God revealed here is *savingly active*. He has "come down to rescue His people" and "to bring them up out of that land into a good and spacious land" (vs. 9). He is now sending Moses as His emissary to do this. He will be with Moses and give him a sign (vs. 12). He will work with the elders of Israel (vs. 16) and the Egyptians (vss. 18, 21) to bring about Israel's deliverance.

The God revealed here is *intent on self-revelation*. He wants people to know Him. He reveals His name, which describes Him. He tells Moses of His past human relationships (vss. 6, 15). He wants His name to be remembered (vs. 15). This God is not a God who hides Himself from His people. He desires to know and be known.

The God revealed here is *close to His people*. He "has come down" to be their active deliverer (vs. 8). He is present with them in their pain. The Christ Child born in Bethlehem was not the first time God had come down to save people.

God tells Moses, "I will be with you" (vs. 12). The promise given to proclaimers of the gospel that the divine One would be present with them to the end of the age (Matt. 28:19, 20) was not a new promise. The proclaimer of deliverance from Egypt had the same promise. The Israelite delegation was specifically told to tell Pharaoh that the Lord "has met with us" (vs. 18). God is close, not only to Moses, but to all His people.

The climax of this revelation of God comes in verses 13 to 15. Moses asks God what His name is. God's answer is, "I am who I am." This answer has provoked endless discussion. Two common explanations that are *not* correct should be mentioned.

First, this is not a statement about God's essence and being or a philosophical statement of preexistence and eternity. Such an understanding is based on the questions and concerns of abstract Greek thoughts. This is not the message here.

Second, this is not a playful, somewhat evasive answer that was meant to be enigmatic and veiled. The context rules this out. Moses is seriously concerned as to what he should tell people. He needs help for his mission. This is not a time for God to play games.

The passage must be seen in its larger context. Moses has just received a powerful promise. God says He is about to deliver the Israelites from slavery to the most powerful nation in the world at that time. This nation has oppressed them for years. How is it possible for deliverance to happen now? Why, after all these years, does their God suddenly become active? Why should they believe this is real? These questions need answering, and the response should be easy to understand.

God replies by using a Hebrew verb usually translated "be" or "become." The form used is called the imperfect, but it does not perform like an English imperfect verb. It refers to incomplete, unfinished, ongoing action. English usually translates such a verb as a continuous or future tense. Thus it could be rendered as "I am," referring to existence and action now and continuing on into the future. It could also be rendered as "I will be," or "I will become," referring to what God will continue to do for Israel. Most likely it is both.

What God means is, You should know Me as the God who is active on your behalf now and will continue to be in the future. Verse 15 points to God's past action with Abraham, Isaac, and Jacob. Putting it all together, God is saying, I have been, am now, and will continue to work for your deliverance. Call Me *Yahweh*, a name based on this verb form, and it will remind you continually of My ongoing saving action on your behalf. That is how you are to identify Me to Israel, and that is how I desire to be known.

The rest of the chapter (vss. 16-22) goes on to explain exactly how the actively saving God proposes to work on Israel's behalf. He will cause the elders of Israel to listen to Moses (vs. 18). He will work with His mighty hand on Pharaoh to let Israel go (vss.

19-22). This will all be proof of the truth of His name.

The enslaved Israelites are not interested in great philosophical speculations about God's essence. They don't want theological discussion. They are not consumed with splitting hairs over law and gospel or justification and sanctification. What they want is help, deliverance, and salvation. They want God to be there for them. The name is given to convince them of that fact about God.

This chapter, epitomized by this wonderful Name, summarizes what the God of the Old Testament is like and what He proposes to do. In many ways, these few verses are the theological center of Exodus and, indeed, of the entire Old Testament. The rest of the book of Exodus is commentary and proof. It demonstrates that God's revelation of Himself in Exodus 3 is indeed true. God really *can* create a new community of people! He *can* deliver Egyptian slaves from oppression, bring them freedom from Egypt, and take them to their own land with their own way of life. He is a living, acting God who does real things in the lives of real people.

Response to "I Am"

Before leaving this powerful chapter, there is one more issue that deserves attention. What is the human response to this revelation? Yahweh has declared Himself as a saving God. What should people do when they find this out? Put yourself in Moses' place. You are probably alone in the desert, and you see a thorn bush ablaze. As you come closer, you realize the bush is not disappearing in the fire. Then you hear your name called and are told that you are on holy ground. God speaks. In awe you drop to the ground, hastily remove your shoes, and hide your face.

Fear, awe, reverence, and worship come from this encounter with God. Does God want to scare Moses into submission? I doubt it. If Moses believes God has the power to save, he must catch a vision of God's holiness and power. His worship is the evidence that he understands the majesty of the One he is dealing with. The very first human response to God's revelation of Himself must be worship.

Not only must Moses worship, but Israel, whom he will teach, must come and worship also at this mountain (vs. 12). When Israel hears Moses' message and comes to believe it, she worships (4:31). That is a clear sign that the people really have faith that God is present.

Moses' initial message to Pharaoh concerns worship. Since Israel has met God, she must go and offer sacrifices and spend some time in worship (vs. 18). While this request may seem strange or at best a trick, such a work break for religious purposes was not unreasonable or exceptional to Egyptian ears. There is an account of a work supervisor who kept a log where he recorded the work habits of his forty-three laborers (Sarna, 56). He recorded the days of the month when they were absent and the reasons they gave for their absences. While illness and laziness account for most failures to appear, "sacrificing to the god" also appears. One log reports that laborers building the royal necropolis enjoyed four days of holiday in order to celebrate a religious festival. When Moses made his request, he could certainly cite earlier precedents and was not asking for special favors. Not only is Yahweh interested in worship, but Egyptian society made an opportunity for it even among slaves. Our culture could learn something valuable from this.

We serve a personal God who loves us, but it is possible to forget that He is also holy fire. We must not forget to remove our shoes and hide our faces. If we fail to do so, we may not yet have seen Him in all His saving glory and power. Slaves (aren't we slaves, too?) need to see and worship. Only then can we gain strength to believe that He, God, gives the power to loose our chains and set us free.

■ Getting Into the Word

Exodus 4

Read Exodus 4 through at least twice. As you read, think about the answers to the questions that follow. Keep your Exodus notebook nearby for writing down answers and ideas.

1. Describe the three signs God gives Moses (vss. 2-9). What are the signs given to prove? Using a Bible dictionary, see if you can find out what snakes, rods, leprosy, the Nile River, and blood mean. What do you think is the symbolic meaning of these signs?

2. Read Numbers 12:3, and compare it with Exodus 4:10-17. Is Moses meek or not meek in Exodus 4? Why? Are Moses' objections valid or not? Why? Is it proper for God to be angry (vs. 16)? Give reasons for your answers.

3. Think about Moses' family relationships. What reason does Moses give to Jethro for returning to Egypt? Is the reason true? Why does he give such a general reason for going? Why does he need to give a reason at all?

4. Verses 24 to 26 are difficult to understand. What do you think they mean? Why are they here? What do they tell us about Moses, Zipporah, and God? Learn all you can about circumcision as practiced in that day. Check a Bible dictionary for information.

5. Before Moses can go before the Egyptians, he must convince his own people of his encounter with God. Enumerate the steps he takes to do this. Tell what the people are convinced of. How do they respond?

■ Exploring the Word

More Signs

Moses continues his questions in Exodus 4 because of his desire for further reassurance. However, the nature of these queries and God's responses change. In Exodus 3, God tells Moses who He, God, is and what He will do for Israel. In chapter 4, Moses raises two other issues. First, how can he, Moses, answer Israel's question when they ask whether the Lord really appeared to him? Second, is he really the man for the job?

In response to the first question, God gives Moses three miraculous signs that he can perform as immediate, visible evidence of his encounter with God.

In the first sign, Moses' shepherd's staff becomes a snake when thrown on the ground. Moses is frightened. At God's command, Moses, probably with apprehension, grabs the snake by the tail, and again it becomes his staff. This sign is the clever use of two very important symbols. The snake in the Near East of Moses' time was widely seen as a symbol of wisdom and healing. Egyptians often worshiped snakes, and cobras were a royal symbol. I visited the British Museum in London recently and viewed their wonderful display of Egyptian mummies. I was reminded again that for a long time Egyptian Pharaohs wore a metal cobra on the front of their headdress. This is one reason Ramm believes the snake in this story was a cobra (Ramm, 32).

Moses' rod—probably his shepherd's staff—is also used symbolically in this story. This rod often reappears in the Exodus narrative. Exodus 4 shows God commanding Moses to take "this staff in your hand so you can perform miraculous signs with it" (vs. 17). Moses obeys, and when he sets out for Egypt, he takes this "staff of God in his hand" (vs. 20).

The staff is constantly used in Moses' work. The same importance is attached to Aaron's staff as well (7:8, ff.). Moses' powerful rod opens a path through the Red Sea for Israel (14:16). Later, Moses strikes a rock with this staff, and water gushes out (17:1-7).

In the Bible the rod is used to symbolize royalty, power, and authority. A scepter is one type of rod, and it has the same symbolic meaning. A scepter belonged to the ceremonial insignia of Egyptian kings (Sarna, 60). Moses' rod becomes his scepter, and he wields it in the presence of Pharaoh, who could not have missed its meaning. God wants Moses to know that He, the Lord, had vested His representative with power, authority, and leadership. The rod is a visible, tangible testimony of God's presence and Moses' important office. Aaron with his rod is also vested with divine authority and office.

The second sign involves leprosy and Moses' hand. After inserting his hand into his cloak, it becomes leprous. A second insertion heals the hand. You can almost feel Moses' apprehension in the middle of this sign and his relief when it is complete.

Unlike the first sign, this leprosy is not mentioned again in Exodus. The significance of the sign is not as clear. Leprosy usually symbolizes sin and/or God's judgment. This sign may be a mild rebuke to Moses for his continued resistance and questions, a simple promise that God can both judge and take away judgment. It could also serve as a warning to both Israelite and Egyptian that God can judge, and serious consequences will result if they reject His messenger and message.

In sign number three, God tells Moses that when he arrives in Egypt he is to take water from the Nile River and pour it on the ground, and it will turn to blood. The Nile was the source of life for Egypt and was considered divine. For Moses (and God) to do this is another symbol of God's power and control over Egyptian life and religion.

What is clear, then, is that these really are "miraculous signs" (vss. 8, 17). They are not just miracles to show that God can do magic. They are *signs* of much greater realities. As Moses must believe he has really communicated with Yahweh, so both Israelite and Egyptian must believe Yahweh has met Moses. These signs show that God is with Moses and active in their midst.

They also symbolize something even bigger—that Yahweh is more powerful than Egypt and her Pharaoh. While Israel is a weak slave people and Egypt is a world power, Israel's God, Yahweh, is able to overcome and defeat Egypt's gods and thus the country and her ruler. Israel is weak, but she has a big God. Applying this lesson, any group of people who really believes in God that way will be delivered as Israel was. Deliverance from slavery comes first in *the mind*. When the mind is liberated by faith in an all-powerful God, then actual concrete deliverance can follow.

Moses and Meekness

In the next section (4:10-17), Moses tries to reject God's call to him, first by claiming he is not a good speaker and finally by asking God to send someone else.

God's response to Moses is direct. In a series of rhetorical questions, Yahweh makes it clear that He, the Lord, is the Creator of humans' mouths and is the One who makes people deaf or mute. "Go," God says, in language that grammatically is a strong command form. "I will help you speak and will teach you what to say" (vs. 12). Moses' job is to do the going. God's job is to take care of the speaking and the message. When God gives the command to act, *He Himself* will provide the ways and means to perform what He has asked.

Moses still replies, "Please send someone else." At this, "the Lord's anger burns." God's response in verses 11 and 12 already hints that Moses is pushing things too far. Moses is making excuses, not showing meekness. In context, the reason is clearly that Moses doubts God's words of enabling. God has said He'll take care of the speaking, but Moses still wants out of his mission. In spite of the inappropriateness of Moses' response, God does give Moses further help by telling him his brother Aaron is on the way and will help him speak.

Many are bothered by the reference to God's anger. This passage clearly speaks of it, as do numerous other passages. To deny the reality of God's anger would require extensive revision of the biblical text. What we must do for those concerned with this issue is give some explanation.

First, we must say that divine anger is not like human anger, which is often meaningless, capricious, petty, and destructive. God's anger shows His real involvement and interaction with people. He is not distant from His people in an emotional sense. If we want God to suffer with us and love us, we must expect anger as well.

We must also realize that God's anger is instructive. Moses learns that he has gone too far. God's anger tells people that they are on the wrong path. When God's anger leads to judgment, it is disciplinary teaching. In the case of Moses, he learns his lesson—no more questions or objections are forthcoming.

The passage is also interesting from the standpoint of prophetic function. Typically in the prophetic process, God speaks to the prophet, and the prophet then gives God's words to the people. However, in this case, God adds another step—Aaron—to the procedure. In this unique situation, Moses becomes "God" (or message giver) to Aaron, and Aaron is "Moses" (or prophet) to the people.

With the divine encounter behind him, Moses returns home to Midian and prepares to go to Egypt. Exodus 4:18-30 is a series of incidents clustered around the theme of Moses' journey from the Mount of God back to Midian and on to Egypt.

The story seems to imply that some period of time after his return to Midian, Moses receives the command to go back to Egypt (vs. 19). Presumably this command means *now* is the time to go. God earlier commands him to go but now reveals His timetable, which is tied to the death of the pharaoh who knows Moses and wants to kill him.

Note Moses' relationship to his family. Even though he is eighty years old, he asks his father-in-law's permission to go back. The reason he gives for the trip is a desire to see if his people (family) are still alive. Such a request and such a reason are strange to our ears. Why does an eighty-year-old man need permission from his father-in-law? Why does he give a reason that isn't the real reason?

We must remember that Moses has been living with his wife's family for years. They have been kind to him, giving him a place to live and a wife when he arrived as an unknown stranger, fleeing from Pharaoh's wrath. We must also note that Moses' culture has a high regard for parents and age. Parental power and authority don't fade with the adulthood of the children. Moses' plans to return seem originally to have included taking his wife and family with him. Zipporah is Jethro's daughter, and her children are his grandchildren. For all of these reasons, Moses acts as an obedient son (in-law) and requests the permission and probably the blessing of Jethro for his journey. People today could learn from such family loyalty.

While courtesy, love, and custom demand that Moses ask permission to go, he is required to give his father-in-law a specific reason for going. The general reason that he wants to see family is not only true, but safer. He can conceal his uneasiness over his God-given mission.

The question has arisen whether Moses' wife, Zipporah, and sons accompanied him to Egypt. Those who say Yes cite verse 20 and verses 24 to 26 as evidence. Those who say No point out that the family is never mentioned later in the narrative as being in Egypt or on the journey out of Egypt. We meet them next in Exodus 18:2-6, when they are in Jethro's care as Moses returns from Egypt. Even in verse 18 Moses says, "Let *me* go," and Jethro says, "I wish *you* (singular) well."

Most likely Moses took his family partway and at a later time thought it better for them and for the success of his mission to send them back home to Midian. They will then be reunited after the Exodus.

The circumcision of Moses' son in verses 24 to 26 seems strange to us. It has elicited many different explanations, some of them too fanciful to repeat here. Apparently Moses had neglected to perform a circumcision (probably two of them—see below), which should have been done earlier. Now he is going to Egypt as God's leader of the covenant people, and he is *not* to perform this ministry unless his own family complies with the covenant requirement of circumcision. Perhaps Zipporah, as a Midianite, whose people did not practice circumcision, had been opposed to the rite earlier. We don't know all the reasons for the delay, but the rite could be delayed no longer.

So Moses' son is circumcised, and the story implies that Moses is also circumcised. If he was circumcised as a child at all, it was probably only partially—a custom that was popular among Egyptians at that time. But now, going on a long journey with an important mission, he cannot afford either to be uncircumcised or to be disabled for a long period by a full circumcision. This is probably the reason for Zipporah taking the excised foreskin of Moses' son and touching Moses' private parts (most commentators believe this is the meaning of *feet* in verse 25) with it. Zipporah's action is a kind of vicarious circumcision, which, given the urgency of Moses' mission, is enough to satisfy the covenant. This may also have been the point at which it was decided that the family should return to Midian while Moses continued on his journey to Egypt.

This section (vss. 21-23) contains the first mention of Pharaoh's heart hardening in response to Moses' message. The issue is an important one, which we will discuss in the next chapter.

Before approaching Pharaoh and the Egyptians, Moses needs to take his deliverance message to his own people. The steps taken are instructive. First, Moses must convince his "prophet" (mouthpiece), brother Aaron. They meet in "the desert" at the "mountain of God" (vs. 27). This is Moses' place of revelation, and one can picture him showing Aaron the burning bush and reliving his conversation with the Lord. Aaron is convinced that God has indeed called his brother to deliver Israel.

Step two is to convince the elders of Israel. Aaron speaks to them (has Moses forgotten Hebrew too?), and Moses performs his miracles in their presence. The elders then call the people together so they can witness for themselves the miraculous signs that Moses performs.

People who claim a message from God would do well to follow this pattern. If they can't convince their family and especially the church's leadership that God has called them, they shouldn't move on to a larger outside group. Unless your own people are behind you, it is not time to go to "Egypt."

Just as God had promised, "They [Israel] believed" (vs. 31). When they *are* convinced that Yahweh is concerned about *them* and has seen their misery, they bow down and worship. Here again, we see the divine process. God demonstrates His love, power, presence, and saving intentions. When people see this and believe, the only thing they can do is worship.

Moses is in Egypt. His own people have been convinced that he has met their God, who desires to deliver them and create for Himself a people. The next step is to go to Pharaoh and the Egyptians. That is the subject of the next chapter.

■ Applying the Word

Exodus 3, 4

1. Are there any "mountains of God" in your life? When and where has God met you and communicated with you? Have you gone back to these places lately? Should you?
2. What do you think God has called you to do? How does your call or the call of those you know compare with that of Moses, Gideon, Jeremiah, or Isaiah? Have you ever felt inadequate, as Moses did? What can you learn about how God works with those whom He has called?
3. When is the last time you took off your shoes and worshiped? What can move you to worship? What might contribute to your ability to sense God's presence and to worship?
4. How does God respond to the questions of people? Is God's response to Moses a pattern for His response to you? Why? How can you tell when questions should stop?
5. Have you ever asked for a sign? Is it right for you to ask God for signs? Why? What circumstances might affect such a request?
6. Who are key religious leaders, in your estimation? Why do you think so? What evidence do you have that God is with them? What kind of evidence would you need to believe in a "Moses" or an "Aaron"? Are there such people today? Who?

■ Researching the Word

1. Do some deeper research into the titles and names for God. Begin by looking up the articles "El," "Yahweh," and "Sabaoth" in the *SDA Bible Dictionary*. From there, you can read some of the Bible texts mentioned in the articles and find more texts by looking under the vari-

ous words in a concordance. What can we learn about how the Old Testament viewed God from a study of these titles? Which titles speak most powerfully to your time and culture?

2. Do a study of how various prophets related to the religious leaders of their times. Two good examples are Jeremiah and Paul. For Jeremiah, concentrate on the narrative parts of his book (you can probably find most of them by skimming). For Paul, read Acts 9 to 15 and Galatians 1 and 2. How did each of these prophets relate to the "church" leadership of his time, and what was the church's response? Did God instruct them how to relate to the church? Compare their experience with God's command to Moses to meet with the "church" of his time. What was the church's response in each case? How were the experiences of Moses, Jeremiah, and Paul similar? How were they different? Make a list of lessons we can learn from this about the relationship to the church of Christians today who feel called by God to carry out a special ministry or to proclaim a unique message.

■ Further Study of the Word

1. For general insight, see Ellen G. White, *Patriarchs and Prophets*, 251-256.
2. On Moses and his call, see William Sanford LaSor, et al., *Old Testament Survey*, 132-137, and Nahum M. Sarna, *Exploring Exodus*, 38-62.
3. On God's self-revelation, see William Dyrness, *Themes in Old Testament Theology*, 30-32.

CHAPTER THREE

God Deals
With Pharaoh

Exodus 5:1–7:7

In the next act of the Exodus drama, Moses and Aaron encounter Pharaoh. God has called and commissioned Moses. The Israelites themselves have just openly acknowledged that Yahweh has visited His people. In response they bow down and worship Him. Seemingly as a united front, God, Moses, Aaron, the elders of the people, and the masses are ready to meet the oppressor, Pharaoh.

Because of all that Yahweh has said and done and because of the quick belief of Israel, Moses expects a positive response from the Egyptian ruler. But he's in for a shock. Pharaoh haughtily asks, "Who is Yahweh?" The oppression increases instead of decreasing. The people and Moses are upset, and the people complain bitterly. In reply God graciously gives renewed messages of promise and hope based on His covenant and who He is.

In the concluding section, the Lord proclaims a clear message of judgment on Egypt. This judgment will deliver Israel and convince Egypt that Yahweh is indeed "the Lord." Moses and Aaron again take courage, obey God's command, and move out to speak with the Egyptian ruler. The stage is set for the plagues, which are God's proof in action of all that He has promised.

While God often gives clear statements about what He will do, the time element is at times missing. Human expectations about the moment God will act often give rise to misunderstanding. These chapters of Exodus encourage us to be careful about predicting exactly when and how God will work out the deliverance He has graciously promised.

■ Getting Into the Word

Exodus 5

Read Exodus 5 through a couple of times. As you read it thoughtfully, consider the following questions:

1. In whose name and by what authority do Moses and Aaron approach Pharaoh (vss. 1, 3)? With what question does Pharaoh respond (vs. 2)? Who does Moses hold responsible for the problems Israel is having with Pharaoh (vss. 22, 23)? What does this tell us about the real nature of this encounter? Who is really in conflict in this story? How does this help us to understand this story better?

2. Note carefully the exact nature of Moses' request to Pharaoh in verses 1 and 3. Compare this with 6:11, 13, 26 and 7:2, 16. Did Moses ask Pharaoh to change? Why do you think so? What are God and Moses trying to do? Why is the request made this way? What does God really intend to do? Is this playing fair?

3. List the various levels of administration that you find in the Egyptian control of their slaves (5:4, 5, 10-18, 21). Did the system seem to work? What role did the Israelites themselves play in this organization? What does this tell us about the plight of the Israelites?

4. Using a Bible dictionary and/or other sources, find out all you can about brickmaking in ancient Egypt. Why was straw important? How much extra work was Pharaoh requiring of the Israelites when they had to find their own straw?

5. Some versions, such as the KJV and RSV, translate verses 22 and 23 to read that the Lord has "done evil" to His people Israel. How does this differ from the NIV? What do you think Moses is really trying to say in these verses about God and His action?

■ Exploring the Word

God vs. Pharaoh

Fresh from their successful meeting with the elders of Israel, Moses and Aaron go to Pharaoh. They seem to think that if God can make Israel and her leaders believe and worship, He can do the same with the Egyptian ruler. The two brothers have a rude awakening. Pharaoh is not moved. God has clearly promised Israel's deliverance, but the *how* and *when* are not yet discerned by Moses and Aaron. They and Israel (as well as Pharaoh) have some learning to do, and this part of Exodus is the story about how that begins to happen.

The two Israelite leaders confront Pharaoh directly, like prophets. What they are saying is what the Lord, the God of Israel, commands. They have met God, and Pharaoh is expected to obey what this God of theirs says (vss. 1, 3). We can only guess at the amazement that must have overcome the onlookers at the Egyptian palace as these two leaders of a slave people speak so audaciously to the ruler of the most powerful nation on earth.

Pharaoh is unimpressed. He does not know this God, and he will certainly not let his Israelite slaves go free (vs. 2). He proceeds to make life more difficult for the slaves by making them work even harder. When they complain, he doesn't soften, but simply calls them lazy.

Note that the same phrase "thus says" is used of both the Lord and Pharaoh (vss. 1, 10). Scholars often called this phrase the "messenger formula." Prophets and messengers of other people in authority are typical users of the phrase. It signals us that two major authority figures are addressing each other.

The Israelite leaders complain to Moses (5:20, 21) and call down judgment upon him for the trouble he has brought to them. Moses, in turn, cries out his complaint to God and asks Why? (vss. 22, 23). He clearly sees God as the One who is behind all Pharaoh's actions.

The narrative thus makes clear that this contest is not being played out just on the human level. Moses and Aaron are not fighting an Egyptian. *The Lord*, the God of Israel, is in direct conflict with the ruler of the greatest nation on earth and his gods. What transpires is to be seen as a cosmic conflict of the gods to prove who really is in charge of things. Yahweh will act decisively in His own way and in His own time, for He alone rules.

Even Yahweh's allies do not understand this clearly. Notice that no command was given to Moses and Aaron to go before Pharaoh at this time. Only later, after the experience and revelations of chapters 5 and 6, does the Lord specifically command the two Israelite brothers to go before the Egyptian ruler (6:29; 7:2). Moses and the Israelites have lessons that they need to learn, and the conflict with Pharaoh must be one in which *all* parties involved come to understand who God is and what He is about. God's timing and procedures are important and must be followed. Even God's messengers must realize that God's timetable, not theirs, must govern actions. In the end, convincing proof of Yahweh's power and salvation will be given, and this is the prelude to that experience.

A Festival for Worship

Moses' initial request to Pharaoh (vs. 1) is that Israel be allowed to hold a festival for worship in the desert. This Hebrew word is usually used to designate a pilgrimage festival with a procession. The aim may have been to return in pilgrimage to the place where Moses had his original meeting with God, since God's earlier promise had been made that Israel would meet Him there (3:12). Exodus 5:3 quotes Moses as requesting permission to take a three-day journey into the desert to sacrifice to the Lord. Sacrifices would have been a natural part of any festival in that culture.

When Pharaoh balks, the two brothers give him an additional compelling reason for the trip: The Lord will strike Israel with plagues and with the sword (death) if they do not go to the desert to worship Him. Nowhere has God made such a statement to Moses. One cannot help but wonder if Moses really believes this, or if he says it to convince the Egyptian ruler to let the people go.

When God spoke to Moses about the deliverance of the people, He clearly said that He was sending Moses to get Israel out of Egypt (3:10; see also 6:11, 13, 27; 7:2). They would then be given their own land to dwell in (6:8). On the other hand, when Moses is given instructions to speak to Pharaoh, he is told to ask permission for the people to go into the desert to worship (3:18; 7:16). Even near the end of the plagues, Pharaoh seems to be operating on the idea that Israel is just going on a worship expedition into the wilderness (10:24).

What is going on here? Is this deliberate deception of Pharaoh?

Pharaoh probably would not have even listened to Moses and Aaron if the initial request had been an outright request for freedom. The simple petition to worship was at least reasonable. Somewhere along the way, the Egyptian ruler would have caught on to what the Israelites were really asking for, but to openly accede to the freedom of the Israelites would have meant weakness and loss of face to Pharaoh. To give permission for a period of worship and then have them flee was easier. Probably all parties knew this and played along because it was to everyone's advantage. It was most likely an adaptation to the prevailing culture.

On the other hand, we should also ask ourselves the reason for Israel's deliverance from Egypt. Why do they need to come out into their own land? Isn't worship the most basic issue? Sacrifice to Yahweh was detestable to the Egyptians, and they could have been stoned for doing it (8:26). Israel must be able to worship the Lord freely. The request to come out of Egypt in order to worship is the most profound and basic of all reasons for the Exodus. If Yahweh is indeed the Lord of all, He must be worshiped.

Bible students cannot help but compare this Israelite exodus for the sake of worship with the final exodus from this world to the heavenly Canaan. The issue in the final conflict is also one of worship. God must deliver His people from the persecution of those who would force the false worship of the beast so that they can worship the true God in the right way (Rev. 14:6-12). The issue for all people in each age is whether they will worship the kings and kingdoms of this world or the King and kingdom of the Lord, the true God.

Slavery and Bricks

The pharaoh and the Egypt that Moses and the Lord confront are formidable enemies. The system of slavery that they have devised is a clever one (5:4, 6, 10-18, 21). Pharaoh is obviously at the top. Below him are slave drivers and foremen. The slave drivers are Egyptian overlords, but the foremen are clearly Israelites (5:15). When brickmaking quotas are not met, the slave drivers who have appointed the foremen beat these foremen. These foremen undoubtedly would also have the prerogative of beating the Israelites working under them. In this sense, at the grass-roots level, Israelites are making Israelites work. These Israelite foremen are undoubtedly given some privileges. At least we know they seem to have had the option of taking their problems to Pharaoh (5:15). The Egyptians have forced the Israelites themselves to become part of the enforcement of their own slavery!

Pharaoh responds to the Israelites' request for time off to worship by requiring them to make the same number of bricks as before but also to find their own straw.

Straw was a vital part of brickmaking for two reasons. First, it was a binding material that made the bricks stronger. Second, the decomposition of the organic straw released a substance that increased brick strength and elasticity. Bricks made with straw were three times stronger than the same bricks without straw. They did not shrink or crack in the same way (Nims, 25, 26).

This being the case, there is no way Pharaoh is going to allow bricks to be made without straw. Previously, the Egyptians had brought in the straw, but now the Israelites must find their own straw, probably by gathering stubble from the fields. The extra work makes it impossible to fulfill the brick quotas set by the slave drivers, which are probably between 2,000 and 2,500 bricks per day per slave.

This makes it easy to understand why the Israelite foremen are so angry with Moses and Aaron. The Israelites as a whole undoubtedly feel the same way. No wonder the two leaders are waiting to see what the results of the foremen's visit to Pharaoh are (5:20). They have a big stake in this issue!

For this reason, Moses is upset with God. Why has all this happened? According to Moses, God has "brought trouble upon" (NIV) or "done evil to" (RSV) Israel. Problems, difficulties, and punishments are often called "evil" in older translations. Remember when reading these translations that "evil" should not be understood as sin but simply as events that the people see as troublesome. When God seems to be in charge, it is easy to attribute everything, even the bad things, to Him. What Moses and Israel are about to learn is that this is all part of God's plan, and soon they will see God work.

We should also notice that God does not get upset by Moses' accusations. Instead, He responds with a long message of hope and encouragement based on what He has done and will do for Israel and to Pharaoh. This message is what we will study in depth in our next section.

■ Getting Into the Word

Exodus 6:1–7:7

Read through Exodus 6:1–7:7 at least twice. As you read it, think about the following questions:

1. **Notice the time-related word that the Lord uses in 6:1 (*now*). In light of Moses' and Aaron's earlier encounter with Pharaoh and all the events of Exodus 5, what significance does this word have? How does this word and the time frame that it sets up influence all that takes place in this section? Why do you think God has waited to use this word until this time?**
2. **List the things mentioned in Exodus 6:2-5 that have not**

changed about God since the days of Abraham, and also note one thing that has changed. What does this change in God's name mean? Why does God mention it here? The word for *God Almighty* (6:3, NIV) is *el Shaddai* in Hebrew. Using a Bible dictionary or concordance, look up other places where this title occurs, and try to discover its meaning.

3. Exodus 6:6-8 gives a list of wonderful promises that the Lord makes for Israel, each beginning with the words *I will* in the NIV. Write down this list of seven specific promises. Ponder the phrase that begins and ends this section. What do you think this phrase means, and why is it stated here twice? What was Israel's response to these promises (vs. 9), and what is the reason for it? What can we learn from this?

4. Compare the genealogy of Exodus 6:14-27 with the one in Genesis 46:8-27. Why does the Exodus genealogy leave out some of the names? What names does it add? Why? Note carefully the introduction and conclusion to this genealogy. How do these verses help us understand the purpose of this list of names?

5. In Exodus 6:30–7:2, the Lord more specifically outlines the way He is going to communicate to Pharaoh. What are the steps in God's methodology? What does this tell us about the nature of prophecy? What does this tell us about how God communicates with people?

6. In Exodus 7:3, 4, God says that He will "harden" Pharaoh's heart. This idea was first mentioned in Exodus 4:21. Using a concordance, look up and list all the references to hardening of hearts in Exodus. There are clearly differences in the way these statements are made. What are these differences? What do they mean? What is really happening in God's encounter with Pharaoh? Does Pharaoh have free choice? Explain your answer. Why does the Bible use this terminology, and what is it trying to teach by using it?

■ Exploring the Word

"Now"

Significantly, this passage opens with God speaking, and His first word is *now*. Hebrew usually puts the most important word in the sentence at the beginning, and this word begins the sentence in Hebrew as well as in English. The word means "at the present moment" or "in the present situation."

The passage does not seek to explain why the problems of Exodus 5 have occurred. No blame is placed, but *now*, as opposed to some other time, God is about to act decisively for His people. Earlier, God has promised certain things, but without specifying *when* they will happen, at least insofar as His intentions regarding Pharaoh are concerned. But at the beginning of chapter 6, He makes it clear that the time has come.

Everything that follows in this section must be read in light of this word *now*. Before, we had future promises; now, we have present action. Before, Moses may have acted in advance of God's timing, but at this time God says *now*—go see Pharaoh *NOW!* Moses obeys the command (7:6). It often happens that God's messengers attempt to do God's will before the divine NOW of God's timing comes, but here, Moses acts within God's timing.

Some have seen this section as a restatement of Moses' call. This may be true from the standpoint that some of the same things are covered. The context, however, is different. Before, we had a general statement of mission and a call to it. Now, we have a specific statement that this is the time for certain things to happen, and immediate action is called for. Further details are also given that apply to the specific situation.

Yahweh Acts

The God who comes to Moses is the same in many ways as the God of Abraham, Isaac, and Jacob, who appeared to the patriarchs as God Almighty (*el Shaddai*—see 6:3). Genesis 17:1; 28:3;

35:11; and 48:3 use this terminology for God. Most scholars believe it refers to His power, although some see it as meaning "mountain." If so, it could well mean "firm," "solid," and/or "high," like a mountain peak. Exodus here clearly sees this term for God as characteristic of the patriarchal period.

This God is also the same in that He has established His covenant with both the patriarchs and Israel and promised to give them the land of Canaan. God has remembered His earlier covenant and has heard the groans of Israel in their slavery.

There is, however, a major difference. God tells Moses that by the name or title *the Lord* (Yawheh) He did *not* make Himself known to the patriarchs. He was known to them as God Almighty, not as Yahweh, the Lord. What does God mean?

Obviously, the stories of the patriarchs in Genesis contain the name *Yahweh*. Exodus wants us to understand that this name/title was put in the story at a later date when Genesis was written down. The *revelation* of the name is first given in Exodus 3:14. The passage we are studying now uses the name often. Particularly it emphasizes the phrase *I am the Lord* (see 6:2, 6, 8, 29). The section seems to come to a grand climax in Exodus 7:5, when, in conclusion to all that the Lord is to do, "the Egyptians will know that I am the Lord."

All this points to the fact that this name/title, the most important name and most basic title for God in the Old Testament, is vitally connected to the Exodus deliverance. God was not keeping something from Abraham, Isaac, and Jacob. They did not know God as Yahweh because they had not experienced the Exodus. This is why the title is emphasized in this section, and forms an envelope of both front and back to the magnificent sevenfold "I will" promises of 6:6-8 and the conclusion to the experience of Egypt (7:5). Yahweh is Yahweh because He both wonderfully delivers Israel and powerfully judges Egypt. Both nations come to know Him and the meaning of His name by the Exodus experience. To say the very name, *Lord*, is to evoke all the memories of deliverance and peoplehood that the Exodus symbolized.

To a slave freed by the Emancipation Proclamation, the name

Abraham Lincoln was not just the name of a president of the United States. That name evoked all the love, respect, and adoration due one who had enabled an oppressed people to pass from slavery to freedom. The name *Yahweh* functioned in this way for the Israelites, who received the gift of peoplehood from the Lord. Just think what this Lord *now* promises to do (6:6-8):

- I will bring you out from under the yoke of the Egyptians.
- I will free you from being slaves to them.
- I will redeem you with an outstretched arm and with mighty acts of judgment.
- I will take you as *My* own people.
- I will be your God.
- I will bring you to the land I swore with uplifted hand to give to Abraham, to Isaac, and to Jacob.
- I will give it to you as a possession.

The emphatic promise, **"I am the Lord!"** closes this section and pledges fulfillment.

I believe that the same God is alive and well and is willing and able to do the same things today for those who cry out to Him in their slavery. Israel was so discouraged by their oppression and their cruel bondage that they could not listen or respond to this wonderful revelation (6:9). Many today cannot respond to the gracious gifts of the Exodus God, because they have been so beaten up they can't even hear the good promises that God gives. They need living demonstrations of God's power, and they need leaders like Moses who are willing to risk moving ahead in the faith that Yahweh is indeed able to do what He has promised.

Leaders

In the first part of chapter 6, we are assured that now is the right time for this deliverance. The genealogy that we find in the verses following (vss. 13-27) declares to us that we also now have the right people for the job—Moses and Aaron.

When we compare this genealogy with the one in Genesis 46:8-27, we see some notable differences. The genealogies are basically the same only for the first three sons of Jacob—Reuben, Simeon, and Levi. The rest of the Exodus 6 genealogy is an expansion that covers the family of Levi. Moses and Aaron are of the family of Levi, and it is clear that they are the focus of this list of names. Both the introduction (6:13, 14a) and conclusion (6:26, 27) make it clear that this genealogy is about these two brothers and that they indeed are the ones whom God is using to deliver Israel.

In the Bible, genealogies are about legitimacy. If these two men are to be leaders, they need to be legitimized, not only by the action of God through them but also by being true Israelites who can trace their lineage back to the patriarchs. This list of names serves this purpose.

The name list clearly emphasizes Aaron over Moses. Aaron is mentioned before Moses. Aaron's wife, four of his sons, and one of his grandsons are named. Even three sons of his cousin Korah are named. No one in Moses' family is named. One could surmise that Moses, by virtue of his leadership, needed little help to be respected and honored. But it seems more likely that there were significant questions about Aaron, and thus greater pains were taken to show how important he really was. Even the summary statement at the end of the genealogy (6:26) reverses the normal order of names and places Aaron before Moses. We should also remember that Aaron's family become the priests of Israel. Proof of lineage is even more important for priests than it is for the average Israelite. God wanted to make sure Aaron and the priesthood he began had proper respect.

Divine Methodology

The right time has come. The right people are in leadership—legitimized by both their action and their lineage. Now it is time to get the right methodology for approaching the ruler of Egypt. God graciously supplies that need in the next section of the text

(6:28–7:7). He also outlines the results that are to be expected from this methodology.

Step one is to see that God is in charge of the whole process. Yahweh says, "*I* am the Lord. Tell Pharaoh king of Egypt everything *I* tell you" (6:28). All the messages that Moses gives as well as their total content are of divine origin. Moses is a leader only in the sense that he is a messenger of the divine oracle.

Moses objects that he has "faltering lips" (vs. 30). Either he is not a good speaker, or he has forgotten so much Egyptian that he feels uneasy expressing himself in public. Never mind, says the Lord, "Aaron will help." Moses will speak, and Aaron will relay the message to Pharaoh.

This passage has often been used to show the true work of a prophet. Moses is like God to Aaron, who is like a prophet to Pharaoh. The clear idea is that prophets don't manufacture their own speeches but only pass on what they have heard from God. In this way, Pharaoh is to receive God's messages and know with certainty that he is to let the Israelites go.

In response to this message, a fourfold sequence of events will take place: (1) God will harden Pharaoh's heart. (2) God will do signs and wonders, and Pharaoh will listen. (3) Through mighty acts of judgment, God will bring Israel out of Egypt. (4) This will cause Egypt to know that "I am the Lord."

This passage is clearly a conclusion to the renewed commissioning of Moses and an introduction to the next section of the book, where God proceeds to do the thing He has outlined.

A Hardened Heart

This is an appropriate place to comment in some detail on step one in the above fourfold series of events—the hardening of Pharaoh's heart. The question has long engaged Bible students in Westen culture, who are concerned about freedom of choice. Did God force Pharaoh to do evil things and then punish him for doing them? Is this fair? What is going on here?

The first thing we can say with certainty is that Pharaoh does have some choice in the matter. God has not just arbitrarily decided something and is now playing with the Egyptian to work things out.

Pharaoh's freedom of choice is clear from the very wording of Scripture itself. While there are nine to ten passages that speak of God hardening Pharaoh's heart, six others say simply that Pharaoh's heart was hardened without naming the hardening agent (see 7:13, 15, 22; 8:19; 9:7, 35). Even more important are three passages that say Pharaoh hardened his own heart (8:15, 32; 9:34). The Bible thus sees both God and Pharaoh as responsible for this heart hardness.

The flow of the story in the Scripture itself makes it clear that Pharaoh had freedom to act. Exodus 10:1 states that God has hardened the heart of Pharaoh and his officials. As you read on, you discover, however, that Pharaoh's officials urge the ruler to give in to the demands of Moses and Aaron (10:7). Pharaoh himself initially gives in and tells the Israelite leaders to go. Only later does he forbid them to go over the issue of who exactly will be leaving (10:8-11). Moses and Aaron themselves make continual appeals to Pharaoh to change. Both the response of the Egyptians and the appeals of the Israelite brothers would be meaningless if both parties understood God's hardening to be some arbitrary act that deprived people of a personal choice.

Why then, you might ask, do God and Moses use this kind of terminology? Wouldn't it have been better to use words that are less open to misunderstanding? I believe God wanted to make a strong statement of His ability to work in the heart of the Egyptian ruler. In Moses' day many people saw their gods working only among their own people and on their own geographical turf. Moses and Aaron needed to have the assurance that the Lord was ruler of Egypt as well as of Israel. He could manifest Himself to Pharaoh as well as to Moses. In their fear and questioning, the Israelite brothers needed to have the unmistakable assurance that God controlled not only their destiny, but could work in Pharaoh's heart as well.

Having taught Exodus and the Pentateuch to North American college students over a period of several years, I have noticed a significant difference in the question they ask about this hardening issue as compared to the question the Israelites themselves were clearly asking. North Americans are concerned primarily . . . about God's fairness. They want people to have a fair chance to make a personal decision. If they think Pharaoh isn't given free choice, they are upset with God.

We must remember, though, that this story was written with Israelite concerns in mind, not the concerns of twentieth century Westerners. The Israelites are helpless slaves who despair of ever escaping from their desperate situation. They are not particularly worried about whether their persecutor, the tyrant Pharaoh, is given free choice. They cry out for deliverance. Their question about God is whether He can deliver on His promise of salvation. Does He really have the will and the power to bring about their deliverance? If we remember that this burning question is the Israelites' concern, we can understand why the story is told in this way. God's hardening of Pharaoh's heart is one way to say that God is at work in a powerful way even in the very soul of their most powerful enemy. Israel's reassurance, not fairness to Pharaoh, is the issue in this story.

God is in control and is clearly at work in the heart of the Egyptians. This control, however, does not destroy Pharaoh's free will. Pharaoh is given many chances to cooperate with God's plan for Israel. As long as he maintains his opposition to God's plan, however, he is bound to fail. God's sovereignty does not destroy human freedom of choice, nor does our freedom to choose leave God less sovereign. Both God's sovereignty and our freedom of choice operate together in this story.

In conclusion, Moses and Aaron in their excitement to act for God have approached Pharaoh with God's ultimatum. They are rebuffed, and as a result, Israel suffers even more. Recriminations follow.

In mercy God again communicates with Moses, and the stage is set for a second try with Pharaoh. *Now* is the time God is ready to act to save His people. *This* is how He will do it. In the next chapter, promised events begin to transpire.

■ Applying the Word

Exodus 5:1–7:7

1. Have I ever launched out to do something I felt was God's will and run into serious difficulties? What was wrong? Was it the wrong time, the wrong action, or something else? What can the story of Moses' first encounter with Pharaoh teach me?

2. Have my actions ever gotten other people into trouble? Has their response been like that of Israel to Moses and Aaron in Exodus 5:20, 21? What can I learn from Moses' response that may help me in such circumstances?

3. Have I ever felt like complaining to God when things do not go well? Did I complain, or did I squelch it? Should I be able to complain directly to God, like Moses did in Exodus 5:22, 23? Why?

4. Do I ever feel the need to hear God's promises repeated to me, or is one hearing enough? Why? Moses seems to need repeated assurances of God's presence. If I need this, is that an indication that something is wrong on my part? How often and in what ways should I be reminded of God's promises?

5. If I wrote my spiritual genealogy listing those who had facilitated my birth and growth in the spiritual realm, who would be on the list? Why? Do I give enough credit to those who have been influential in helping me in my relationship with God?

6. Have I ever seen God "harden" someone's heart? What were the circumstances? Do I really believe God can work on the heart of major opposers of divine truth? How does God work with such people, and how could I facilitate such work in my life? In the lives of others?

7. How does a person harden his or her heart against God's will? How can I recognize the temptation to do this when it comes to me? How can I best guard against yielding to such a temptation?

∎ Researching the Word

1. Read Romans 9:1-24, which deals with God's choice and hardening. Compare this passage with the Exodus verses on hardening. Do the answers given in this chapter for the Exodus hardening passages also apply for Romans? Why? Read what the *SDA Bible Commentary* says on both passages as well as the section in Fretheim's book mentioned in the Further Study section. On a Bible basis, how would you respond to someone who questioned God's fairness?

2. When Moses and Aaron asked Pharaoh to let the Israelites spend a few days in the wilderness sacrificing to their God, the Egyptian ruler responded by giving the people more work to do. Moses and Aaron were upset and complained to God: We spoke to Pharaoh as You commanded, but so far, only trouble has resulted. You haven't delivered Israel at all (5:22, 23). Scan through the Psalms, looking for those in which the songwriter expresses disappointment and frustration with God. Look also for those in which the songwriter feels frustrated but seems to understand God's way of working. Construct an answer for Moses and Aaron that is based on what you have learned.

3. Have you ever felt frustrated or angry with God for the way you felt He was leading in your life? Think of several Bible characters who felt frustrated because God did not act in the way they expected Him to. Reflect on all the circumstances of each one's life—the before and the after. With which Bible characters do you identify the most? What experiences in your life cause you to feel this identity? What lessons do these stories teach that can help you with your questions about God? Among the Bible characters you might study are the disciples at Christ's crucifixion (Luke 24:21); Job (esp. Job 1–3 and 38–42); Jonah (the book of Jonah); Habakkuk (the book

of Habakkuk); the Shunammite woman (2 Kings 4:8-37); John the Baptist (Matthew 11:1-3); Judas (Matthew 27:3-5).

■ Further Study of the Word

1. For general insight, see Ellen G. White, *Patriarchs and Prophets*, 257-263.
2. On bricks and brickmaking, see any Bible dictionary under "brick" or C. F. Nims, "Bricks Without Straw," *Biblical Archaeologist* 13, no.1 (1950), 22-28.
3. On the hardening of Pharaoh's heart, see Terence E. Fretheim, *Exodus*, 96-103.

CHAPTER FOUR

God Judges Egypt

Exodus 7:8–11:10

The contest now begins in earnest. On one side God has prepared His leaders and His plan of action. He clearly states that now is the time for things to happen. Past promises will become present realities.

On the other side, Pharaoh is already aroused. His first encounter with Moses and Aaron has left him convinced that the Israelite slaves and their God are no match for him. He has taught them a lesson about laziness, work, and who is in charge. He considers himself ready for whatever may come.

The ten plagues are the story of the critical part of that contest. They are like a championship boxing match that goes ten rounds. The struggle is not easy, because both contestants are tough and determined. The suspense builds with each round.

The Israelites and the Egyptians are not just bystanders. This struggle between Yahweh and Pharaoh affects the followers of both, for two peoples are locked in battle. Believers have no doubt that Yahweh will win. He does triumph gloriously and judge Pharaoh decisively, but the battle is real. The struggle teaches us many lessons about God and humanity. In this chapter we look at the contest in detail and study what God wants us to learn from it.

We must prepare ourselves for the meting out of judgment. Most modern people have trouble relating to this concept. Punishment is out of style. As you contemplate judgment and the ten plagues, ask yourself what the biblical concept of judgment is and what it means to you.

■ Getting Into the Word

Exodus 7:8–11:10

Please read Exodus 7:8-13 carefully. Then read 7:14–11:10
rapidly two times to get an overview of the plagues. When
you have done that, answer the following questions:

1. List the steps involved in the rod-to-serpent episode in
   7:8-14. Note in particular the reason for the event (6:9)
   and the final end of the Egyptian rods (vs. 12). Recall
   what has earlier been said in chapter 2 about the meaning of rods and snakes. In light of all this, what is the
   real significance of this event? Why does the Bible seem
   to be amazed that Pharaoh's heart is hard after this? Note
   the key role the rod plays in the story of the plagues by
   noting 7:17, 19, 20; 8:5, 16, 17; 9:23; 10:13. What might
   be comparable to a rod today?
2. Although God and Pharaoh are the key characters, they
   each have helpers. God has Aaron and Moses. Pharaoh
   has his wise men, sorcerers, and magicians. List the actions that Moses, Aaron, and the Egyptian magicians
   perform in the story. Who tends to drop away, and who
   comes on strong in the end? Do you see any pattern?
   What does it mean?
3. Find all the places where a specific purpose of the plagues
   is mentioned. What are the purposes named? Are the
   plagues accomplishing their purpose? Why? What is the
   nature of the plagues? Are they miraculous?
4. Some have suggested that the plagues were at least partially natural. Hail, frogs, locusts, etc., were natural occurrences in Egypt. On the basis of your reading, do
   you agree or disagree? Why? Could there be some mix-
   ing of the natural and miraculous? What is the evidence
   from the Bible text? What is the difference between the
   natural and the miraculous?

5. **Many patterns and progressions for the plagues have been mentioned. Some Bible students see them as beginning fairly mildly and then getting more and more destructive. The outline given in the book suggests another kind of grouping. What is that? Others have seen them as divided into three groups between the ones Aaron brings on, the ones Moses brings on, and the ones God directly brings on. On the basis of your reading, are any of these true? Do you see any other possible progressions, groupings, or patterns in these ten plagues that speak to why they are in the order given? What might a pattern mean?**

■ Exploring the Word

Of Rods and Snakes

Some students actually understand the story of the rods that become snakes as the first of the plagues. Those who do, consider the last judgment of Pharaoh—the killing of the firstborn—as a unique, separate judgment outside of the ten. Most, however, see this rod-and-snake story as a prelude or introduction to the ten judgments, and this is how we will understand the matter.

God gives Moses and Aaron the rod-to-snake routine as an answer to Pharaoh's possible desire to see them do a miracle. Since they perform it, we assume that Pharaoh asks them to do it. It is clear that such a practice is almost like a presentation of credentials. If you purport to speak for the divine or for some major authority, you are expected to show that you can do something miraculous as a demonstration of your power. God doesn't leave Moses and Aaron without their credentials.

Pharaoh, not to be outdone, calls his own magicians, and they do the same thing. Aaron's staff promptly swallows all of their staffs.

In the earlier account of the rod-to-snake demonstration, the Hebrew word used for *snakes* is the common generic term *nachash*.

In Exodus 7, although the English word is the same in the NIV and most other translations, it is different in the Hebrew—*tannin*. This word refers to a reptile of horrendous proportions, like a sea monster. Pharaoh is connected with this word in Ezekiel 29:3 and 32:2 (Durham, *Themes*, 33).

Picture the scene. Monstrous reptiles moving around the great audience room of the Pharaoh and the aggressive Aaronic reptile pursuing and devouring the Egyptian-created monsters. Not only is the scene vivid and somewhat humorous, but the message is clear. Rods represent rule, power, and authority and are like the scepters that kings use. Pharaoh is the Egyptian monster. Pharaoh's authority, represented by all those Egyptian monsters, is devoured by Aaron's single rod, representing Yahweh's power and authority. No one present should have missed the symbolism. Yahweh's power is greater than Pharaoh's and in a contest will devour and destroy it. A shiver should have gone up and down the spine of every Egyptian there. The only other reference to "swallow" in Exodus is 15:12, where the sea swallows the Egyptians. Those who fail to learn the lesson of the snake swallowing other snakes are *swallowed* by the Red Sea!

You can almost hear the amazement when Exodus comments, "Yet Pharaoh's heart became hard and he would not listen to them" (vs. 13). The result of his opposition to Yahweh has been clearly portrayed in chilling terms, yet he ignores it.

This incident directly introduces the judgments on Egypt which follow. Pharaoh has been given a chance. His end has been portrayed in striking drama, yet he refuses to listen. The only way left for God is to bring pressure on him through the plagues. Now they begin.

Before leaving this story, it is interesting to note the critical role the rod of God's leaders plays in the stories of the plagues. In at least eight verses, the rods of Moses and Aaron are the instrument of the plagues (7:17, 19, 20; 8:5, 16, 17; 9:23; 10:13). It is also clear when God says "stretch out your hand" that the rod of authority is usually assumed to be in their hand (compare, for example, 10:12, 13). By the end of these judgments, the Egyptians must have quaked when they saw the rod of Yahweh. One wonders what the rod of Yahweh's authority can be compared to today. Who wields it? How does it go into action?

The Contestants

We cannot emphasize too much that this whole section is a battle or contest between Yahweh and Pharaoh, between truth and falsehood, between freedom and slavery, and between good and evil. Yahweh and Pharaoh, however, use other people. We now turn our attention to them.

Moses and Aaron are God's representatives. The differing roles they play are fascinating. In the first three plagues, God gives His commands to Moses, but Aaron actually is the agent to bring the plagues (see 7:19; 8:5, 6, 16, 17). In plagues four and five, God is the direct agent (8:24; 9:5). In plagues six, seven, eight, and nine, Moses acts as the direct agent of God (9:8, 10; 10:12, 21). Finally, in plague ten, God works directly again (12:12).

We are not sure exactly what this means, but the section of the story that we are now considering does seem to give an increasingly important role to Moses, and Aaron fades somewhat into the background. Perhaps Moses is remembering more and more of his Egyptian and gaining confidence in his leadership. If this is the case, his dependence on Aaron as a spokesman decreases. Both, however, continue to function as a leadership team.

Another factor to consider is that Aaron is especially active when the Egyptian magicians are on the scene. This means that when the first three plagues are over and Pharaoh's miracle workers disappear, so does Aaron's prominent role. With these competitors gone, Moses seems able to care for things himself.

These "magicians" of Pharaoh with their "secret acts" come as somewhat of a surprise in the story (7:11, 22; 8:7, 18, 19). They are able to duplicate the introductory miracle of the rod-to-snake change and the first two plagues. They fail, however, to turn dust into gnats and thus reproduce the third plague. After that, they disappear from the scene.

We know that magic played a very important role in Egyptian life and religion. It ranged all the way from protective magic against evil to productive magic to ease childbirth and aid in lovemaking (see Douglas, 766-771). The wonder working mentioned here was common and is found in other ancient literature. Other contests between Egyptian magicians and foreign wonder workers also appear. Yahweh evidently felt it important to defeat the Egyptian magicians as part of the Exodus process. It only took three plagues to do so. At that time they recognize the finger of God (8:19) in the work of Moses and Aaron, but their leader's heart remains hard.

We cannot tell from this Bible text whether they did their work by sleight of hand or the use of spirit powers. There is, however, some evidence that the rod-to-snake trick may have had some natural basis (Douglas, 769-770). Similar feats are still performed in Egypt today. The magicians are not named in Exodus, but Jewish tradition and 2 Timothy 3:8 call them Jannes and Jambres.

Why These Plague Judgments?

If you look closely at the passages on the plagues, you will be amazed at how rich and varied are the reasons given for these events. The most obvious reason, as well as the most often stated, is that Pharaoh is unyielding. God wants to see His people free, and Pharaoh keeps refusing or saying Yes and then changing his mind. Thus God must keep sending judgments.

Beyond that, a wide number of reasons are stated. God wants the Egyptians to know who He is and see His power (7:17). They must come to realize there is no one like Him (8:10). And the scope is even broader: God desires His name to be known and proclaimed in "all the earth" (9:16). Thus the plagues have worldwide "evangelistic" purpose. God wants the world to respond to Him.

The plagues also let both sides know that there is a distinction between Israelites and Egyptians (8:23). Beginning with the plague of flies, the land of Goshen, where the Israelites reside, is spared the plagues. Judgment and plagues fall on Egyptian territory only.

God also performs this large number of judgments to "multiply wonders" (11:9) so the Israelites can tell their descendants what God did (10:1, 2). In the end, the plagues also make it possible for the Israelites to collect a great deal of wealth from the Egyptians as they leave (11:2)—perhaps as "back pay" for their years of service as slaves.

Clearly the God of Exodus wants to give unmistakable reasons for His actions. He is not arbitrarily inflicting the Egyptians with pain and suffering. His hand is forced by Pharaoh and his negative response. God can take these very judgments, which He wishes were not necessary, and turn them into powerful lessons, not only for Egypt and Israel, but for the whole world.

Plagues—Natural or Miraculous?

Wide discussion has taken place among Bible students as to the exact nature of the plagues (see Ramm, 62, 63). Are they miraculous, natural, or some combination of both? Are they acts of God directly, or are they acts of nature that God uses to secure the release of His people?

Some have viewed the plagues as highly dramatized natural events that led to problems in Egypt and to the release of Israelite slaves. These people have pointed out that all of the plagues outside the death of the firstborn were events that took place fairly often in Egypt. For example, the water-to-blood plague could have been caused by an algae that typically turns the water of the Nile red. Others have tried to combine the natural and the supernatural. The plagues were natural phenomena that were heightened and timed by the addition of miraculous factors coming from God's direct intervention.

The problem with all this is that it doesn't really fit with the Bible. It may help some twentieth-century people feel better about Exodus to believe that these were natural phenomena, but this is not what the Bible says. The Nile water did *not* become *like* blood, but was "changed into blood" (8:17). Fish died, and the river stank.

Each of the plagues is attributed to the direct action of God or

His work through Moses and/or Aaron. The whole point of this is that these are acts of God to deliver His people. Thus to call them natural not only violates the story as told in Scripture, but it lessens God's ability to save.

God is, after all, a good communicator. He deals with items that are part of the Egyptian setting. He does not turn the Amazon to blood or bring diseases to polar bears. All the plagues deal with things that relate directly to the Egyptian experience. The point is that God miraculously uses things relevant to the Egyptian setting so they will make sense to His audience.

Patterns to the Plagues

Scholars who have studied the plagues have found numerous possible patterns and progressions to them. In this section we look at some of the suggestions they have made.

Since most commentators argue that the whole plague sequence is related to the contest between Yahweh and Pharaoh and his gods, they note a religious pattern to the plagues. They see all the plagues as striking in some sense or another at the gods of Egypt. Some possibilities are as follows: The Nile was worshiped; therefore, turning the Nile to blood insults the divine river. There was a frog god called Heket who was related to midwives and childbearing. The plague of frogs struck against that god. The list could go on (for one list, see Ramm, 61).

While in general it is true that Yahweh worked against the Egyptian gods, scholars are by no means agreed. Exactly which gods were acted against and how each plague destroyed their influence is not clear.

Various ways to group the plagues have also been suggested. My outline of Exodus suggests that they are in pairs, with each pair dealing with a similar problem. As mentioned earlier, some divide the plagues into those with Aaron as agent (1-3), God as agent (4, 5, 10), and Moses as agent (6-9).

Others point out that in the first five plagues, Pharaoh's heart "became hard." Only beginning in plague six does God make

Pharaoh's heart hard. Thus Pharaoh's heart is only made hard by God after he has hardened it himself.

While all these patterns are interesting and do have some element of truth, the one most obvious to me is that things get progressively worse. The first several plagues are basically a nuisance rather than harmful to people. As things progress, each plague, with the possible exception of the darkness, seems to get more serious and more injurious. The climax, of course, is the death of all the firstborn. God in a sense is progressively turning up the heat on Pharaoh, giving him a chance to respond each step of the way. He refuses until his own son is taken from him.

Of major importance is the length of the process: It gives Israel time to begin understanding the power of God as it is repeatedly shown. It proclaims Yahweh's long-term commitment to Israel's salvation. The process demonstrates to the Egyptians God's patience and His desire for them to let Israel go before He has to do something more drastic. The plague judgments are a lengthy process that take increasingly drastic turns as Pharaoh refuses to obey.

In this section we have looked at the larger picture of the plagues as a whole. In the next section we will focus on the individual plagues. We have seen the forest. Now we examine the trees.

■ Getting Into the Word

Exodus 7:15–11:10

Read Exodus 7:15–11:10 at least twice, with attention to the details of the plagues. As you read, write down on a piece of paper for each of the ten plagues:

1. What exactly took place in this plague?
2. Who was the agent causing the plague, and how did this agent operate?
3. What was the result of the plague?
4. Are there any statements about how the plague was relieved or stopped? What are they?

5. **Are there any unique or special elements in this particular plague?**
6. **Is there any statement about the significance of this plague?**

■ Exploring the Word

Plagues One and Two—Water Problems

In the first plague the Nile and other Egyptian water is turned into blood. The interesting thing about this plague is that Pharaoh has no idea how God will act. Thus Moses and Aaron intercept him as he goes to the bank of the Nile. Pharaoh must be at the scene to see with his own eyes the reason for the blood.

What a powerful way to open the series of Yahweh's judgments! At the river, in the presence of Pharaoh and his officials, God's messengers say exactly what they are going to do, and they do it. The predicted results follow. The water turns to blood, the fish die, the river stinks, and the water cannot be drunk.

Pharaoh's magicians also turn water into blood. One wonders why Pharaoh didn't ask them to turn the blood back into water! Be that as it may, Pharaoh does not listen to Moses and Aaron but returns to his palace.

Ezekiel 29:3 quotes Pharaoh as saying, "The Nile is mine, I made it for myself." We cannot be sure whether this particular pharaoh said this, because it was probably a common idea in Egypt. The point is that this plague should have given him pause to think about the truth of his "theology."

While we cannot in any scientific or historic sense prove that this plague really happened, we do have some interesting Egyptian texts. The river Nile as blood is mentioned in a catalog of catastrophes that describes disastrous conditions in Egypt during the middle kingdom (2300–2250 B.C.). The particular text in which this is found dates from about the time of the Exodus and recounts an earlier event. A line from the text says, "Why really, the river is blood" (Durham, *Exodus*, 98).

The first plague concerns what happens to the water itself. The second plague has to do with what comes out of the water—frogs. When Pharaoh refuses to let Israel worship, God uses Aaron to bring the amphibians everywhere. If we can picture the scene at all, it must strike us as funny. Pharaoh's bed, bedroom, and kitchen do not escape the onslaught. Yuck!

Again, Egyptian magicians duplicate the feat and simply add to the problem. Why can't they get rid of the frogs instead of making more of them? But they can't, because Pharaoh has to ask the hated Israelite leaders to get rid of the frogs. Pharaoh's servants apparently found ways to get uncontaminated (nonblood) water to drink, but frogs in bed is too much.

Pharaoh promises to let Israel go and worship, but then he reneges on his promise. This comes after Moses gets rid of the frogs exactly at the time Pharaoh specifies. The Lord has struck again, but Pharaoh sees relief coming and hardens his heart. As we look at these first two plagues, we begin to get a clear idea of the message that is portrayed: Yahweh's word is all powerful. Even though Israel and her leaders appear in the rational eyes of humans to be powerless, as people of God they have His word, and that is all they need. In the face of that power, the worldly power of Pharaoh is worthless. He can only ask for help and relief. We also see how hard it is for the oppressor to give up on his oppression. Oppressors don't let go easily. Pharaoh reverses himself the minute the pressure is off. Only as pressure increases again do we begin to get another positive response from him.

Plagues Three and Four—Insect Problems

The NIV calls the third plague gnats. Aaron strikes the dust of the ground with his staff, and swarms of gnats come upon people and animals.

The Hebrew word has been variously translated as gnats, swarms of gnats, lice, mosquitoes, and maggots. The harvester gnat, the anopheles mosquito, and the sandfly have all been suggested.

For the first time, the Egyptian magicians are said to fail. They cannot produce gnats, much less get rid of them. Since they cannot replicate this activity, they warn Pharaoh that God or a god is in action here. They do not name Yahweh, but rather, say that this is "the finger of God" or "a god," as some believe it should be translated (Durham, *Exodus*, 106). They do not yet know the true God, but they recognize divine power when they see it. Pharaoh's heart remains hard even though his own magicians see the hand of God in the work of Moses and Aaron.

The Hebrew word *flies* in plague four comes from the word *mix* or *mixture* (Durham, *Exodus*, 107). While this mixture of flying insects is usually translated as flies, some say it would be biting or stinging flies, though nothing in the text says they sting.

For the first time in the plague story, the land of Goshen is specifically said to be spared. God says He will put a distinction between His people and the Egyptians. This is a "miraculous sign" (8:23). Interestingly enough, the Hebrew says that God will put a "deliverance" between His people and Pharaoh's people. What a powerful way to state the case! Deliverance from these flies is a powerful sign of Israel's ultimate deliverance from their bondage as slaves.

Under the onslaught of the flies, Pharaoh shows his first signs of weakening. Israel can sacrifice and worship, he says, if they do so inside the country. Moses bargains for more, and Pharaoh says, OK, you can go to the desert, but not very far!

On this basis, Moses prays for God to remove the flies. When the flying nuisances disappear, so does Pharaoh's promise of freedom to worship. Pharaoh hardens his heart. More pressure and plagues must follow.

Plagues Five and Six—Disease on Animals and Humans

The march of plagues continues with bodily afflictions on humans and animals. The disease on domestic animals, which causes death, afflicts only Egyptian livestock. Pharaoh sends inspectors to Goshen to see if any Israelite animals have died. They haven't, but Pharaoh still has a hard heart, even though his own flocks and herds are clearly afflicted.

The text says, "All the livestock of the Egyptians died" (9:6). The question has arisen as to where the animals of plagues six (9:10) and seven (9:19) come from. First, the animals involved in plague six need not necessarily have been the livestock mentioned in 9:20. They could be types of domestic animals like dogs and cats. It should also be noted that 9:3 specifically says "livestock *in the field*." A careful reading of the text implies that while livestock in the field all died, stabled or penned livestock may not have. This would be one way to explain the existence of livestock after plague five. It is also possible that the Egyptians bought new animals from the Israelites, whose flocks and herds were spared the disease of plague five.

Plague six has several unique twists. First, this plague of boils on animals and humans is caused when Moses tosses two handfuls of soot or ashes from a furnace into the air. The symbolism is clear: As the fine dust settles over the land, so will the boils settle on living beings in Egypt.

Also, this plague is the last one that uses Aaron's name. In the last four plagues, only Moses is mentioned. Aaron is not the only one disappearing from the scene, however. Although the magicians have not been mentioned since their failure in plague three, they are probably present at the interview that Moses and Aaron have with Pharaoh in plagues four and five. This is suggested by the fact that the author of Exodus calls attention to their absence in the sixth plague. The reason they are not present seems obvious: they are so afflicted by boils that they can't appear before Moses and Aaron. Yet in spite of the humiliation of his magicians, Pharaoh still doesn't listen to God or Moses.

Plagues Seven and Eight—Crops Destroyed

These plagues have the longest descriptions of the ten. The seventh, hail, is the longest, and the eighth, locusts, is the second longest.

The seventh plague begins with a warning. Pharaoh is told to let the people of Israel go, or God will send the full force of His plagues (note the plural, vs. 14) against Pharaoh, his officials, and his people. Pharaoh has done enough to deserve death. The only reason he is still around is that God wants to use the situation for the purpose of teaching people who He is (9:15, 16). Still, Pharaoh does not respond, so God must finish the matter. This introduces the last four plagues. They will strike the people of Egypt, and they will complete God's purposes.

However, God still offers a way of escape to those who are willing to obey Him. He warns the people to find shelter for themselves and their livestock before the hail begins to fall. Those who ignore the warning suffer the consequences. The land of Goshen is again spared the terrible hailstorm. Hail kills the animals and people who are caught outdoors and destroys many crops and much vegetation. Wheat and spelt are spared, however. For the first time, human lives are lost.

For the first time, also, Pharaoh acknowledges that he has sinned and asks Moses to pray for "a lifting of the plague." Moses prays for the plague's lifting, even though he knows the Egyptian officials and their leader do not really fear Yahweh.

Sure enough, when the hail stops, Pharaoh and his officials harden their hearts and do not let Israel go. Even loss of life and crops does not bring them to stop their oppressive ways. How hard it is for oppressors to release their slaves!

In the eighth plague, whatever crops escaped the hail are eaten by locusts. This devastation of their food supply must have sent a collective chill of fear down the backs of the Egyptians.

The plague begins with the statement of Pharaoh's hardness of heart (and the hardness of his officials' as well). This is a change, since previously the mention of hardened hearts has occurred at the end of each plague. The eighth plague also opens with a statement of what the plague means to the Israelites and their posterity—they will know who Yahweh is.

Moses gives prior warning to Pharaoh, and for the first time, his officials beg him to let Israel go. Their argument is the progressive ruination of their country. And Pharaoh agrees—on condition that only the men go. Women and children must stay. Moses says everyone must go. Pharaoh retorts, "The Lord would *really* be with you if I let women and children go!" (my interpretation of 10:10). "No!"

Moses responds by stretching his staff over Egypt, and God causes a strong east wind to blow the rest of the day and throughout the night. The following day the ground is black with locusts. The creatures devour every plant that remains from the hail, so that the land is stripped of its vegetation.

And again the familiar pattern comes into play. Pharaoh asks for mercy, and Moses and God oblige. God reverses the wind to a strong west wind, and by the following day, not a locust remains. Yet Pharaoh's heart is hardened. He will not let Israel go.

By now we can clearly sense the impending doom of Pharaoh and Egypt and the irresistible, unchanging will of Yahweh to deliver His people.

Plagues Nine and Ten—Darkness and Death

Plague number nine commences abruptly. No warning to Pharaoh is recorded. On God's command, Moses stretches out his hand (probably holding the rod!) to the sky, and an oppressive "felt" darkness covers Egypt for three days. Israel again escapes the plague.

This plague causes Pharaoh to temporarily weaken and agree that all Israel except their livestock can go. Moses refuses, saying that the livestock will be needed to make sacrifices when they worship.

Instead of hardening at the end of the encounter in this plague, Pharaoh's heart is hardened while he is still talking to Moses. He orders Moses to leave his presence and never appear before him again. If he does, he will die. Moses replies ironically, "Just as you say, I will never appear before you again" (vs. 29).

The question arises as to what is so terrible about this plague. After the devastation of animals and crops, what is so bad about a few days of darkness. Why does it push Pharaoh to make concessions he has never made before?

Part of it must be the fear factor. The supernatural darkness is so dense that people can't see each other. The effect must have been terrifying, especially since no one knew how long the darkness would last. Imagine how you would feel if the sun should fail to come up tomorrow morning!

Probably even more important was the symbolic nature of the act. The eternally rising sun was a given in Egypt. People thought the sun could not be destroyed. Re, the sun god, was the chief source of creative life. Something stronger than Re and the sun was obviously at work in this darkness. Not only the physical darkness but the theological meaning of the darkness and its practical implications must have totally unnerved the Egyptians. Their lives were literally and symbolically thrown into chaos.

Plague ten is anticipated but not spelled out in detail in this passage (chap. 11). Plague ten will be an act of Yahweh. As Aaron was once prominent but gradually gave way to Moses, so Moses begins to fade, giving Yahweh the limelight. Plague ten is His direct act. No negotiation with Pharaoh takes place. Moses simply declares that at midnight the firstborn of both animals and people will be struck. Before that happens, the Israelites are to ask the Egyptians for gold and silver. God will see to it that the Egyptians respond favorably.

The result of all this will be that instead of the Israelites asking to leave, they will be driven out by the Egyptians themselves. Egyptian officials will bow down to Moses and beg him to leave. Pharaoh alone will be in opposition, and even he will finally capitulate.

Conclusion

This long saga, which seems so drawn out to us, has inexorably led to Israel's deliverance and the crushing defeat of Pharaoh, his gods, and official Egypt. It has become unmistakably clear that Yahweh is powerful—more powerful than anyone or anything in Egypt. Not only is Israel's God powerful, but He has an unshakable resolve to deliver His people and will abide no opposition to that plan. Pharaoh has opportunity after opportunity to obey, but he resists them all and pays a dear price. Israel will not only come out from Egypt but will come out with all their livestock and much gold and silver from the Egyptians as well. The stage is set for the next act of the drama—the Passover and the actual coming out of Egypt.

■ Applying the Word

Exodus 7:8–11:10

1. Why were there so many plagues? Why did the process of getting Israel out of Egypt take so long? Does it ever seem to you that God takes a long time to act, to judge, and/or to save? What things in these chapters can help you understand why God takes His time? Could some of these same things be part of His reason for acting slowly or seemingly so slowly in your life?

2. God's judgments against Egypt all related to their situation and life. If God was sending plagues on our society, what would He do? What would judgments against the oppressors of God's people today be like if they paralleled the plagues? Can you think of anything in recent history that would be like these plagues? Explain.

3. The rods of Moses and Aaron were mighty instruments of God's power. What today would be a comparable rod of God's authority? Do present day church leaders have a "rod"? What would it be?

4. Pharaoh's poor leadership made his country and his people suffer. Are things like that happening today? Where? Does this story teach us anything about how we should react when such things happen?   .

5. When Moses and Aaron first confronted Pharaoh, few rational people would have given them much chance of winning the contest. But they did triumph through God.

What can this teach us about how we should relate to the political situation in our world? Not long ago, people were afraid that Communism was invincible, yet few of us worry about that now. Who are the Pharaohs and Moses of today? What seemingly powerful rulers or countries or movements do you expect to fall under God's judgment? Will Christians also suffer from these judgments?

■ Researching the Word

1. Psalm 78:42-52 and Psalm 105:28-37 in poetic form tell the story of the plagues of Egypt. Compare these two accounts with the Exodus account you have just studied. How many plagues are there, and in what order do they occur in each account? What are the similarities and differences between these various accounts? How do you explain the differences? Are they significant? Why was each account written? What can this comparison teach us?

2. Make a list of the key words in the plagues of Egypt; then read through Revelation looking for these key words. (As an aid, find these key words in a concordance, and then look up their occurrences in Revelation.) To what extent do you think these symbols in Revelation are a prediction of real events that have happened or will happen? Look for clusters of these symbols. Do you find them primarily in parts of Revelation that have already been fulfilled, in parts of Revelation that have yet to be fulfilled, or in both kinds of passages? What is happening in these cluster passages? What is God doing? What are the people doing? Are the people God's people or the wicked? To what extent are these passages eschatological (having to do with end-time events)? Does Revelation give any suggestions of how God's people should relate to what is happening? How can Christians

today apply these principles in their day-to-day lives? How does the story of the plagues in Egypt help you to understand these passages in Revelation?

■ Further Study of the Word

1. For general insight, see Ellen G. White, *Patriarchs and Prophets*, 263-272.
2. On Egyptian gods and the plagues, see Bernard L. Ramm, *His Way Out*, 60-62.
3. On Egyptian magic and sorcery, see J. D. Douglas, ed., *The New Bible Dictionary*, s.v. "Magic and Sorcery" or any available Bible dictionary or encyclopedia.

CHAPTER FIVE

God Delivers His People

Exodus 12:1–13:16

The first eleven chapters of Exodus have all been a buildup to what happens in chapters 12 to 15. The oppression of Israel and Yahweh's plans to save His people and judge Egypt culminate as Israel actually escapes from slavery.

The decisive event leading to this escape is the death of the Egyptian firstborn, both humans and animals. Chapter 11 has only predicted this event. Now the event actually takes place, and Israel escapes.

The Exodus event is so central that the author gives much more space to the ways the people are to remember and experience it than he does to an actual description of what happened. No one questions the Exodus event. The issue is how to celebrate and commemorate it. The answers to this question give rise to a passage that is rich in meaning, symbolism, ritual, and theology. We do well to ponder it, for this exodus is the pattern for all future deliverances and exoduses that God performs for His people.

■ Getting Into the Word

Exodus 12:1-30

Read Exodus 12:1-30 through carefully twice. As you read, consider and answer the following questions. Remember to keep your Exodus notebook nearby.

1. Exodus 12:2 seems to give the Israelites a change in the yearly cycle or calendar. Name the things in the story that would make dates important. List other dates given in this section. Look in a Bible dictionary under "year" or "calendar," and find out more about the Hebrew yearly cycle. At what time of our year would this first month be? Why do you think this month is made the first one?

2. Much prominence is given to the animal used in the Passover. List the steps to be taken in its choice, preparation, usage, and possible disposal. Why is so much care and detail necessary? What does the animal signify?

3. Where is the blood of the animal placed (vss. 7, 22)? What would this imply about how the animal was slaughtered? What does the passage specifically say the blood does (vss. 13, 23)? Why would blood do this? Look up blood in a Bible dictionary. What do you think blood means in this passage?

4. Besides the Passover, the passage talks about a Feast of Unleavened Bread. How long does this feast last? What happens during it? Why is it so crucial to get rid of all yeast? Could Exodus 12:39 give a hint as to the meaning of this festival?

5. Notice the overall timing of this Passover. Does this first Passover come *before* or *after* the actual deliverance? Are the Israelites looking *back on* deliverance or *forward to* their salvation? What significance does this have for the meaning of the event to Israel? What if they had refused to observe Passover? What does this say about the importance of God's festivals?

■ Exploring the Word

Shifts in Focus

As we enter this crucial new phase of the creation of God's people in Exodus, two major shifts in focus take place. First, the emphasis shifts away from the battle between Yahweh and the gods of

Egypt to the people of Israel. During the plagues, the Israelites have been in the background as Egypt is judged. Now they move to the forefront. This passage is about God's people directly. In fact, 12:3 uses a new term to describe them. They are now the "whole community" of Israel. Their deliverance experience is binding them in a special way into a new community—a people of God.

Besides the shift in focus from Pharaoh to Israel, there is a genre switch from story to liturgy. What has been a description of contest and conflict becomes a call to liturgy, festival, worship, and commemoration. Only thirteen verses directly describe the circumstances of the actual release from Egypt (12:29-42), while fifty-two describe in detail the Passover, the celebrating of unleavened bread, and the consecration of the firstborn (12:1-28, 43-51; 13:1-16). All of these are rituals connected with the Exodus story. Now that the long-awaited event is happening, the emphasis shifts to ways it can be recalled and relived.

We would do well to take heed and follow similar procedures, but more on that point later. First, we should examine the details of the story.

A New Calendar

The words "this month is to be for you the first month, the first month of your year" (12:2) speak volumes. The events that are about to transpire are so crucial that the Israelites are commanded to reorder their yearly cycle. *First* in this case probably means not only numerically but also in importance. Israel is to begin the year by remembering the very events that made her a people—God's exodus deliverance.

The importance of giving a month and a day (the tenth day— see vs. 3) becomes obvious. If any event is to be a "lasting ordinance" (vss. 14, 24), then there must be a set time to celebrate it. Not only is the Passover tied to a specific time, but any future celebration of it must also be dated. And, as we would expect, the timing of the Feast of Unleavened Bread follows. It, too, must be specifically dated (vs. 18).

As far as we can tell, there were at least two calendars used by Israel. We in the West have different calendars as well. We have a regular calendar beginning in January, a school calendar beginning in August or September, and a fiscal year beginning most often on July 1.

Israel's religious and ceremonial calendar began according to the instructions given here in Exodus. Month one, which was named Abib or Nissan, fell during our March-April. It was the time of the later (spring) rains and, of course, of the Feasts of Passover and Unleavened Bread.

We actually have the names of only four of the months in ancient Hebrew—the first, second, seventh, and eighth (see Sarna, 82, 83). The months were usually called simply by their number. Later, after the exile, the Jews seem to have adopted the Babylonian names for the months.

The Israelites also had a civil year. It began in the seventh month of the religious sequence and was equivalent to our September-October. This month saw the autumn (early) rain, the Day of Atonement, and Feast of Tabernacles.

The key lesson in all of this is simply to notice how central the Exodus is. To remember it and give it prominence, a whole new calendar is needed. Time begins with deliverance. A newly created people needs a new calendar that identifies them and their unique experience.

The Passover

In preparation for their deliverance, all Israel is commanded to participate in the Passover. The whole community is to obey if they desire to escape the judgment on Egypt. To be Israelite is to do Passover. Later regulations make it clear that others who are not ethnically Israelite may participate, but birth as an Israelite doesn't compensate for nonparticipation.

The ritual is a *family* one. In contrast to later times, when thousands of pilgrims flooded Jerusalem for the Passover, the first Passover celebrations were for stay-at-homers. They did the Passover as families and households.

The central core of the ritual required a "flock animal" (Durham, *Exodus*, 151). Most versions translate the animal in verse 3 as "lamb," but both Hebrew words used in verses 3 and 5 make it clear that either a lamb or a kid would do. The choice probably depended on availability.

The animal was to be a year-old male without defect, and it was to be slaughtered at twilight on the 14th of the month. The slaughter obviously needed to have taken place in such a way that blood could be caught in a basin (vs. 22). Skilled herdsmen like the Israelites undoubtedly knew how to bleed animals. I believe the implication also is that they were following regulations later mentioned in Leviticus about not eating blood (Lev. 17:10-12). They were also, of course, preparing for the sprinkling of blood on the doorposts of their homes.

To Western minds, the whole process seems gory and distasteful, but such slaughter was commonplace for the Israelite herdsmen and their families. We must not attribute our sensibilities to those of other cultures and times.

The meat is to be roasted, not boiled or eaten raw. Along with the roasted meat the Israelites are to eat bitter herbs and unleavened bread. All the roasted meat is to be consumed before morning or else burned up. All this eating is to be done in haste, with clothing prepared for immediate flight.

What does all of this mean? Clearly, the way the story is told and the numerous details that are stressed all have significance. But before tackling the meaning of Passover, I think it best to briefly describe the Feast of Unleavened Bread, which, though less familiar to Christians, was a separate feast for the Jews.

The Feast of Unleavened Bread is so closely tied to the Passover feast and the departure from Egypt that the two almost seem to be one. However, a close reading of the text does point out a major difference, and that is the reason for its mention here. The Passover was actually celebrated for the first time as a *prelude* to the Exodus. The Feast of Unleavened Bread was at best only partially celebrated at that time, since a full celebration required seven days, and Israel left the night of the Passover. They didn't *have* seven days in which to celebrate the Feast of Unleavened Bread.

No specific command is given to celebrate the Feast of Unleavened Bread now, as is done for the Passover (vs. 21). The reason for the unleavened bread on the trip out of Egypt is that Israel must hurry and leave so quickly that they take their bread dough before yeast is added (12:34, 39). The unleavened bread feast thus begins *after* the exodus from Egypt.

The feast is celebrated by removing all yeast from the house and for seven days eating only unleavened bread. On the first and last days of the feast, no work except for food preparation is to be done, and there are to be sacred assemblies. Anyone who eats anything with yeast in it during those seven days is to be cut off from the community of Israel. Israelites and aliens are subject to the same regulations.

Now the big question: What does all of this mean—both the Passover and the Feast of Unleavened Bread? Let us deal first with the major points and then discuss some of the specific issues in more detail.

First, the Passover is clearly meant to protect those who practice it. Each time its significance is explained in this passage (vss. 12, 13, 23, 27), the main theme is that the blood of the slain animal placed on the doorposts is a sign to God. When He brings judgment on Egypt, He will see the blood and pass over the house, not bringing judgment on it and thus sparing it from death. The destructive plague will not strike, and the destroyer will not enter the house. Those who participate in the Passover are safe.

Second, the Passover emphasizes preparedness, readiness, and haste. The Passover is to be put into effect at once (vs. 21) and eaten in a state of readiness and in great haste (vs. 11). The dress of the people says this as well as the eating of the unleavened bread. The people not only eat in haste, but must leave in haste, taking bread, their staple diet, with them before they even have time to add yeast (vss. 33, 34, 39). Those who eat the Passover expect and are prepared for deliverance, which comes very soon.

Much has been written about the symbolism of the various elements in this Passover celebration, so some discussion here is merited.

Leaven (or yeast) was typically used by Hebrews with five grains—wheat, barley, spelt, rye, and oats. Other grains like rice and millet rot but don't ferment. (For a good discussion, see Sarna, 90, 91.) Most sacrificial rituals ban the use of leaven (see Exod. 23:18; Lev. 2:11; 6:9, 10). However, there are some exceptions, such as the wave offering and the sacrifice of thanksgiving for well-being (see Lev. 23:17-20; 7:13). The Jewish explanation for this is that these two offerings were eaten by the worshiper or priest and were not offered to the Lord on the altar.

Because leaven was prohibited on such a wide scale, it is likely that the process of leavening was associated with decomposition and putrification and thus symbolized corruption and sin. Several texts in the New Testament point to this negative meaning of leaven. Jesus warned His disciples against the leaven (false teaching) of the Pharisees (Matt. 16:6, 11, 12), and 1 Corinthians 5:6-9 actually interprets the unleavened bread of the feast as purity versus the leaven of sin (see also Mark 8:15; Luke 12:1; and Gal. 5:9). The Exodus is the great national liberation of Israel. When it is celebrated, it must not be tainted by anything that symbolizes evil. Removing all leaven from the house symbolizes putting away all sin from the life so the celebrant can remember and experience God's gracious deliverance.

The bitter herbs are also symbolic. The only other passage in the Bible mentioning bitter herbs is Lamentations 3:15. In that passage it clearly means cruel suffering. Since the herbs would probably not be mentioned unless they were symbolic, one can assume that these herbs probably referred to Israel's bitter suffering under Egyptian oppression (see Sarna, 91). Exodus 1:14 speaks of their "bitter" life and uses a Hebrew word coming from the same root. Later Jewish writings make the same connection. The most widely used bitter herb since the time of the Jewish Talmud is lettuce.

The most prominent symbol of all is the slain animal and its blood. The initial description of the ritual mentions all parts of the ceremony (vss. 3-11). All subsequent descriptions of both the Passover and/or its meaning clearly emphasize the animal and, in particular, the blood (see chaps. 13, 21-23, 26, 27). Thus the passage makes it unmistakably clear that the heart of this ceremony is the animal sacrifice and, in particular, the use of the animal's blood. This is also the heart of the protection and deliverance that come to those who observe the Passover.

For Christians, Jesus is "our Passover lamb" (1 Cor. 5:7). He is the One who makes our protection and deliverance possible in our exodus from sin. His shed blood protects our households from judgment and death. We must continually remember and re-experience this as did the Hebrews.

Some have gone into great detail on symbolism. They see the Christian Communion elements of bread and wine in the unleavened bread and blood of the Passover. Things break down, however, on careful examination. The unleavened bread is not the sacrifice. A closer parallel would be the roasted flesh. The blood of the Passover was most likely not eaten. Hebrews were forbidden the eating of blood in no uncertain terms (Lev. 17:10-12). It is best to see the parallel between the Passover meal and the Lord's Supper in a more general way.

Others have seen exact parallels to the crucifixion in this ceremony. The blood of Jesus shed in His head (by the crown of thorns), His two hands, and His feet is paralleled, they say, by the Passover blood. It is put above the door (head) by the two sides of the door (hands) and on the threshold (feet). The problem is that nothing is said in Exodus about the threshold. Their response is that the animal is slain at the feet, so blood is certainly present there (Durham, *Exodus*, 145)! I think it is better to say in a more general sense that as the sacrifice and blood of the Passover animal saves Israel symbolically, so the death and blood of Jesus Christ delivers us in reality.

Sacrifice and blood are prominent in the Old Testament system of rituals. The meaning of sacrifice and blood is multifaceted. We must be cautious about trying to pin its meaning to one specific thing or precisely defining the way it accomplishes its work.

Blood saves, protects, delivers, and cleanses, among other things. Exactly how this happens is not as important as realizing that it does. (Those who are interested in pursuing this question further are encouraged to see the "For Further Study" section at the end of this chapter.)

As I studied this passage, I was impressed by its organization and overall time sequence. The first Passover clearly comes *before* the great deliverance, *not after*. The original significance of the Passover is thus not a looking back but a *looking forward* to salvation. It is an act of obedience and faith to believe in the very imminent act of God's deliverance. Passover participants said, "We believe the act of God's salvation is at hand. It is so close that we are dressed and ready to move out *now*." To have refused to participate in that first Passover would have meant death that very night. Passover saved people from death and preserved them for the future.

The Lord's Supper, in its initial occurrence, was the same. Jesus had not yet died and been resurrected, but those wonderful saving events commenced the very night the supper was eaten. The emphasis is on *now* and *future*. It was (and is) an act of faith in present and future salvation.

Too often we think of Exodus and Calvary as *past* events. Passover and Lord's Supper are indeed memories of the past, but even though these events are history, I believe we need to catch the spirit of the first Passover and first Lord's Supper. They were *now* and *future* oriented as well. For Israel, during all its history, the Exodus, deliverance, and covenant happened for them *now*, whenever now was (see, for example, Deut. 5:2, 3). The people spared are *us*; the homes passed over are *our* homes (see 6:27—*our* homes). The God who acted is still saving and acting *now*. Each deliverance is a new exodus.

The same is true for the Lord's Supper. Jesus is alive *now*. He is saving us *now* just as much as He did back then. Our only hope for the future is in Him. We are in the upper room. In a very real sense, we are still staring ahead to His death and resurrection, even though the events themselves are in the past. These things must still be happening for us, and in us, or we are hopeless now. We eat and drink and thus obey Him and declare our faith in His continuing action for us.

In a biblical sense, this is the meaning of these rites. They are not, as we often see them, just an important way of reliving the past and pondering its meaning for us today. Now and future are also strongly present. The rituals in a time sense *recreate* the original event. This is not some pious fiction but is based on at least two concepts. First is the sense of ongoing community solidarity. Without the disciples and the early church, we wouldn't be here. They are our fathers and mothers, and what happened to them happens to us as well.

Second, all of Scripture and life tell us that each new generation needs to be delivered. Unless God is continually at work to save now and complete His work in the future, the past is meaningless. Our faith only has the power if we believe that God is active in the present the same way He was in the past.

One can only say in conclusion that our religious life and, in particular, the way we respond to and practice baptism and the Lord's Supper would be revolutionized if we grasped these ideas. No longer would Communion Sabbath be the most sparsely attended service. May God teach us how to see the power of these celebrations now. How precious these divine ordinances would be to us if this were the case!

■ Getting Into the Word

Exodus 12:31–13:16

Read carefully Exodus 12:31–13:16 at least twice. As you read, answer the following questions:

1. **Notice the contrast in the attitude and action of Pharaoh and the Egyptians between verses 31 to 36 and the earlier parts of this story. For each statement of Pharaoh, cite an earlier statement or action that is different. Do the same for the Egyptians. Was it fair for the Israel-**

ites to "plunder" (vs. 36) the Egyptians? Why?

2. Exodus 12:37 gives the number of Israelites leaving Egypt as 600,000. Compare these figures with Numbers 1:46, 47; 2:32; 11:21; 26:51; Exodus 30:12-16; 38:25, 26. Are they similar? Should they be? If there are this many men, what do you think would be the total number of people if women and children were counted? Try to imagine what the logistics of moving such a group of people would be. Do you think these numbers are meant to be taken literally? Why?

3. Compare Exodus 12:40 with Genesis 15:13, Acts 7:6, and Galatians 3:17. What are the differences? Why are they there? See what the *SDA Bible Commentary* says about this in comments on Genesis 15:13 and Exodus 12:40. Read the passage in Exodus 12:40-42. What really is the emphasis? Is it the 430-year period or something else?

4. As a postscript to the coming out of Egypt, the regulations for the Passover are given in 12:43-51. List the rules for foreigners and aliens. What do they tell us about how a foreigner became part of the Israelite religion? List the rules of Israelites. Why do you think these rules were made? What do they teach us about the Passover?

5. Describe in detail the regulations about the consecration of the firstborn. Give the reasons for this set of rules. How do the reasons compare with the reasons for the Passover and Feast of Unleavened Bread? How are they the same, and how are they different? What does all of this tell us about the meaning and importance of the Exodus?

6. Firstborn animals are mentioned along with firstborn humans. Why are animals included? What do these regulations say about beasts? What does it mean that "all first-born males of your livestock belong to the Lord" (13:12)? What do the statutes about the donkey tell us about how animals were ranked?

■ Exploring the Word

Israel Comes Out

What a change comes over Pharaoh! The death of the first-born all over Egypt awakens him. During the night, he summons Moses, whom he has threatened to kill if he appears before him again (10:28). The man who has done all he can to make Israel *stay* now says, "Up," "Leave," "Go," "Take," and "Go" again. Five verbs are used in two short verses to tell Israel to get out of Egypt.

He now allows them to take even their flocks and herds, which before he had forbidden. They are to do "as you [Moses and Aaron] have said," which I assume meant "Take anything you want, and do as you wish."

Most poignant of all, he asks for a blessing! He who at one time said, "Who is the Lord?" (5:2) asks for God's blessing! More than anything, this simple statement signifies his defeat by God.

The Egyptians join with their leader and urge the Israelites to hurry and leave. They are afraid for their lives. As the Lord had promised earlier, the Egyptians were ready to give the Israelites gold, silver, and clothing—whatever they asked.

Some have suggested that this was fair play because it was fair pay for all the work the Israelites had done as slaves. Whatever the case, it also became a treasure store to draw on when Israel built their tabernacle in the desert. Also, if Israel needed to buy things on their journey and during their sojourn in the desert, this Egyptian treasure could well have been their source of "funds."

The Exodus Numbers

As portrayed in Exodus, the scope and logistics of the Exodus are staggering. If we take the 600,000 men as a literal figure, we would have a minimum of two million people and perhaps as many as three million. Many non-Israelites ("other people"—vs. 38) went with them, as did "large droves" of livestock.

Such things as organization, transport of goods, food for animals and humans, to say nothing of sanitation, would have been massive undertakings. Serious commentators have seen other problems with these large numbers.

The land of Goshen, where the Israelites lived, could hardly have supported two million or more people. It measured only thirty-eight miles by less than three miles. Large numbers of Israelites may have lived elsewhere outside of Goshen.

Another question that has been raised is Israel's relationship with the Egyptians, if their numbers were that large. Scholars estimate the population of Egypt during that period to have been about five million (Sarna, 97). Can five million completely dominate two and a half million people? Possibly.

The numbers given in Exodus 12 are roughly equal to the figures given later in Exodus 38:25, 26 and in the initial census in Numbers (1:46, 47). They also parallel those in Numbers 11:21 and those from forty years later in Numbers 26:51. Some scholars feel that the same numbers are historically true for the united monarchy of David and Solomon (see Sarna, 101, 102 and his list of sources in an endnote). This would suggest that the population of Israel remained fairly constant from the Exodus to the united monarchy, if we take these figures seriously.

There have been many suggestions for dealing with this question, three of which I believe merit consideration for those who take the Bible record seriously.

The first option is that the numbers are to be taken literally as they are translated now. The Exodus record emphasizes the blessing of God and the great fertility of Israelite women. The Israelites dwelt not only in Goshen but all over Egypt, and Egyptian power and oppression kept them slaves in spite of their large numbers. Problems in the wilderness and in settling Canaan kept their numbers from growing appreciably over the years.

The God who provided miraculously for their deliverance miraculously provided organization and food for the animals and humans during their wanderings. All that they needed was graciously supplied, and the wilderness sojourn manifested the power of God in the same way the Exodus did.

The second suggestion depends on the translation of the He-brew word *'eleph*. Exodus 12:37 translates this word as "thousand." The word has numerous other meanings. It can mean subdivision of a tribe, and, more precisely, a military group comprised of members of an extended family. If one takes this translation and substitutes it for the translation "thousand," the text reads 600 military groups. Using Numbers 1 as a guide, there would be an average of eight or nine men per group, for a total of about 5,000 men. The total population would then be 20,000 to 30,000 people (see Sarna, 98, 99 and his endnotes for more details). Deuteronomy 7:7, which calls Israel the "fewest of all people," would seem to support this viewpoint of smaller numbers.

This solution would lessen the miracle of the provisions in the desert but make greater the miracle of the Exodus from Egypt. It seems to fit more with the territory of Goshen and the wanderings in the Sinai desert.

This solution works in this passage and some of the passages in Numbers, but not in others. There are problems with the total in Numbers 1:46 and the sum of the firstborn sons in Numbers 3:43. Though ingenious and helpful in some passages, it fails to explain all the census numbers in the Pentateuch.

A third option is based on a broader definition of the Exodus than usual. Some believe that Israel understood the Exodus to be an era stretching from Moses to Solomon—from the exit out of Egypt to the building of the temple in Jerusalem. The temple is the supreme consummation of the Exodus. Pharaoh released Israel so she could worship Yahweh as she wished, and that departure culminates in the temple on Mt. Zion.

There is some biblical basis for this definition. When Israel sings God's praises after the Red Sea deliverance, the song/poem of celebration concludes in Exodus 15:17 with these words:

> You will bring them in and plant them on the mountain of your inheritance—the place you made for your dwelling. The sanctuary, O Lord, your hands established.

The same idea is echoed in Moses' farewell address when he speaks of the site the Lord will choose to establish His name (Deuteronomy 12:9-11; see also Sarna, 100, 101). Solomon seems to refer to the same things when he engages the services of Hiram and when he dedicates the temple (1 Kings 5:17-19; 8:16, 56).

These texts make it possible to say that the temple is the culmination of God's redemption begun in the Exodus. In a sense, then, all Israel at the time of Solomon were exodus people. They saw themselves as coming out of Egypt. If understood this way, the figures represent the literal number of people alive at the time of the temple rather than at the departure from Egypt. This would imply, however, a late date for the writing of Exodus, or at least later dates for these numbers.

This would explain why the numbers remained constant from the first Passover to the building of the temple. All Israel was present all the way through the entire Exodus experience.

Whichever solution one chooses, it must be remembered that the numbers are not emphasized in this passage. They are only mentioned once. Whether God wanted to tell us that 25,000 people or 2.5 million people escaped is not the crucial point. The issue is God's power to deliver, save, and preserve His people.

Whatever the exact number was, the fact remains that in the Exodus, God's power is amply proven. The basic issue of Exodus is not in question. This should free us to consider the question of numbers without fear because we know that what really matters is secure.

Exodus 12:40 says that the Israelites lived in Egypt 430 years. Genesis 15:13 says that they were to remain there 400 years—a statement that was quoted by Stephen in Acts 7:6. Galatians 3:17 says the law comes 430 years after the covenant. Why the difference?

I suggest that the Genesis 15 figure is meant as an approximate statement of time, which was quoted again in Acts. The Egyptian sojourn was 400 years, in round numbers. In more exact figures, it was 430 years.

As I read the passage, the emphasis again is not so much on the number of years but on the fact that God was right on time—"to the very day." God's timing is impeccable. The Lord even kept a vigil that night to make sure His promise was fulfilled on time. For that very reason, Israel is to keep a vigil on Passover night to honor the Lord for His vigil in future generations. This adds a further element to what it means to keep the Passover.

Passover Regulations

Now that the Passover has been observed and the Exodus has literally come to pass, it is appropriate to point out certain key regulations in connection with the feast.

Interestingly enough, the regulations begin with foreigners. In fact, rules concerning foreigners and aliens are the largest part of the passage. The reason could well be that right from the beginning non-Israelites were in the midst of God's people and "exodusing" also (see 12:38). Non-Israelites may not eat of the Passover, be they foreigners, temporary residents, or hired workers. *Anyone*, however, who is circumcised and has all males in his household circumcised may celebrate the feast. The text goes out of the way to say that the same law applies to both Israelite and alien. Equality of entrance requirements is based on willingness to submit to covenant requirements.

This fairness and openness should impress us. Many have seen the Jews as racially prejudiced snobs. This legislation made it simple for non-Hebrews to join the Israelite community. The joining had nothing to do with race or ethnic background. All that was asked was submission to the covenant requirement of male circumcision.

Besides the circumcision requirement, several details of observance procedures are added to the earlier explanation. This Passover is not a progressive house-to-house party. It is to be eaten inside one's own house. No meat is to go outside, and none of the bones of the animal are to be broken.

It is important that community solidarity be practiced. "The *whole* community of Israel must celebrate it" (vs. 47). Again the passage emphasizes "all the Israelites" (vs. 50) did what God commanded through Moses and Aaron regarding the Passover. Since *all* Israel was saved (and will be delivered), it is important that *all* take part in the celebration. It is not one option to choose among many, but a definite requirement.

One gauge of the importance of the Exodus is the tremendous amount of commemorative ceremony and liturgy that comes about because of it. We have already discussed the Passover and the Feast of Unleavened Bread. Both are practiced because of the Exodus. We now come to a third type of ceremony directly related to the Exodus—the consecration of the firstborn. This rite is mentioned numerous times in Exodus (22:29; 34:20) and the Pentateuch (Lev. 27:26; Num. 3:13; 8:17). Jesus Himself was presented by His parents in accordance with this ordinance (Luke 2:22, 23). Every Jewish family with one son or more was thus in their own family reminded of the Exodus deliverance. This act is a "sign on your hand" and a "symbol on your forehead" (13:9) that Yahweh brought you out from Egypt.

The firstborn regulation required the actual sacrifice of all firstborn males of the animals. Since donkeys were especially precious and harder to come by, the Lord allowed a lamb to be sacrificed as a redemption for firstborn donkeys. If, however, the donkey was not redeemed by a lamb, its neck had to be broken (34:20).

Human firstborn males are not sacrificed but "redeemed" (vss. 13, 15). *Redeem* in this case means "obtain release by means of payment." This payment could be in money (Num. 3:50) or by sacrifice of some animal, such as a lamb.

Again the meaning of all this is made very clear. It all has to do with the Exodus. The Lord killed the firstborn of Egypt to obtain the release of His people but spared all the firstborn of Israel. All Israel's firstborn thus belong to Him in a special way. As these rites are performed, the reality of Exodus is again vividly brought before the people, and their own ongoing deliverance by God is celebrated and recreated.

The reality, power, and meaning of the Exodus is thus celebrated

and recreated in three ways that represent different but complementary perspectives. One day each year, as a family, the Israelites recreate the sequence and redemption of Exodus night. For
one week each year, the Israelites, by the very way they eat their
most basic food—bread—relive Exodus food and Exodus experience. Any time any female in Israel, human or animal, gives birth
to her first male offspring, the slaughter of the Egyptian firstborn
is reexperienced.

How could Israel forget? God wanted to make certain she remembered. That remembering must be made sure before the story
can go on. The story can only continue if the original story is
carefully remembered. God has taken great care to make sure that
that happens.

■ Applying the Word

Exodus 12:1–13:16

1. **What does my yearly calendar emphasize? What are the
   most important times or days of the year? What is the
   "first" or primary month for me? Why? Does my faith
   shape my calendar, or does my secular calendar shape
   my faith? Should we change our calendar to fit our religious experience, like Israel did? If so, what yearly and
   monthly spiritual observances might I celebrate?**
2. **Passover and the Feast of Unleavened Bread are portrayed as family celebrations of faith. Does my family
   have any celebrations of our faith? How did they begin,
   and what do they mean? If we were to begin such a celebration, what might we celebrate? How would we celebrate?**
3. **What role do religious rituals play in my life? Are they
   important? Why? If they are not important to me, could
   my attitude be based on a weak understanding of what
   rituals meant in Bible times? How could the Hebrew
   idea of ritual explained in this chapter contribute to the**

power of ritual in my life and church?

4. Christians often connect the Passover with the Lord's Supper. Do we have anything in the church that might be comparable to the Feast of Unleavened Bread or the consecration of the firstborn? If not, realizing the meaning of these rites, would it make sense to establish Christian ceremonies that are like them? Why or why not? What would such ceremonies be like?

5. According to the Exodus account, the deliverance took place right on time. Can I think of instances in which God acted right on time for me or those I know? Is it possible to know God's timing ahead of time? Why? Did knowing God's timing help Israel? Would it help me?

6. How do I relate to the killing and sacrifice that takes place in these and other passages? Does the slaughter of the Egyptian firstborn and of sacrificial animals bother me? Why? Do I think this bothered Israel? How does my reaction compare with theirs? How does God fit into all of this?

■ Researching the Word

1. The Passover is the first major passage in the Pentateuch where blood is specifically utilized for saving purposes. Using a concordance, look up all the references to blood as it relates to sacrifices in the Pentateuch. What are the different ways blood is used? Are explanations given as to its meaning? Why? What can you learn from this about the meaning of blood in the sacrificial system? How might Christians apply this to their understanding of Jesus and the New Testament?

2. With the aid of a concordance, look up all the occurrences of *passover* and *lamb* in the New Testament. Where are the largest number of references to each of these words found? What general significance do you see to this in each case? Did Jesus keep the Passover?

What relationship is there between the Passover and His establishment of the Christian ordinance of Communion? Having completed your study of the chapter in Exodus dealing with the establishment of the Passover, what relationships do you see between the Passover and the Communion service? What are the similarities, and what are the differences? What is the meaning of the lamb in the New Testament? How does the Passover festival in the Old Testament contribute to the New Testament understanding of the lamb? What spiritual lessons do you find in this study that can be helpful in your life?

■ Further Study of the Word

1. For general insight, see Ellen G. White, *Patriarchs and Prophets*, 273-282.
2. For more detail on the Passover, the Feast of Unleavened Bread, and the consecration of the firstborn, consult a Bible dictionary like the *SDA Bible Dictionary* or *The New Bible Dictionary*.
3. For a detailed discussion of the options and evidence in connection with the number of Israelites in the Exodus, see Nahum M. Sarna, *Exploring His Way Out, Exodus*, 94-102; Bernard L. Ramm, 81-83; and Francis D. Nichol, ed., *SDA Bible Commentary*, 1:556.

CHAPTER SIX

God Vanquishes Pharaoh's Army

Exodus 13:17–15:21

The center of Exodus is God's gracious deliverance of Israel from Egyptian slavery. That is the basic way God creates a people. The core of this deliverance takes place in two separate but closely related events. The first is the exit out of Egypt after the death of the firstborn Egyptians. That event was the subject of the previous chapter.

The second event is God's victory over Pharaoh's army. That is the subject of this chapter. Israel is not safely out of Egypt until Pharaoh's capacity to bring them back is destroyed. Liberation from Egyptian slavery can only be celebrated when redemption from Pharaoh's army is accomplished.

The climax to both events comes in the powerful song of praise in chapter 15. When Israel knows she is truly free, she can sing and dance and play instruments in glory to the Exodus God. When God creates a people, they are a people who naturally worship and praise, for that is the consequence of free salvation.

■ Getting Into the Word

Exodus 13:17–14:12

Read Exodus 13:17–14:12 at least twice. As you read, look for answers to the following questions. If you write them down, it will help you remember.

1. Using a map in your Bible, Bible dictionary, or Bible atlas, try to trace the route of the Exodus. List the names of the various sites mentioned, and see if you can find them. Which ones do we know the location of, and which don't we know? Why are there problems in locating these sites? Who decides on the route? What are the reasons given for the choice (13:17, 18; 14:3, 4)? What does this say about God?

2. What did Moses take with him from Egypt? Read Genesis 50:24-26. What is Joseph saying by making this request? What is Moses saying by keeping this promise?

3. What are the prominent visible symbols of God's presence (13:21, 22)? Can you think of other places where cloud and fire symbolize God's presence? (See, for example, 1 Kings 8:11 and Isa. 6:4-6.) This cloud could perform other functions (14:19, 20). What do you think these symbols meant to the average Israelite? Why are they important?

4. List the specific preparations Pharaoh made to go after Israel. Does he sound serious? Why would he need to do so much? Do you think Israel planned to fight? See 13:18 before you give your answer.

5. Enumerate the specific steps in Israel's response when they realized that Pharaoh and his hordes were after them. Was this response typical? See Exodus 16:3; 17:3; Numbers 14:3; 20:3, 4; 21:5. What do you think were the reasons for such a response? What does this response teach us about effects of slavery and human nature?

■ Exploring the Word

Route of the Exodus

Where did Israel go when they left Egypt? This passage makes it sound like we can easily trace their path because descriptions and place names are given. The task is, however, not easy.

We actually know more about the route that was not taken than we do about the route that was. The way through the "Philistine country" (13:17) was the coastal Mediterranean route, which was the most direct way. God did not lead them that way because they might have faced war and become discouraged. That route, because it did have several major Egyptian military outposts along it, was the favorite path of invaders, and Egypt wanted to be prepared. The route by which God did lead them was called the "desert road" toward the "Red Sea" (13:18). This path ran south and east toward the Sinai desert.

Most of the cities named in the account, however, are not possible to locate. Over time, place names often change. While Rameses (12:37) is fairly certain, and many think they know where Succoth (13:20) is located, all the other cities (places) named are unknown. We simply do not know precisely where the Israelites went. The location of the "Red Sea" has also been much discussed. The words in Hebrew are not the technical name for the actual Red Sea (Gulf of Suez), but mean "Reed Sea" or "Sea of Reeds." There are several (some say as many as five) shallow lakes with many reeds in the lowland between the Mediterranean and the Red Sea. Three prominent ones are Lake Sirbonis, Lake Timash, and Lake Manzaleh. Various of these lakes have been suggested as the site of Israel's wonderful deliverance.

There are those even among recent commentators, however, who defend the traditional interpretation of the actual Red Sea (see for example, Fretheim, 153). Even though the Red Sea does not contain reeds, there are several places in the Old Testament where it is clearly called "Sea of Reeds" (see, for example, 1 Kings 9:26; Jer. 49:21; and probably Exod. 23:31).

When God says He will lead Israel on the desert road toward the Red Sea, He is describing major geographical features. The small reed lakes do not fit this category of important geographical locations. In my opinion, the nature of this event for Israel and the description of what happens fit better with the Red Sea interpretation.

Before leaving the subject of the Exodus route, one other issue needs consideration. The story says God makes route choices for Israel based on two things. First, He doesn't want them discouraged by war (13:17), and second, He has Israel double back to encourage Pharaoh to pursue them (14:2-4).

This constitutes clear evidence that God takes human, earthly situations into consideration when He leads. The psychological state of Israel and Pharaoh as well as the sociopolitical situation in the country affect God's actions. While it is true that Yahweh is so powerful He could smash through all obstacles and need not take into consideration the human condition, that is not the way He chooses to operate in Exodus theology.

Providence considers the human situation. Providence and wise planning are not mutually exclusive, but ideally walk hand in hand. In love the all-powerful God notices our fears and feelings and the situations that surround us, and He acts accordingly.

Joseph's Power

In the haste surrounding the Exodus, Moses does not forget to keep an old promise. An oath had been sworn to Joseph to take his bones out of Egypt and presumably rebury them in Canaan (Gen. 50:24-26). The extraction of the oath by Joseph was in essence a powerful act of faith. Joseph really believed the promise that God would deliver His people from Egypt and get them back to Canaan. The oath would have been a waste of time had he not held that strong hope. The fulfilling of the oath is an act of faith on Moses' part. It clearly signals his belief that what is happening in the Exodus *is* the fulfillment of the promises and that Israel will make it back to Canaan.

The event has wonderful symbolism as well. Joseph had been the first one to go down into Egypt. Israelite theology saw God behind that move, for it was through Joseph that God preserved Israel in the time of famine.

There had been a time to go into Egypt, but now it was time to come out. Joseph was in a sense the first one in and the last one out. To take him out means closure to the Egyptian-sojourn part of Israel's history. That was something temporary. The real place of home is Canaan. Now even the one who had helped them survive in Egypt is going back home.

Light and Shade for the Journey

God does not just bring Israel out of Egypt and then leave her to fend for herself. He gives a constant reminder and evidence of His presence. The daytime reminder is a pillar of cloud, and the nighttime is a pillar of fire. One or the other is always present.

The stated purpose of these twin "pillars" is to guide the people and give them light. They can thus know *where* to go and at night have light to go where guided. Underlying all this, of course, is the surety that God is there, and where they are going is where He wants them to be.

The cloud and fire can provide other services as well. In Exodus 14:19, 20, the cloud moves from the front of Israel to their rear. It brings darkness to the Egyptians, making it impossible for them to find Israel during the night of the Red Sea crossing. The cloud thus *protects* as well as guides.

The cloud becomes a powerful symbol of God's presence in Exodus and the rest of the Pentateuch. Counting the initial mention in Exodus 13:21, the word appears eighteen times in Exodus. All of the usages apply to the cloud of God's presence. The cloud figures prominently in Moses' visit with God on the mountain and in connection with the tabernacle. The cloud is mentioned in Leviticus in connection with the Day of Atonement and is utilized twenty times in Numbers.

Beyond manifesting the presence of God, the exact meaning of the cloud is not clear. Probably it symbolizes power, since clouds bring storm and rain. The Canaanites called their storm god Baal, which means "cloud rider." Psalm 68:4 calls Yahweh the same thing. Yahweh certainly is God of the weather, the storm, and the rain. The name may well have evoked a sense of mystery as well. In a cloud, seeing is hampered, and vision is not clear. God reveals Himself, but we cannot see all of Him, for He is so much more than we can "see" or comprehend.

The use of fire for a symbol of God's presence is also prominent in Exodus and the Pentateuch. Particularly vivid is the fire
on Mt. Sinai (19:18), when God comes near, and the fiery glory in
24:17.

Christians, of course, are familiar with the fire of the Holy Spirit
that descended on believers on the day of Pentecost (Acts 2). This
experience shows that the vivid fire symbolism was not limited to
Old Testament times, but carried on into the New Testament.

Both cloud and fire were powerful, evocative manifestations
and symbols that meant much to Israel. Time could well be spent
in a careful study of their meaning all through the Bible (see the
Researching the Word questions at the end of this chapter).

Pharaoh's Pursuit

It was no trivial matter when Pharaoh decided to pursue Israel.
He took a major step in committing a large force to his attempt to
bring his escaped slaves back. This was serious business.

Some commentators have seen a conflict between 13:17 and
14:5. They say 14:5 sounds as if Pharaoh has just learned that
Israel has fled, while 13:17 (and other passages) portray him as
letting them go.

What I believe happens is that Moses has been asking all along
simply for permission to go into the wilderness to worship Yahweh.
Moses' original request to Pharaoh was for a three-day trip into
the desert for worship (5:1-3), and throughout his repeated con-
tacts with the Egyptian ruler, he consistently asked for time for
him and his people to worship God. He never did tell Pharaoh
that Israel intended to leave and never return. Thus when Pharaoh actually allowed the people to leave, he said, "Go, *worship* the
Lord *as you have requested*" (12:31). He permitted them to go on
those conditions. While he perhaps suspected that they would
leave for good, he may not have told his officials. In 14:5 Pharaoh
learns for the first time that Israel is not just going to worship but
has indeed fled the country. That fact, plus the knowledge that

the Israelites seem confused (they even returned partway), plus God's hardening of the monarch's heart, leads him to make a major miliary commitment to bring Israel back.

Pharaoh prepares his chariot (he himself will go as commander) and his army. Six hundred of his best chariots along with all the other chariots of Egypt are to go. The army includes chariots, horsemen, and troops. Typically chariots had three men manning them, with one being the commander. One man drove and two fought.

The implication seems to be that this was a two-part force. The best crack chariot units were commanded directly by Pharaoh, while the larger chariot force operated somewhat independently under its own commanders (see Durham, *Exodus*, 191). Other troops and cavalry could also have been attached to each section of the force.

Did Pharaoh need all this? He must have thought so. He must have surmised that he would have a battle on his hands, for 13:18 says that Israel went out of Egypt "armed for battle." Perhaps Pharaoh thought a big show of force would mean quick surrender without a battle. Whatever the case, the bigger the army, the larger the victory for Yahweh. I think the impressiveness of the force is mentioned for that very reason (14:17).

The large force has its desired effect on Israel, as far as Pharaoh is concerned. Israel is intimidated and more. First, they are terrified—not an unnatural reaction for slaves as they face the full military might of their oppressor! In their fear they cry out to God and confront Moses. They accuse him (and God) of bringing them out into the desert to die. They say in essence, "Didn't we tell you earlier not to do this?" They claim that in Egypt they had asked to be let alone, for serving Egypt was better than death in the desert.

Several things can be said about this Israelite "murmuring." First, such urgent pleas to return to slavery are typical for people who have had an extensive period of oppression. Such people do not need a word of condemnation, but rather a word of good news, which Moses, in fact, proceeds to give.

Second, such murmuring is a recurring theme in the pentateuchal story of Israel (for example, see Exod. 16:3; 17:3; Num. 14:3; 20:3, 4; 21:5). While not the response of faith, it is an understandable human response. What believer hasn't at some time or another wondered if the journey of faith, which seems at times so insecure, is not worse than "life in Egypt"? The choice is always between the land of promise, often seeming a bit distant, and life in Egypt.

Israel complains for several other very practical reasons. First, not all the group are Israelites. A "mixed multitude" that included many Egyptians came out of Egypt (12:38). Besides that, not all Israelites are Israelites of faith. Some undoubtedly are only ethnically Israelite and question God and the covenant. Furthermore, slavery has deprived many Israelites of any real knowledge and understanding of life and God. They have a slave mentality, which makes it difficult for them to see things in a broad perspective. Recognizing where they are in their spiritual development, God deals with them mercifully, reassuring and delivering them. The details of how that happens is our next subject.

■ Getting Into the Word

Exodus 14:13–15:21

Read Exodus 14:13–15:21 carefully twice. As you read it, look for answers to the following questions:

1. Examine thoughtfully 14:13, 14. List in detail the parts of Moses' response to the complaints of the people. What are the reasons behind each of these statements? The story that follows is a commentary on some of these statements. What might these verses teach us about how God deals with complaining people?
2. Exodus 14:19 mentions the angel of God for the first time in Exodus since the burning-bush episode in 3:2. Compare these passages with Genesis 18:7; 21:17; 22:11,

15; 24:7, 40; 31:11; 48:16; Exodus 23:20, 23; 32:34; 33:2.
You may also want to look the term up in a Bible dictionary. What does it mean? Who is referred to? Why does
the term appear in this passage?

3. Write down the various steps in the deliverance that take
place in 14:15-31. Note especially the purpose of this
deliverance. How does the deliverance make this purpose happen? Find also the results of this deliverance.
What change does it make for the complaining Israelites?

4. Who sings the first song in 15:1-18, and to whom do
they sing it? Why? Who sings the second song (vss.
19-21), and to whom? Why? Is 15:19-21 different from
15:1-18? In what ways? Why do you think Exodus included this long song in the story? Is it important? Why?

5. Examine carefully the content of the long song in
15:1-18. List all the ways it describes God and His actions. How does the song conclude? How would you
describe the song's content in one sentence? In modern
terms, what would you call this kind of song?

■ Exploring the Word

How to Face Fear

The reason Moses' answer to Israel in 14:13, 14 should be so
carefully examined is that it represents a model or paradigm of
how God typically responds to the distress of His people. Let us
examine it part by part.

The first command is, *"Do not be afraid."* God begins here because this is where the people are emotionally. Their first response
to the Egyptian army is terror, so God starts at their level. Fear
paralyzes and makes us irrational. It must be dealt with.

The reassuring command to "fear not" is very common when
God appears to people. God spoke these words to many other
people throughout biblical history: Abram (Gen. 16:1), Hagar

(Gen. 21:17), and Isaac (Gen. 26:24). He said it to a suffering Israel at a later time (Isa. 41:10-14), and He spoke it to the shepherds in the field (Luke 2:10). He still says it to people who are afraid. He says it because He knows that to be human is to fear, and He wants to reassure us of His loving presence. We may think the worst is about to happen, but God says, "No, it won't!" "Fear not." Fear is an evidence of unbelief. To abandon fear is to trust God's word.

The second command Moses gives is, "*Stand firm.*" This follows logically on the first command. When fear flees, you can stand your ground. Moses did not mean fight, but rather station yourselves *where you are now* at the ready. There is no need to retreat. If you believe that where you are now is where God has led you, why move? Stay put, because where you are is where you should be! Retreating would give the wrong impression.

The third element is a *promise*, which like element two, proceeds from the preceding two commands. If you cast out fear and stand firm, *you will see* the deliverance that God will work on your behalf. By obeying God's commands, the Israelites will view with their own eyes the salvation of God, and the Egyptians they see today they will never see again. It will happen today.

The fourth element is a *second promise*, which builds on the first promise. The *Lord will fight for you*. Israel may have brought weapons along (13:18), but they are *not to be used* at this time. Israel need not fight, for God as warrior and leader in battle will fight for them (14:25; 15:3). What a relief that must have been to the people to hear this as they looked at Egyptian chariots!

The final element comes back again to instruction. Not only is Israel to fear not and stand firm; she need only *be still*. The order does not mean be motionless. Israel must walk across the sea. Israel must do what God asks. No, the call is for *silence*. Shouting, complaining, cursing, lamenting, crying—battle cries—will do no good. Israel need not fight or talk. God needs no weapons or words. In silence Israel will see the mighty deliverance of Yahweh. A similar silent observation of the mighty acts of God is called for in Psalm 46:10.

This simple five-part statement by Moses contains the essence of God's word to fearful saints. Present-day "slaves" who obey His commands and believe His promises will also experience victory in the process of escaping their own "slavery," whether that slavery is to sinful habits, relationships, debt, or seemingly impossible circumstances.

Angel of God

Exodus 14:19 portrays the angel of God as moving from the front of Israel to her rear when the Egyptian army draws near. The passage makes it clear (14:19b) that this angel is *not* identical with the cloud of God's presence, which also moves to the rear of Israel to separate her from Egyptian forces.

A perusal of the concordance on the texts given in the Getting Into the Word section will tell you that the term is fairly common in Genesis and Exodus. It is also fairly common in other parts of the Old Testament, especially Judges. What is its meaning and significance?

The word translated *"angel"* in Hebrew means "a messenger or attendant" (see Durham, *Exodus*, 163). It can refer to human beings who are messengers. The exact meaning of the word must be understood by the context in which it is used.

The careful reader may have noticed that the Exodus 14:19 passage actually says angel of "*God*," while many of the texts in the Getting Into the Word section say "angel of the *Lord*." Some commentators have tried to argue that the meaning of these two is different. However, even though the Hebrew words for *Lord* and *God* are different, I think the terms *angel of God* and *angel of the Lord* are synonymous.

It is hard to tell exactly why the angel of the Lord/God is said to do certain things when often God Himself does the same things. In fact, in some texts the angel of the Lord is almost identical to God Himself (see, for instance, the story of Hagar in Gen. 16:7, ff; 21:17, ff; the "sacrifice" of Isaac in Gen. 22:11, ff; and the story of the burning bush in Exod. 3:1, 2, 13, 14, where the angel of the

Lord and Yahweh seem to be the same Being). The angel seems to be particularly present in destruction and/or judgment and in protection and/or deliverance, such as this story in Exodus 14.

Because at times the angel seems almost to be God Himself, and because of His powerful and gracious acts, some have equated his mention in the Old Testament with Jesus. While this may be true in some cases, we need to be careful not to insist on this interpretation in every instance.

God Finishes Pharaoh

The time has come to look at the actual story of how Israel is delivered as God finishes Pharaoh off. As is often the case, the story begins with God telling in outline form what He *will* do (14:15-18) and continues in more detail by telling exactly what He *does* do (14:19-31). Whenever this occurs, comparing these two sections often gives a fuller view of the story than either part considered separately.

God begins by using His angel and His pillar of cloud to bring darkness on the Egyptians and light to the Israelites. This keeps the two sides apart during the night.

Then Moses stretches his rod over the sea, and God parts the sea, using a strong east wind, which turns it into a path with dry ground. Note that in several parts of this story God uses what we would call "natural means" to execute His will. All nature is at His command.

The Israelites cross through the sea on the dry path the wind has made. Walls of water are on each side. The Egyptians try to pursue Israel by entering the sea. But God throws the Egyptians into confusion and makes their chariots fall apart. They recognize that God is fighting for Israel, but before they can escape, Moses raises that mighty rod. The parted sea comes flowing back together and covers the army with water. All the Egyptians who have followed Israel into the sea perish.

What reason does Exodus give for this turn of events? The Lord says He will gain glory through what happened to Pharaoh and his army (14:17, 19), and the Egyptians will "know I am the Lord." The same reason is stated earlier in 14:4.

We would most naturally expect to see the reason have something to do with Israel's salvation. That is stated at the very beginning of the Exodus story and is almost certainly assumed here. God's covenant, faithfulness, and desire to deliver His people are the basic reasons for the whole story, but God's purposes are wider and more comprehensive. Part of what God wants to do concerns Egypt, and beyond that one nation, the world.

Honor is something public and open. This very open destruction of the Egyptian army declares the activity and power of God in a way that all can see. It gives Him a *name* that none can question. This is the reason why the deliverance takes place in this way. The Exodus not only saves God's people but declares to the world who God is and invites belief.

The result of all this for Israel is clearly stated in 14:30, 31. Israel unmistakably sees the power of God when they experience salvation and see the Egyptian army dead on the shore of the Red Sea. They are moved to "fear" the Lord, that is, to reverence and worship Him and hold Him in awe. They put their trust in Him and in Moses, His servant. Terror and bitter complaints against God and Moses have given way to worship and trust. The people are now ready to sing their song of response, which follows.

Songs of Moses and Miriam

Those who realize their salvation naturally turn to praise of the Saviour. Rather than a brief statement of the fact that Israel praised and sang, we have the actual songs—the first such examples in Scripture.

In reality Exodus 15 has two songs. The first, in 15:1-18, is said to be sung to the Lord by Moses and the Israelites. In this song the singers praise in the first person: "*I* will sing" (vs. 1). Except for the first short section (14:1b-5) and the last verse (vs. 18), which address the Lord in third person ("The Lord," "He/Him"), the song actually is sung to God directly in the second person ("O

Lord," "You/Your"). This latter form is more personal and fits the opening verse, which says that the song is sung "to the Lord."

The second song is given in brief form in 15:21. Miriam sings this song "to them," which the context makes clear means all the women of Israel. They sing and dance in praise and joy to the accompaniment of tambourine. The content of the song is very close to the song of Moses (compare 15:1 and 21), except that Miriam's song says "Sing!" which is a command imperative in the second person plural. She is saying to the women, "You all sing!" What we have is either a specific command to them to sing or a kind of antiphonal singing with Miriam leading and the women answering in song. It could well be true that the men sang the first song and the women the second. "Israelites" in 15:1 literally says "*Sons* of Israel," but that phrase typically means all the people. Whatever the case, the main point is clear. *All* men and women take this opportunity to sing praise to God for His mighty deeds. This act of singing is so important that the Scripture reports not only the singing but the content of the songs as well. We will now turn our attention to the song itself.

The long song can be easily divided into two parts. Part one (vss. 1-12) praises God for His redemption from Egypt. Part two (vss. 13-18) describes in faith what God will do as Israel enters Canaan. Both parts praise and exalt God for His past, present, and future acts on behalf of His people.

Notice what some of these acts are. The specifics of Yahweh's victory over Pharaoh are described, including chariots and horsemen. The breath of God's nostrils piles up the water of the Red Sea and then brings it back on the Egyptians. God leads and guides His people. He will cause the enemy nations around to be terrified and silent. God will in the end bring them to the Promised Land and to the sanctuary or temple He makes for them. The song concludes with the clear statement that "the Lord will reign forever and ever." If He really has done and will do all this, there is no one at any time capable of challenging His rule. He will be King of all forever.

This song can best be described as an exultant song of praise for the Lord's past and future actions for His people. It is an extended and detailed doxology, sung as only a people just delivered could sing.

In the introduction to this book, I discussed how central the book of Exodus, and in particular the Exodus story, is in the Bible. Time and time again, when God's people are in need, the Exodus is recalled and alluded to. The return from the exile and the salvation given them by Jesus were and still are new exoduses to believers. At this point it is good to expand this idea.

The chapters of Exodus that we have just studied give us a pattern of how God works in salvation and how humans respond. We can call this an exodus model or paradigm. What are the parts of this pattern model or paradigm?

First, the *situation of the people* is *seemingly hopeless*. By natural means there seems to be no hope. The people are oppressed slaves in Egypt or refugees caught between the sea and the Egyptian chariots. Humanly speaking, doom seems inevitable.

Second, the response of the people is *fear, cries for help,* and *bitter complaint*. The people turn to God and His chosen leader and then desperately cry for help or blame others for the situation. This is the natural response of slaves, past and present.

Third, *God graciously delivers*. In the midst of this hopeless situation, the Lord steps in with His salvation. The plagues fall, and the firstborn of Egypt perish. The cloud moves between Israel and the Egyptian army, and the waters of the sea bury horse and rider. The enemies of God's people are defeated. Yahweh wins.

Fourth, *God delivers in a very public, dramatic,* and often somewhat odd manner. When God delivers, it catches attention. It *witnesses to unbelievers*. He desires people to come to faith and give Him honor. That can only happen when all Egypt sees the firstborn die and when Pharaoh's large army is publicly drowned. The story also makes it very clear that the victory is God's doing and not humans'. The Lord, not humans, deserves the honor.

Fifth, *people respond in faith and worship*. As Exodus 4:30, 31 says, when the people realize that God is about to save, "they believed" and they "bowed down and worshiped." When God finishes with

Pharaoh, the people "feared the Lord and put their trust in him" (14:31). They proceed to sing because it is the true sign of such recognition. It is the public demonstration of faith that the graciousness of God has indeed delivered and He alone deserves the glory.

This five-part model is still the way God works today. Whatever our private and/or public Egypt and slavery may be, the procedure is the same. Seeking God in our slavery is the key. Whether we beg or complain is not the crucial part. The key is seeking Him. That allows Him to begin His work. When we truly recognize that work, we, too, will sing and praise and probably even dance for joy.

■ Applying the Word

Exodus 13:17–15:21

1. **In choosing the route of the Exodus, God took into consideration the situation and feelings of the Israelites. How has God taken account of my situation and feelings in the way He has led me? Have I taken time to notice? How should this affect the way I deal with other people?**
2. **Have there been pillars of cloud and fire in my life, which have been constant symbols of God's presence and guidance? Should I look for such things? Why? If they were present in the lives of Christians today, what would they be?**
3. **Have I ever murmured against God, a Christian leader, or my situation in life? Why did I do it? Was it justified? As I look back on it now, do I see the situation in the same way? What can I learn from Israel's murmuring that would help me in relationship to the people and circumstances I tend to complain about?**
4. **Have I ever been terrified about circumstances that looked hopeless? What were/are those circumstances?**

Is it a sin to be afraid? Why or why not? What can Moses' answer to Israel's fears in Exodus 14:13, 14 teach me? Can I use a similar approach today?

5. Is it right for God to do things to "gain glory" (14:4, 17, 18)? Why? Am I to do things to gain glory for God? Why? If I am, what might such things be?

6. How often do I sing praises? Do I do it because others do or because I am in church, or do I do it because I want to? Whom do I sing to? Do I ever really sing to God? What might happen that would cause me to sing in the way Israel did in Exodus 15?

7. Miriam and the Israelite women danced in procession with singing and tambourines. Should I do something like that today? What could I do that would portray the same meaning and response to God's great salvation? Does my response to God really show how I feel, or do I have to tame it down for the sake of others? How should I show true religious celebration and joy?

■ Researching the Word

1. Cloud and fire are both widely used symbols for God's presence in the Bible. Using a concordance, look up all the references where fire and cloud are used in connection with the presence or manifestation of God. What can you learn about their meaning? Does the meaning develop over time? After reading these passages, why do you think God used these as means to show Himself? Do you think God still uses these things today? Can you think of modern experiences in which they are used? If God came to us today, would He use cloud and fire or something else?

2. In many ways the exodus of Israel from Egypt is a type of the greater "exodus" of God's people from the world of sin. Review the "exodus paradigm" in the section of the chapter titled Songs of Moses and Miriam. (For con-

venience, you may find it helpful to write it down.) Next, read through Revelation, looking for the various aspects of the paradigm. What aspects of the paradigm do you find? Are there some parts that you do not find? If so, why? In what parts of Revelation do you find that the paradigm applies the most? What spiritual lessons for your own life does this research suggest?

■ Further Study of the Word

1. For general insight, see Ellen G. White, *Patriarchs and Prophets*, 282-290.
2. For the route of the Exodus, see Siegfried H. Horn, et al., *SDA Bible Dictionary*, 332, 333; William LaSor, et al., *Old Testament Survey*, 128-130; and Nahum M. Sarna, *Exploring Exodus*, 103-106.
3. For the deliverance at the Red Sea, see William LaSor, et al., *Old Testament Survey*, 141-143.

CHAPTER SEVEN

God Provides
in the Desert

Exodus 15:22–18:27

The momentous two-act deliverance is past. Israel is out of Egypt and free from the threat of Pharaoh's army. What next? Is that all the Exodus is about? In reality, Exodus and the creation of a people has just begun. Israel knows Yahweh can deliver from Egypt. The question now is, What can He do in the harsh, unforgiving desert of Sinai? Can He care for their needs? Can God keep on working for His people?

The answer is a resounding Yes! Do the people need water? He can provide it, and three specific ways are described here. Are they hungry? Manna and meat are provided. Do enemies threaten them? God can provide victory in the most amazing ways. Do they need leadership, organization, and guidance? God can provide the people and the methods to turn a motley crowd into an organized army. Everything Israel needs, God can take care of. Before the next step in creating a people can take place, the assurance of God's power and willingness to give constant provision must be present. This section of Exodus makes that clear.

■ Getting Into the Word

Exodus 14:22–17:7

Read Exodus 15:22–17:7 through at least twice, and then answer the following questions. Record your answers in your Exodus notebook.

143

1. Make a list that includes every instance when Israel cries out to God, grumbles, or tests Yahweh and/or Moses. How many times are there? At what stage in their experience does Israel tend to respond this way? How do God and Moses respond to their grumblings? What does this teach about God, Israel, and the way people learn?
2. In this passage God supplies water three times. What are the three methods He uses to supply water? Which of these are miraculous, and which are not? Why? What are these stories meant to teach Israel and us?
3. Read carefully Exodus 15:25b, 26. What commands and decrees of God are referred to here? What promise does God make? On what condition? Is this legalism or bribery? Why? What do you think are the Egyptian diseases referred to here? What do you think "I am the Lord who heals you" means in this context? See 2 Chronicles 7:14, and compare it with this passage.
4. What is the reason given for the provision of quail for meat to eat? Is this a valid reason for God to give them? What does this teach about God? Does God's response have anything to do with Moses and Aaron? Why?
5. A large part of the instruction about manna deals with the Sabbath. List all the things we can learn about the Sabbath by studying the manna regulations. All of this takes place before Mt. Sinai. What does that teach us about the origin of the Sabbath? Was the Sabbath commandment in Exodus 20 new? Why?

■ Exploring the Word

Israel's Response

If anything is clear in this passage, it is that Israel is not shy about showing a frank response to God and Moses in every situation. These reactions, as portrayed in this passage, are without exception negative.

The pattern begins at Marah. When the water is bitter, the people grumble against Moses (15:24). In the Desert of Sin, they grumble against Moses and Aaron (16:2) because they miss Egyptian food and are afraid of starving. This grumbling, Moses tells them, is really against God (16:8).

The same thing happens at Rephidim. First, the people quarrel with Moses and say, "Give us water to drink" (17:2). Moses replies rather directly, but the people go on and grumble against him. This is serious grumbling, for Moses believes they are about to stone him (vs. 4)! Later in the passage the people's action is described as, "They tested the Lord" (vs. 7; see also vs. 2).

In every single instance of need, Israel complains! The complaining comes, not after asking and being denied. Whenever a need arises, the grumbling arises. One would think that they could at least seek God and ask His help *before* complaining. From our point of view, they had already seen enough of what God could do to at least be somewhat patient. But no! At the onset of their troubles, they start their grumbling. One can sense how troubling this is to Moses. His response is to cry out to God (15:25; 17:4). He doesn't know what to do with the people, so he seeks the Lord. Reasoning does not seem to work (17:2). Only the action of God will suffice.

This response of Israel to their problems is, I believe, an evidence of unbelief. They simply don't see that God can and will work to provide for them. They have short memories and have already forgotten all He has done to deliver them. Unbelief and the slave mentality have a powerful grip on these Israelites.

But most amazing in all this is God's response. Although Israel complains against Moses, the grumbling is ultimately against God. As we have already seen, it is a testing of God (vs. 7). Shockingly, God responds by taking care of their needs with no questions asked. He supplies the *needed* water. He supplies the *special* food of quail meat—a luxury, even, rather than a necessity. He gives them manna as daily food. No punishment comes on them for their unbelief. There isn't even a word of reproof. God simply responds to the needs of His people through their leader Moses. What a testimony to the gracious patience of God! He responds to the complaints of unbelief. It is well to remember that *all* the gracious provisions in this chapter take place in this context.

Water in the Desert

Anyone who has ever experienced the desert knows the importance of water. Not only did the Israelites need to drink, but the story makes it clear that large numbers of livestock needed water as well. Some water could be taken along, but most people can carry only so much at about sixty-two pounds per cubic foot! It is natural that the first crisis over God's provision should arise over water.

For three days the people travel without water. When they come to the oasis of Marah, the water is bitter, and the people complain. When Moses cries out to God, he is shown a piece of wood. When he throws the wood into the water, it becomes sweet and drinkable. This is water-supply incident number one (15:22-28).

Incident number two is the simple account of 15:27. The people travel to Elim, where there are twelve springs, and camp there near the water. Since we have already been told that the pillar of God's presence is leading Israel, we assume that God supplies this water by leading His people to it.

Incident number three takes place at Rephidim (17:1-7). Israel camps there, but there is no water for the people to drink, and they complain.

God responds by leading Moses and the Israelite elders on ahead of Israel to the rock at Horeb. There Moses takes his rod and strikes the rock. Water comes forth in the presence of the Israelite elders. The place receives the names Massah ("testing") and Meribah ("quarreling"), because of what has taken place there.

The three incidents portray three ways God supplies water: by a piece of wood, by His leading, and by Moses striking the rock. There has been much debate as to how to understand these incidents, especially the Marah and Rephidim stories. Are they to be seen as direct miracles of God, are they naturally occurring events, or are they some combination of the two?

Proponents of the first view point to direct statements about God's presence and His leading and say that they are miracles. The story does not say that the wood made the water sweet. The wood might just be the way Moses exercised faith. Even if the wood did bring about the change, the direction to the wood was a miracle. The arrival at Elim is a miracle, because God has clearly guided them to water. At Rephidim the striking of the rock is clearly portrayed as a miracle. Theologically, this viewpoint is important, because the argument of the passage is God's divine presence and provision. Exodus wants to make it clear that God is the One who provides, and the way to do that is to have Him work miracles that show His power.

The proponents of the natural view have their arguments as well. There are several kinds of wood that are known to sweeten bitter water. One type of wood is appropriate for this particular water, and Moses finds it. Elim is a naturally occurring oasis, and Moses, from his past experience as a shepherd in that area, knows where it is. As to water from the rock, Moses knows where a stream or spring flows just beneath the thin layer of rock. He goes to the place and with his rod breaks the thin layer, and water comes forth. If God had not intended for us to understand these events naturally, so the argument goes, He would not have mentioned the wood or oasis or rod and rock.

I personally prefer the third option—a combination of the natural and the miraculous. I believe it is correct for two reasons. First, the stories clearly mention God at work *and* natural things such as wood, springs, rod, and rock. Both are clearly taught in the story, and we must not neglect either.

Second, I find this option to be both theologically and practically more true. Time and again in Exodus God works but takes into account the human and natural condition. He uses wind and wood. He takes into account the people in His choice of the Exodus route, and He knows where oases are. He doesn't perform a special miracle in each place. Both the natural and the human are taken into account as the divine works. In a practical sense, that is how life is. God often works in and through natural circumstances to care for us each day. Some see everything as a miracle, while others see only the natural. I suggest that *all* of life for the people of God is under God's control, but that control is a gentle, benevolent control that often works quietly in the background and uses the resources of His good creation. Indeed, I believe that a major reason Israel goes through these experiences is to learn their lesson.

God Heals

One of the most provocative and profound texts in Exodus is the short passage in 15:25b, 26. At Marah God is said to make a decree and a law for Israel to test them. If they obey "his commandments and all his decrees," He will not bring upon them the diseases of the Egyptians. He says this for, He declares, "I am the Lord who heals you."

This brief passage is a foretaste of Mt. Sinai and the covenant. What is called for is total obedience to Yahweh's commands and *all* His decrees. The words *commands* and *decrees* are general terms. They do not have in mind any special body of law, but refer to all that God might require. This passage is good evidence that Israel knew God had commandments before Sinai. This is simply the first reference to them.

The point here is not the specific content of these laws, but rather the principle of *obedience*. The "test" (decree or law) has to do with whether Israel will obey God or not. If she obeys she will escape Egyptian diseases, a probable reference to some of the plagues that fell on the Egyptians.

Pharaoh failed to obey God's command to release Israel and as a result suffered the plagues. God is fair. The same principle is in place for Israel. If she now fails to obey God, she will suffer plagues like Egypt.

The first response of many is to call this legalism, bribery, or blackmail, but careful examination of the text will show that these allegations are not true. First, the passage must be seen in the context of the whole book of Exodus. God is not saying, "If you obey, I will do something for you." He has already, with no calls for obedience, saved Israel from Egypt and Pharaoh. They stand as free people in Sinai. There must be a response to deliverance. A relationship with God must be established. This is the first hint of what that means.

In the Old Testament, obedience and faith are very close to each other. To obey is to manifest true belief. To have true belief one must demonstrate obedience. To obey God's commands is a sign you believe what He says and acknowledge who He is and what He has done for you.

At Marah God has shown that He can "heal" bitter waters. If Israel wants to see that kind of healing continue, she must show her response in faith and obedience. More of what all that means will be spelled out as Israel covenants with God at Sinai.

The working out of this principle will show who God is. The plagues showed Pharaoh who God really is. The plagues and/or the healing will for Israel also demonstrate who God is. As He operates by this principle, Israel will learn more fully about Him and His ways.

Meat, Manna, and the Sabbath

The next major requirement of humans after air and water is food. It is natural, then, that the second major test of God's ability to provide develops over the issue of food. In the process of providing food, God teaches other vital lessons that Israel needs to learn.

The first way God provides for food is by sending quails to cover the camp. This is in response to Israel's complaint that they miss the meat of Egypt and that it would be better for them to be eating meat in Egypt than starving in the desert. The meat is given (16:8, 12) so Israel may know that the Lord has heard their grumbling and so they will know that He is the Lord their God.

This meat is obviously something extra. The manna is called "bread" or "food" (vs. 15). This is the basic staple of life and is provided throughout the people's entire desert sojourn (vs. 35).

The quails are different, for they are flesh food—something added, something special. They are not provided on a regular basis but are given now just because the people want them. How gracious!

This entire episode occurs to teach the people that Yahweh is a providing God. Just before the gift of this food, a special theophany or manifestation of God takes place. All Israel is called before Him (vs. 9). As Aaron speaks to them, in the distant desert they see the glory of the Lord appearing in the cloud. Yahweh then says that the immediate gift of food that evening (quail) and the next morning (manna) will show them God.

At this initial period of Israel's experience in the wilderness, God goes to special lengths to meet not only their needs, but their wants. He desires that their faith be built and that they learn who He really is. Later, the situation may change (see Num. 11:31, ff), but for now, God is very patient with the people.

The story emphasizes two major themes. First, God provides for the food needs of His people. That issue we have already discussed. The second theme is the Sabbath. To that issue we now turn our attention.

Numerous facts about the Sabbath can be learned from this description of the manna.

1. The Sabbath is a day of rest (vss. 23, 30).
2. Everyone is to stay where he is on the Sabbath. No one is to go out (vs. 29).
3. The Sabbath is the seventh day (vss. 22, 23, 26, 29).
4. The Sabbath is a holy day (vs. 23).
5. No manna falls on the Sabbath (vss. 25, 26).
6. On the sixth day, a double portion of manna is to be gathered, and half of this is to be saved for the Sabbath (vss. 22, 23).
7. Manna can be kept overnight for the Sabbath. Any other day, manna that is kept over spoils (vss. 19, 20, 22, 23).
8. This Sabbath is a command of God (vss. 23, 28).
9. This Sabbath is to be kept "to the Lord" (vss. 23, 25), probably meaning "for the Lord's honor."

This passage lets us know clearly that the Sabbath existed before Sinai and the covenant made there. Most of what we learn in the fourth commandment we already see clearly taught here and in Genesis 2:1-3. The Sabbath commandment was thus not something new to Israel but reached back to the earliest days of their history. Sabbath keeping was taught weekly in the gift of the manna. The manna was God's bread from heaven, which by its very manner of coming reminded the people of God's command concerning the Sabbath.

Conclusion

At the very beginning of their wilderness wandering, God sets out to teach Israel that He can provide their most basic needs—water and food. He is even willing to give some gracious extras like meat to satisfy homesick ex-slaves. He is willing to do this in the face of grumbling and unbelief. He graciously blesses, not because of but *in spite of* the response of the people. He knows their humanity and their past, so He is patient.

God makes it clear that He is doing all this so their trust and belief in Him can grow. The gifts of food and water are given in such a way that other lessons are learned as well. The people can see that God can work in a multitude of ways that combine divine power and natural circumstances. Sabbath keeping is learned from the manna gift. Does Israel realize what a gracious and wise God she serves?

■ Getting Into the Word

Exodus 17:8–18:27

Read through Exodus 17:8–18:27 carefully at least two times, and then answer each of the following questions from the Bible text:

1. Using a Bible concordance and dictionary, find out all
   you can about the Amalekites. Where did they origi-
   nate? You will want to check Genesis 36:12; Numbers
   24:20; Deuteronomy 25:17, 19; and 1 Samuel 15:2; 27:8
   for information also. What was the final end of the
   Amalekites?
2. In Exodus 17:10 two new characters are introduced into
   the story: Joshua and Hur. Using this passage, a Bible
   dictionary, and a concordance, find out all you can about
   these men. What do their names mean? What role do
   they play in Israel? What can we learn from this about
   leadership training?
3. List the specific steps that Israel uses to gain victory
   over Amalek. Why did God use these steps, and why did
   they work? Give the specific steps that followed after
   the victory. What might this teach us about how to respond to the times God gives special triumphs to us?
4. What specific things does Exodus 18 teach us about Israelite family and hospitality customs? Note carefully
   how Moses, the Israelites' top leader, receives his
   father-in-law. What do they do together? Do we or
   should we follow similar customs today? Why?
5. Draw a diagram that describes the organizational structure that (a) Moses first used and (b) Jethro, Moses'
   father-in-law, suggested to him. What are the advan-
   tages of the second system? What can we learn about
   leadership and organizational principles from this passage?

■ Exploring the Word

Battle With Amalek

God has already shown His gracious willingness and awesome
power to supply the needs of Israel for water and food. In this
particular section, He shows His ability to provide for two other

needs: victory over attacking enemies and good organization and governance. The methods by which Yahweh works to do this are most interesting.

The Amalekites are descendants of Esau's grandson Amalek. Culturally and linguistically, they are closely related to Israel. They live mainly in the desert between Sinai and southern Palestine, though some seem to live in an area later known as the Ephraim mountains (Horn, 33). Rephidim is at the edge of their main territory, and they undoubtedly understand the Israelite presence as an invasion.

Their encounter here in Exodus is the first in a long series of encounters with Israel. Because of this first encounter, Exodus says that "the Lord will be at war against the Amalekites from generation to generation" (17:16). God also promises to completely blot out the memory of Amalek from under heaven (vss. 14, 15).

This blotting out seems to have taken a long time. A year after this first encounter Israel attempts to enter southern Palestine against God's will, and Amalek defeats her at Hormah (Num. 14:43, ff.). Two encounters between Amalek and Israel occurred during the period of the judges. On one occasion they, along with Eglon, king of Moab (Judg. 3:13) attacked Israel, and later they combined forces with the Midianites to raid Israel's crops and herds. Gideon drove them out (Judg. 6:3-5, 33; 7:12; 10:12).

During the period of the monarchy, Saul defeated the Amalekites (1 Sam. 19). David also fought against them. Later they seem to have declined, and the remnant seems to have been destroyed in Hezekiah's time (1 Chron. 4:43).

Thus in spite of their similarity in background and culture, Israel and the Amalekites were formidable foes. Amalekites were determined fighters, protecting their home turf. In spite of God's word against them, they persisted in bothering Israel for a long time. A defeat by Amalek at this juncture would have made it extremely difficult for Israel to move around the desert as she saw God leading her.

On the Israelite side, the battle with Amalek introduces us to two new characters: Joshua and Hur. Hur (meaning "free" or "noble") is the lesser of the two figures, both here and in later history. Hur assists Aaron in holding up the hands of Moses during Israel's battle with the Amalekites. Later (24:14) Aaron and Hur are left in charge of governing Israel while Moses and his assistant Joshua ascend the mountain to meet with God. Jewish tradition says that Hur was Miriam's husband, which fits his close association with Moses and Aaron. The same tradition also considers him to be the grandfather of Bezaleel, the chief artisan in the construction of the tabernacle.

Joshua means "Yahweh is salvation" or "deliverance." This is an appropriate name for someone of his prominence, since Exodus is a deliverance story. The name is, in fact, the name of Jesus—Jesus being the Greek form of the Hebrew/Aramaic name. Joshua was a young man at the time of the Exodus and seems to have served as a personal assistant to Moses (33:11). In this passage he has direct control of Israelite military endeavors. Joshua was, with Caleb, one of the two spies who actually believed Israel could take the land of Canaan (Num. 13, 14). Later, of course, on the plains by Jordan, Joshua was formally consecrated the military and civil leader of Israel as Moses' successor (Num. 27:12-23).

This capped a long period of apprenticeship, which began here and continued through many experiences, including visits with God on Sinai and waiting on the Lord at the Tent of Meeting (24:13; 33:11). He assumed leadership at about seventy years of age and after faithful work in leading Israel during the conquest period died at age 110.

The details of the actual battle with Amalek are amazing. A trained military strategist would be scandalized by what happened. Although Exodus does not tell us the details of the Amalekite attack, Deuteronomy 25:17-19 adds some facts. Evidently the Amalekites plan their raid against Israel well. They attack when Israel is worn out, and they begin by cutting off the laggards in the Israelite line of march. This kind of attack shows "no fear of God" (Deut. 25:18). The probable meaning is twofold. First, their attack demonstrates that even though the Amalekites are related to Israel and thus have some knowledge of God, they actually have no fear of Him. Second, their attack from the rear on the most weary of the Israelites offends common standards of human decency (see Sarna, 120, 121). The same terminology is used in Leviticus to refer to taking advantage of the deaf, the blind, and the aged (Lev. 19:14, 21). This vicious attack from the rear at a vulnerable time for Israel is what provokes the words of judgment on Amalek.

After this raid, Moses instructs Joshua to pick some good men and go out to fight Amalek the next day. During the battle, Moses promises to stand on top of the hill with the staff of the Lord in his hands.

The next day Joshua goes into battle, and Moses, Aaron, and Hur go to the top of the hill, probably overlooking the site of the fighting. As long as Moses holds up his hands, Israel wins. If he lowers his hands, Amalek gets the upper hand. Aaron and Hur assist Moses and make sure his hands remain raised—we assume, with his staff in his hands. The fight lasts till sunset, and Joshua overcomes the Amalekite army. Such tactics would seem preposterous to any modern general, but God's battles are never like human battles!

What does this raising of the hands mean? Why does Israel win by Moses' upraised hands and rod? There are several possibilities. Some have suggested that the reason was psychological. The hand in ancient Near Eastern society symbolized power. The rod had been used powerfully before by Moses. Moses may have used a military ensign or standard as well (17:15). Any combination of hand, rod, and/or ensign would have served as a perpetual lift to the Israelite fighters in the valley. Looking to these symbols of power would have made them confident of victory. However, while some element of this may have operated in this situation, my feeling is that it is not adequate to explain the powerful effect of the raised hands.

The second possibility is that the raised hands refer to an attitude of prayer. Uplifted hands was a common posture of petition and/or prayer. As long as Moses prayed, God blessed Israel's army with victory. If Moses stopped praying, Israel stopped winning.

While prayer would be important, again, I think this explanation is not the true one. The word used to describe Moses' raised hands in this instance is not the word commonly used for lifting the hands in prayer. Certainly Moses could have continued to pray when his hands were lowered. This posture wasn't necessary for prayer.

What really happened, I believe, is something different. The staff was not *Moses'* staff but *God's*. It symbolized the power and sovereignty of Yahweh that had been active all through Israel's exodus from Egypt, as we have seen. The staff brought plagues and stopped plagues. It parted the waters of the Red Sea and brought them back together again. It visibly and vividly represented Yahweh's presence and power. Lifted high, it meant Yahweh's power in action. Lowered, it meant human power in action alone.

The key lesson for Israel is that victory is provided by God, not by their own military prowess. The raised hands and rod make that clear to all Israel. The *Lord* is Moses' banner, and the *Lord* will be at war with the Amalekites (17:15).

Israel takes specific steps to follow up this battle. The Lord commands the first step: The story is to be written in a book, and Joshua must hear it. Why? Because God will blot out the memory of Amalek. The story of what happened is the rationale for what is to happen to Amalek in the future.

This instruction is interesting for various reasons. This is the first mention of writing in the Bible (the possible exception is Gen. 5:1). *Book/scroll* has the definite article (*the*) in the Hebrew, so the author seems to refer to a specifically known book. Some have suggested that it may refer to the "book of the Wars of Yahweh" (see Durham, *Exodus* 237, and Num. 21:14). Key events in Israel's history were recorded in this book. Some have equated this book with the book of Jashar mentioned in Joshua 10:13 and 2 Samuel 1:18. Joshua is to hear this—we assume by someone reading it to him. (Perhaps he could not read.)

The next step in response to the battle is that Moses builds an altar, which he names. He calls it "Yahweh is my banner." Banners (standards or flags) were the symbols that nations carried into battle, giving their identity and symbolizing allegiance. The Lord is Israel's flag of identity because the power for the victory rests with Him. Moses says his hands are "lifted up to the throne of the Lord" (17:16). This is a clear reference to his raised hands during the battle. For this reason, an altar in honor of Yahweh is made. A place of worship memorialized the work of God in giving victory through His power.

Thus the Lord's victory for Israel is remembered or memorialized in two tangible, lasting ways: in a book and in an altar. Human minds are quick to forget. The Old Testament emphasizes memory as an important key to a vibrant faith. Because of this, special action is taken to keep memories alive. God commands it, and Moses initiates it.

We can each well afford to ask the questions, How well do I remember God's acts for me? How good is my memory? Have I taken steps to help my memory by erecting tangible memorials to the graciousness of God?

Jethro's Visit

The urgent needs of water, food, and protection from enemies have now been met. Now the time comes to address a vital need that is crucial for Israel's long-term life. How should Israel be organized? God provides this organization through the agency of Jethro, Moses' father-in-law. However, before considering the issue of organization, it will be helpful to notice the family and social interaction that takes place in this chapter.

Exodus 18 gives an interesting and, in many ways, touching picture of ancient Semitic family life and custom. The story also gives a respite from the rush of battle in chapter 17 and a breather before the climactic events that will take place on Sinai.

Jethro has heard how God delivered Israel from Egyptian slavery. Moses' wife, Zipporah, and their two sons have been staying at home with him—a common practice for an extended family in Semitic society. Now that Israel seems safe and is in fact nearby,

Jethro comes to visit and brings Moses' wife and children back to him. As is customary, he sends advance notice of his arrival.

Moses doesn't just sit and wait. He goes out to meet his father-in-law, bows down before him, and kisses him. These are clear signs of respect, honor, and affection. Interestingly, nothing is said about Zipporah and the two sons. Jethro is the center of attention here!

They proceed into the tent after these greetings, and Moses shares the Exodus experience. Later there are sacrifices to God, over which Jethro presides. Moses, Aaron, and the leaders of Israel then eat bread together in a religious setting.

The next day Moses performs his duties as judge for the Israelites. From morning till night, he hears and decides cases. After observing everything, Jethro gives his son-in-law some very practical advice about governance and organization. Moses listens respectfully to his father-in-law and does "everything he said" (18:24). Finally Moses "sent" his father-in-law on his way, probably going a distance with him, as was a common custom (vs. 27).

It is clear from the story that Moses as top leader takes second place to Moses as proper son-in-law. Moses shows the utmost courtesy and deference to Jethro and willingly follows his advice. This gives us some insight into what "honoring your father and your mother" (20:12) meant to the typical Semite. We might learn some lessons in a society that often treats older people with little respect.

We can learn other lessons from this story. Jethro is a Midianite (2:15, 16; 18:1). The Midianites are descendants of Abraham through his wife Keturah (Gen. 25:1, 2) and are thus related to Israel in a similar, though even more distant way, than Amalek. Amalek attacks Israel, while in contrast, at least one part of the Midianite tribe makes peace with them. Some scholars even see this passage showing how two main branches of the family of Abraham are brought together after many years.

The passage also seems to be telling us that Jethro comes to have faith in Yahweh and joins the people of God. After Moses' testimony describing the salvation God wrought for Israel, Jethro confesses, "Now I know that the Lord is greater than all other gods" (18:11). Immediately, he brings a burnt offering and other sacrifices to God—an obvious act of worship—and then proceeds to eat in the presence of God with the leaders of Israel. He thus not only verbally confesses his faith, but worships God and communes with the leaders of Israel before God. And they accept him as a fellow believer.

If this is true, Moses has just performed the first recorded act of cross-cultural missionary work, and the result is that he gains an important convert. The testimony of Moses about God's gracious deliverance has brought a Midianite to faith. The Exodus has barely been completed. Much remains to be done to make Israel into a full-fledged people of God. But the message has already crossed some cultural barriers. This people that God is creating is *not* based on rigid ethnic purity but on faith in the delivering Yahweh. What had been God's purpose for the world before the Exodus (9:16) is already beginning to take place. Regardless of race, anyone who believes can be part of Israel.

Moses may have been called by God, but according to this story, he is a rather inept administrator. He is trying to do everything himself. Jethro gives him great advice, which he says is, in fact, God's command (18:23). Here we have the first described convert giving divine advice to the top leader. This is an interesting commentary on the honesty of the Pentateuch about Moses and the way God works. Yahweh can miraculously give victory as well as organize Israel through the counsel of a Midianite father-in-law.

Note carefully the counsel Jethro gives. First, he critiques the old system and tells Moses it will wear him out. He cannot handle everything alone. Actually, Jethro uses the plural when he tells who will be worn out. The implication is that both Moses *and* the people will be unable to handle the stress for long. This idea is also implied in Jethro's final remarks about Moses standing the strain and the people being satisfied (vs. 23).

Jethro then outlines a plan of action. It has four basic parts to it.

1. Moses is to be (remain?) the people's representative before

God and the one who brings their disputes (special ones?) to Him (vs. 19).

2. Moses is to have a major teaching role. He is to teach all laws to the people and show them the way to live. The idea is that if the people understand these principles, there will be fewer problems and disputes. Prevention is the best medicine for the heavy burden of judging.

3. Moses is to select capable people who are honest and trustworthy and appoint them as officials. Jethro recommends four levels: thousands, hundreds, fifties, and tens. Although it is not altogether clear, evidently an injured party would begin his appeal at the lowest level and move up the chain if he felt justice was not done. This would make the system much like the modern court of appeals, where cases move from lower courts to higher ones.

4. Moses is to be the judge only in the most difficult cases, which the other appointed judges cannot decide themselves.

The system seems remarkably wise. Moses is spared, and the people get quicker service. Moses remains top leader, but the responsibility for leadership and justice is widely shared with the people. An educational system is instituted to instruct the people, which in the end will prevent unnecessary litigation. All we can say is that the University of Egypt must not have had leadership and administration courses at the time Moses attended—or perhaps the only system they taught was the one used by the pharaohs! In any case, we can thank God for Jethro, because we can still learn from him!

Conclusion

Israel now knows by experience that God can provide. Water, food, victory over enemies, and now organization, have been provided. These blessings have come in a variety of ways. Some, like the water from the rock, appear to be quite miraculous, while others, like Jethro's counsel, are "natural." In *everything*, though, we see God's hand. He works with people and through people to bring about that which will meet needs. Deliverance and Exodus are not one-time events. They are ongoing, constant provisions from the hand of a gracious God.

■ Applying the Word

Exodus 15:22–18:27

1. In this passage Israel's complaining does not seem to stop God from helping them. How can I apply that to my life? Does complaining to God bring results for me? Would there be a better way to relate to God? What would that be? Are there special circumstances in these stories that apply to me? Could complaining be an expression of my faith? Why?

2. Does God still protect His people from "Egyptian diseases"? How? Has God protected me? Is the Lord still a healer for me? If He is, on what basis does He do it? Is health a reward for obedience? Does God's promise in Exodus 15:26 still apply today? How?

3. In this passage God supplies the basic needs of Israel—food, water, protection, and guidance. Does He do these things for me today? In the modern age, should we still look to God for these things? Can I think of instances in which I believe God supplied my needs? What are they? Have they been many or few? Why? What can these stories teach me today about God's provision for me?

4. Have I ever recorded in a book what God has done for me or built an altar of remembrance? How well do I remember important spiritual events in my life? What could I do that might help me remember God's acts? What would a modern scroll of the "Words of Yahweh" or an altar look like?

5. Moses led Jethro to faith by testifying about God's acts of deliverance for Israel. Do the missionary methods I

use follow that pattern? If I were asked today why I believe, what would I say? Has God done anything in my
life that I can tell about? What is it? Do I naturally share
it? Why?

6. Do I know divinely called people who are inept in key
areas like Moses was? How about me? Do I ever let my
belief get in the way of my efficiency? How teachable
am I? Am I willing to learn from others who are not
longtime "Israelites"? What can I learn from Jethro's
wisdom about organization that applies to me?

■ Researching the Word

1. Exodus 16:23 contains the first mention in the Bible of
the word *Sabbath*. (Note: Gen. 2:1-3 uses the term *the
seventh day* but not the word *Sabbath*.) Exodus 16 tells
us much about the Sabbath. Add to that knowledge by
looking up all the references to the *Sabbath* in the
Pentateuch (not counting Exod. 16, where there are 39
references). Find out all you can about the Sabbath and
its observance from these passages. Often we only read
the Sabbath commandment in the Ten Commandments
in Exodus 20. What added things do we learn by broad-
ening our scope? Putting it all together, what do you
learn that you can apply today?

2. Use your concordance to find all the references to manna
in the Bible outside the book of Exodus. Study each reference in its context (read several verses before and
after each one). What spiritual lessons do the Old Testament authors draw from manna, and how do these
lessons enlarge on what we learn in Exodus? Which is
the primary New Testament passage on manna? What
difference do you find between the lessons the New Testament draws from manna and those in the Old Testament? What relationship, if any, do you see between the
reference to manna in the central part of John 6 and the

story at the beginning of the chapter? How does Jesus apply the lesson of manna to Himself? What help for daily living can we gain from the total biblical teaching about manna? Use the *SDA Bible Commentary* and the *SDA Bible Dictionary* as resources to help you understand what manna was and its spiritual meaning.

■ Further Study of the Word

1. For general introduction to the material, see Ellen G. White, *Patriarchs and Prophets*, 291-301.
2. For deeper understanding of the people involved in the story, see Siegfried H. Horn, et al., *SDA Bible Dictionary* on "Amalek and Amalekites," "Kenites," and "Midianites." Use a map or atlas to see where their territory was.
3. For a discussion of the meaning of Moses' upraised hands, see Bernard L. Ramm, *His Way Out*, 105, 106.

PART THREE

God Makes
a Covenant

Exodus 19–24

CHAPTER EIGHT

God Initiates the Covenant

Exodus 19, 20

The deliverance phase of Exodus is finished. Now comes the time for formal commitment. Deliverance compares to premarital courtship. Israel has become acquainted with the gracious saving power of God. Now it is time for "marriage"—for covenant and commitment.

Impressive marriages help cement the marital relationship. A certain amount of ceremony benefits all parties. The Sinai marriage of Yahweh and Israel is fitting, for it comes with cloud, fire, thunder, smoke, and trumpets. The Lord Himself comes to meet His bride. Solemn vows are exchanged and the Ten Commandments spoken. The occasion is awesome and memorable.

Now we must become students of marriage and examine all this closely. It can teach us much about what happened, *but it can also instruct us as to what* happens now. *What does "marriage" to God entail, and how does one do it right? Such instruction makes commitment more meaningful and helps prevent "divorce."*

■ Getting Into the Word

Exodus 19

Read Exodus 19 carefully at least twice, and then answer the following questions, keeping your Exodus notebook handy for writing down your answers:

1. What is the geographical setting of these events? Compare 3:12 with 19:1-3. What is the significance of this place? What is the *time* setting of these events? Compare 19:1 with 12:2, 3, 17, 18. How long had Israel been gone from Egypt? Why do you think the time is mentioned?

2. Exodus 19:3-6 outlines the basic terms of the covenant. List the specific elements in God's instruction to Moses about the covenant. What has God done for Israel? What specifically does God require of Israel? If Israel accepts, what will she be? Do other people besides Israel have a place in God's concern? Why? How does Israel respond to these terms of covenant?

3. Specific regulations govern Israel's meeting with God. Enumerate the specific regulations governing Israel's interaction with God. What are the reasons for them? What is God trying to teach by giving them?

4. God manifests Himself on the mountain in a multitude of ways. List the various ways the presence of God is shown at Sinai. Why are there so many natural phenomena? Using a Bible dictionary or commentary, see if you can find out the significance of these phenomena. What impact do they have on Israel (20:18, 19)?

5. Count the number of times Moses goes up and down the mountain. What happens on the mountain? Who can and who cannot go with Moses? Why? What is the importance of all of these trips?

■ Exploring the Word

Covenant Background

Since momentous events are about to occur, a sense of setting in place and time become crucial. The people have left Rephidim and come to the desert (wilderness) of Sinai. There they encamp "in front of the mountain" (19:2). As discussed in an earlier chapter, although we know approximately where this mountain is, the exact location is not certain.

What is most crucial is that the arrival at this place fulfills God's word to Moses spoken in 3:12. The sign that God's promise was true is the worship of Israel at the mountain where God first appeared in a burning bush to Moses. The place is thus a sign of the trustworthiness of God's word. This location is, in fact, where the rest of the book of Exodus takes place. No more movement occurs until the book of Numbers.

We learn in 19:1 that arrival at Sinai comes in the third month after Israel left Egypt. We are not told what day this is. The probable reason for mention here is not simply to give the time frame but to connect it with the Feast of Weeks or Pentecost. Israel had been gone from Egypt about seven weeks, or fifty days. In the Jewish liturgical calendar, the giving of the Torah, or Law, was celebrated at the time of Pentecost/Weeks, seven weeks after the Passover (see Williams, 82). Thus the time between the exodus from Egypt and the arrival at Sinai fits the calendar of Israelite feast celebrations. Story and feast are closely linked.

Israel has experienced all manner of special blessings from God. The time is now right to begin asking what obligations the people have in response to God's grace and deliverance.

Most Bible translations connect the phrase "on the very day" with the third month, pinpointing the arrival of Israel at Sinai. The only problem is that the *number* or day of that very time is not given.

Some have connected the phrase with the ascent of Moses up the mountain in 19:3. If this is true, then verse 2 is a parenthetical statement giving information about Israel's travel and location (see Durham, *Exodus*, 256, 257). The purpose of the passage (vss. 1-3) is to show Moses' eagerness to go up the mountain. He wants to meet God immediately. As soon as Israel arrives in Sinai, "on the very day," Moses ascends the mountain. This understanding has merit.

What did God say when Moses went up the mountain? The

short summary we are given in 19:3-6 is really the essence of the divine-human relationship. The rest of the Old Testament, and in fact the New as well, is simply an expansion and a working out of this relationship. It deserves careful consideration as we look at its three main parts.

Part one declares what *God has already done* for Israel. The orientation is mainly to the *past*. The second section deals with what Israel is to do *now* and in the future. On the basis of part one, a commitment is called for. The third segment is the result of the first two parts. The orientation is to the *future* and concerns *what Israel will be* if she agrees to this covenant with Yahweh.

Part one receives its punch from the fact that Moses and Israel have personally experienced God's deliverance in the immediate past. The message begins with the words *you have seen.* Their own eyes have seen and their own minds have been impressed with the acts of God. He has judged Egypt and totally demolished Pharaoh's army.

He has also carried Israel on eagle's wings. This wonderful picture of God's care as a mother eagle over her young is most fully described in Deuteronomy 32:10-12. Here the mother eagle hovers over her young and spreads her wings to catch them as they learn to fly. This is how God has watched over His people. He has not only given them birth but has cared for and trained them. Those looking for powerful maternal images for God should surely appreciate this one. It occurs often in the Psalms as well (see, for example, Ps. 17:8; 36:7; 57:1; 61:4; 63:7; 91:4).

Finally God says, "I have brought you to myself." The whole emphasis is *personal*. God wants intimate personal relationships with His people. Deliverance is not enough. Care can be impersonal. The climax of what God has done is to bring Himself in close communion to His people. This is what He desires!

This is what God has done, so now we must ask what Israel is to do. Two things are mentioned: "Obey me fully," and "Keep my covenant" (19:5). Every word in these two responses or conditions is crucial to fully understand what God desires of His people.

Israel is to *obey*. Christians have listened far too long to a theology that makes a monumental difference between *faith* and *obedience*. Faith, to this way of thinking, is good, and obedience is unpleasant and legalistic. In the Semitic mind, such a difference did not exist. People who really had faith would obey and follow. If you followed/obeyed (the Hebrew word literally means to "hear" or "listen"), it signified that you had faith. The two words and ideas are not opposites but rather complementary. One signifies an *attitude* of trust and acceptance (faith) and the other an *action* of following (obedience). Obedience is *not* legalistic in itself. It is the wrong attitude that can turn obedience (or faith, for that matter), into legalism.

Israel is not just to obey, she is to obey *"me,"* that is, Yahweh. The obedience is not a slavish following of an abstract legal code but a heartfelt response to a saving Person.

I am glad that in this basic statement of covenant God makes it clear that obedience is personal. Of course, Israel is told to obey laws, ordinances, regulations, etc., in many places. The law words, however, are usually prefaced by the adjective *my*. The laws are *Yahweh's* laws. To obey is to lovingly follow the One who bears us up on His wings.

Israel is not only to obey Yahweh personally but also to obey *fully*. There is something exclusive and complete about the obedience Yahweh asks. He brooks no rivals. No other god can claim such obedience. Selective obedience to *some* of what Yahweh wants is not acceptable. *All* Yahweh says is to be followed.

The second phrase in this section dealing with Israel's response is *Keep my covenant*. The first two words closely parallel the phrase we have just examined. Israel is to "keep"—that is, follow and live by—the covenant. This keeping of the covenant is a personal response because it is *my*—Yahweh's—covenant.

The word *covenant* deserves some special consideration. The debate as to the origin, meaning, and theological significance of the covenant has raged for years in both the church and the scholarly world. I do not expect to answer all the questions that have been raised over the years, but I do believe we can find some guidelines that will help us understand the meaning of the word *covenant* in Exodus.

Where did the covenant idea come from? We know that the word *covenant* (and ideas connected with it) was quite common in the culture of the ancient Near East. The particular setting we know the most about was political treaties, in particular, international treaties.

We have large numbers of documents that deal with the covenant form in treaties from three main eras: The Hittite Empire (ca. 1450–1200 B.C.), Aramaic treaties from Syria (ninth century B.C.), and Assyrian treaties (ninth to seventh centuries B.C.) (Sarna, 135 ff.). The period closest in time to Exodus and the era where most scholars have concentrated is the Hittite Empire.

These treaties fall into two general categories. First, there are parity treaties between parties of roughly equal status. Second, there are sovereign/vassal treaties between superior and inferior powers.

Some scholars have tried to show that what we have in the covenant at Sinai is a sovereign/vassal treaty of the Hittite type. We must remember, however, that while there are many similarities with these Hittite treaties, there are also significant differences (Sarna, 140-144). Some of these differences are that the Old Testament is unique in seeing God make a covenant with an *entire people* rather than with an individual, like a king. The Exodus covenant is also unique in that God is the source and the sanction for the law connected with the covenant.

Much more could be said, but those who are interested are encouraged to work through the material in the "Researching the Word" and "For Further Study" sections at the end of the chapter.

What should be said in conclusion to the question on the source of the covenant concept is that ancient Near Eastern culture had a covenant concept that was known to Israel, but God took that idea and built on it. He used the familiar to move to the unfamiliar and lead His people to a unique and powerful covenant relationship that made similar political treaty/covenants look shallow and poor by comparison.

What did this covenant at Sinai mean? We must be careful lest we make it too new and/or unique. While it is true that the Exodus is a powerful event and Israel's situation is new, we must remember that the roots of this go back to former times. The basic reason given in Exodus for God's exodus-deliverance is His remembrance of the *earlier covenant* with Abraham, Isaac, and Jacob (2:24, 25). Thus the Sinai covenant has its roots in the covenant with the fathers.

God used the same language with Abraham about keeping the covenant (Gen. 17:9, 10) that He uses with Israel at Sinai. The concept of obedience is not new (see Gen. 22:18; 26:5). It has even occurred earlier in Exodus (15:26; 16:28).

Thus this Exodus covenant is not totally new and different. It uses similar terminology as God's earlier covenant with Abraham. It owes its existence to that earlier covenant. I believe it is, in fact, a development of that covenant. The basic principles involved are the *same*.

The new elements of this covenant, based on the specific historical situation, are, however, important. God makes this covenant with a people, not with a single person. Although earlier covenants had a wider group in mind (Abraham's descendants), the patriarch was the one with whom God made the covenant. Now the whole people respond. A freed slave people in a new situation require special attention. Laws that earlier were assumed are not to be specifically stated, and regulations that relate to new situations must be spelled out. The principle of obedience, however, has always been present.

Although it should be clear by now, I will state it so no questions will arise: The covenant God talks about here is *not* a legalistic covenant of works. The very basis of the covenant is God, who has delivered freely and graciously. He merely asks for a response to see if Israel wants to continue their growing relationship. He has been courting her. Israel is *not* asked to obey as a condition of deliverance. She stands free at Sinai now. Is she willing to continue with God?

If Israel is willing to continue, then wonderful things will happen. God makes a threefold promise about what she will become.

First, out of all the surrounding nations, Israel will be God's "treasured possession." Israel will belong to Him in a way that other nations do not. She will be special. The exact nature of that specialness has often been misunderstood. It certainly does not mean that God would care for this nation only. The probable meaning has to do with *God's purpose*. Israel will be especially used to fulfill God's plan for the world.

This idea is strengthened by the second phrase: She will be a "kingdom of priests." Priests are mediators between God and humanity. Priests have both status *and* responsibility. All Israel will be priests in a sense. The theology of the priesthood of all believers did not begin with the New Testament. At Sinai, God promised that Israel would be a kingdom of priests to mediate the power and presence of God to others.

She is also to be a holy nation. Again the term combines special "set-apartness" with duty and responsibility. Holy people are revered, but they can only have that status if they live in a holy manner.

Israel thus is promised *privileges and responsibilities*. She is summoned to status and service at the same time. With her specialness comes her mission.

It is crucial to notice that in these verses discussing Israel's glorious role, twice the author mentions a widening of the scope. "All nations" and the "whole earth" are part of God's plan (19:5). He hasn't forgotten them. While at this time He is preparing Israel for her special role, and that is the point of emphasis, it is clear that at the same time God has in mind all those nations that He promised to bless through Abraham. The great missionary God always has the whole world in view.

Moses brings this great threefold message of past deliverance, present response, and future blessing down the mountain. He summons the elders and presents it to them. What do the people want? Do they want to continue their relation with Yahweh? Will they "marry" Him?

Yes! They all respond, "We will do everything the Lord has

said" (vs. 8). There seems to be no hesitation. Moses hastens back up the mountain to tell God.

Israel has often been criticized for this response. I think much of the criticism has been unfair. I find something charming and transparent here. Actually, the response is amazing. The people have not yet heard the specifics of what God will command, yet they still say Yes. They are willing on the basis of what they have seen of God to trust Him with their response.

Clearly they don't understand everything. They may be hasty, but they quickly say Yes because God has done all this for them. It all sounds reasonable and good. The stage is set for the next stage in the drama.

God Meets Israel

When Moses takes the people's answer back to God, God pledges to meet him in a dense cloud. That is a clear demonstration to Israel that God is speaking to their leader. As a consequence, the people will trust Moses *and* allow him to fully play his role of messenger between them and God. God also wants to care for His leader and give him the respect he needs to function.

The Lord now reveals the conditions under which He will meet with Israel. The regulations and requirements are specific. Moses is to "consecrate" the people today and tomorrow (vs. 10). The exact significance of this term is not clear. Literally, it means to set them apart for holiness. They are to cease their normal activities. The text seems to imply that the washing of clothes (vss. 10, 14) and the abstaining from sexual intercourse (vs. 15) is part of that consecration command.

Not only that, but access to the mountain is to be strictly regulated. The people are not to go up the mountain or even touch the base of it. Breaking this regulation means death by stoning or being shot with arrows. No one is to touch the offender. Animals are to be governed in the same way. Only when the ram's horn sounds are the people to approach the mountain.

On the third day, when God descends on the mountain, the

people are again warned against forcing their way through to see Him or to go up the mountain. Even priests need to consecrate themselves and refrain from going up the mountain on pain of death.

The whole tenor of this instruction, it seems, is to balance nearness and distance. God wants His people to respond to Him personally. He wants to come near, and He wants to bring them to Himself. He desires the people to see His cloud and hear Him talk to Moses. On the other hand, He must maintain some distance. God is to be loved, but He is to be worshiped and not trifled with. This is no "buddy-buddy" relationship. The power and majesty of God must be preserved lest the people lose respect and a sense of awe.

Part of the dynamic also involves Moses. This whole Sinai experience lifts him higher in the eyes of Israel. He is the communicator with God. He is the instruction giver, and above all, he alone can go up the mountain. Later Aaron is allowed to go up (vs. 4), but at first Moses is the only one.

Although it is hard to tell exactly how many times Moses goes up and down prior to the giving of the Ten Commandments, there seem to be at least four (vss. 3, 7, 20, 24, 25). Three of these four times Moses goes himself. The clear implication is that Moses is a special link between Israel and God. God and Moses are exalted together.

After Israel has consecrated herself for two days, God comes down on the mountain on the third day in the sight of all the people. Everyone needs to see the Covenant Maker. It is quite a spectacular show.

First, there is thunder and lightning and a thick cloud on the mountain. All this is accompanied by a very loud trumpet blast. The people appropriately tremble. Then Moses leads the people out of the camp to the foot of the mountain. Mt. Sinai is covered in smoke because the Lord came in fire. The smoke billows out like smoke from a furnace. The whole mountain trembles and the trumpet blasts grow louder and louder.

Then Moses speaks and God answers. What an awesome experience! The ultimate sound and light show takes place. Later we are told that Israel trembles with fear (20:18). Who wouldn't have? God had their attention!

Why all of this? It is obvious God wants everyone to realize that this is a special time. This is, in fact, the only instance in the whole Old Testament where the gathered community of Israel meets God directly and hears His voice without a mediator. The purpose of this ultimate theophany (appearance) of God is to center the reverence and attention of the people on the covenant relationship and the Ten Commandments or the ten words that are so central to it.

In a sense, some reverence and fear are good. Israel and we, the children of the twentieth century, need to meet the God of the covenant and law before we meet the covenant with its accompanying commands. We are called not so much to an abstract law code but to the God of law. We are not so much keepers of a legal covenant as reverers of the covenant God. The ground for faith and obedience is a Person—an awesome Person who can meet us and speak to us. Israel meets that Person directly on Sinai, and He calls them to fear and obey Him.

Is there a symbolic meaning to all the natural phenomena accompanying the descent of God to Mt. Sinai? It is hard to assign specific meaning to all the things that happened. Some have suggested that there was a thunderstorm and a volcanic eruption taking place at the same time. We have no record of volcanic activity in this area during that era. Besides, the story wasn't written that way. This is not a volcano or a storm, but God. All the imagery is used elsewhere to describe God and His presence. The difference is that this is the climax of all theophanies, so it uses *all* the imagery at once. Usually it's cloud and/or storm or fire. Here it is both, plus trumpets thrown in for good measure. All of it says, "Yes, in fact, God is here!"

Now the question comes—what has all this built up to? With all this amazing show when God comes, what does He actually say? That is the subject of our next section.

■ Getting Into the Word

Exodus 20

Read Exodus 20 through slowly at least twice. As you read, think about and then answer the following questions:

1. What is the very first thing God says in Exodus 20:2? Is this part of the following Ten Commandments? Why is this verse here? In light of our study so far, what is its significance?

2. Compare Exodus 20:1-17 with Deuteronomy 5:6-21. Make a list of all the differences. How many differences are there? In what commandments? Are the differences significant? Why do you think the differences are there?

3. Exodus 20:5, 6 is a statement about the way God behaves toward people. Compare the New International translation with the King James. What key word is added in the NIV? How does it change the meaning? What contrast does this verse make? See also Exodus 34:6, 7; Numbers 14:17-19; and Deuteronomy 7:9.

4. Exodus 20:18-21 records the response of the people to the voice of God. What is that response? According to Moses, why should the people not be afraid? What does the test consist of? What would sinning in this case be?

5. List the wrong ways to worship that God warns Israel against in Exodus 20:22-26. What will be the results of proper worship? Why does this passage occur here right after the Ten Commandments?

■ Exploring the Word

God's First Words

When Yahweh proclaims His word from the mountain, the first words are vital. They set the crucial context for the Ten Commandments that are to follow. "I am the Lord your God who brought you out of Egypt, out of the land of slavery" (vs. 2). He identifies Himself clearly as the delivering Exodus God. The commandments that follow are not some abstract code but the will of the delivering God, who is establishing a relationship with His redeemed people.

In many churches I have seen a picture of the two tables of stone with the Ten Commandments written on them. Sometimes this picture is in the foyer of the church, but often it is in a prominent place at the front of the church, on the wall behind the pulpit. Never have I seen such a picture that clearly contained this verse (vs. 2). What a tragedy! To study the Ten Commandments without knowing that this verse comes first is a sure way to invite misunderstanding and legalism into the church. It is interesting to note that for the Jews this verse is the first commandment.

In a very real sense, this verse is a summary of all that has gone on in the first nineteen chapters of Exodus. This one verse states in capsule form everything that has led up to Sinai. Everyone who memorizes the commandments should memorize this verse first. The only ones who can keep the commandments that follow with the right spirit and attitude are those who know that the One requesting obedience is the Lord, who has delivered them from slavery. This deliverance is what gives God the right to ask His people to obey.

This verse is also important because the commandments come to an already-delivered people. The commandments are not a way to earn salvation. Salvation has been accomplished. The commandments are instruction to guide delivered people into a proper style of life and behavior.

This is a good point in this chapter to discuss an interesting structural feature of Exodus that is unique. Most law codes are just that—law codes. Exodus contains law codes, but they are interspersed with story or narrative. This point was mentioned in the introduction to this book, but it needs further exploration.

Every segment of Exodus that is a code of laws, regulations, or commands is bracketed by story. There are four such blocks of law: the Ten Commandments (20:1-17), the covenant code (20:22–

23:33), the priesthood code (25:1–31:1-18), and the tabernacle code (35:1–40:33). Each block is preceded and followed by story. The laws cannot be understood properly without the story and vice versa. The very structure of the book makes law and story an integrated whole.

This unique feature in Exodus has important implications and teaches us much (see Fretheim, 201-207, for a full exposition). Notice a few of the things this way of organizing can show.

God is the dominant force in both story and command. In the story we can see God's acts, and in the laws we hear His words. This combination is a full picture of the God who acts and speaks.

The laws are more clearly seen to be the gracious gifts of God when tied to the story of His mercy and deliverance. Since the story is a saving/helping story, it is easier to see the law as saving and helping as well.

Not only are the laws seen to be helping, but the motivation for keeping the law is contained in the story. The reason for keeping the law is not rational ethical explanation but the Exodus.

Putting narrative and law together helps integrate life. The divine action in saving and the human response in law keeping are joined. Law and daily life as seen from the story are joined. The laws fit with the personal experience of people. Parts of life that some have put in separate boxes are joined when statute and story go hand in hand.

This is why the entire Pentateuch is called "Law" by the Jews. Law, of course, means instruction. Instruction in the Old Testament is *both* story and statute, history and command, narrative and regulation. The two must *never* be divorced. To do so would violate the most basic fabric of Scripture and the way God deals with us.

The Ten Commandments

Before looking at each command individually, several preliminary observations will be helpful. The commandments are given in an *apodictic* form—a straightforward command or declaration of basic principle. This form of law was quite rare in the ancient Near East. The most commonly used form of law in the region at that time (and in Israel) was the casuistic or case law. Case law simply states a case—"if" such and such is to happen, "then" such and such should take place. This means that the Ten Commandments, as apodictic laws, are meant to be broad general principles and not the narrow form of case law that applies to specific instances.

Eight of the Ten Commandments are negative: "Thou shalt not...." This means that they open up possibilities and life rather than closing it down. There are all kinds of positive things that *can* be done and only a few that *cannot*. The focus is on creating a fence that defines outer limits rather than in giving detailed instructions about positive duties. Thus they are short. The two positive commands remind us, however, that there is a positive side to the commands as well.

The commands are clearly designed to build community. They are given to the newly created people of God. Their purpose is to keep these people together and protect them from behavior that would disrupt relationships and tear them apart. They are meant to be kept by the group.

The commandments are brief—easy to teach, remember, and recite. Israel probably did this often in her worship life. It is also clear that the commands were meant to be understood and practiced by everyone, and in a time when few were literate, that meant memorizing and reciting them.

The First Commandment

"You shall have no other gods before me."

This command forms the basis for all the others. Yahweh demands an exclusive relationship with Israel. He can tolerate no rivals to His claims on Israel. They are to worship and obey no one else.

Debate has raged as to whether this command exhibits belief in pure monotheism or shows henotheism or monolatry. Pure monotheism denies the existence of other gods, while henotheism and monolatry demand the worship of one god while not denying the existence of other gods.

Actually, for the purpose of this commandment and the covenant, the question is not important. Probably most Israelites at the time were theoretically henotheists. The issue, however, is not theology but priority, worship, and allegiance. Yahweh is to be first and above all in every area of life. He alone deserves allegiance, obedience, and worshipful devotion. That is what matters for the covenant and the God-person relationship.

The first commandment has a universal relevance. Not only did Israel often stray after others gods, but even "unbelievers" today worship various gods of this world. The life of allegiance is the crucial issue, not some abstract theology. In this sense the first commandment is right on target both for Israel and for us today!

The Second Commandment

The first commandment has shown clearly *who* is to be worshiped and who is not. The second, third, and fourth commandments describe *how* this Yahweh is to be worshiped.

"You shall not make for yourself an idol." This idol refers to the form of anything in heaven, on the earth, or in the subterranean realm. Humans, animals, spirits, angels, etc., cannot be used as part of worship. Israel must not bow down to them or worship them. The commandment is obviously referring to representations of Yahweh, for the worship of idols of other gods would have been forbidden in the first commandment.

Throughout history, the definition of idols has been strongly debated. The typical Western definition of idols has been that they are images of *three* dimensions. Muslims and some Christians have defined idols as *two*-dimensional representations of the divine. By this definition, *pictures* of God or Jesus in books or on walls would be idols.

To be fair to those using images and pictures, we must admit that few of them would say they are worshiping the image. They would explain their actions as worshiping God *through* the image, the image being merely a worship aid. What is wrong, then, with "idols"?

The real danger of images is that God becomes localized. We capture Him, so to speak, by a creation of our own hands. We "meet" Him most easily in places and things that we have set up. We can begin to control God and use Him for our purposes in our ways.

If this is true, then many things can become idols. Shrines, a special church, a private ritual that becomes *the* means that we use to worship, can take the place of the real God, who can show up whenever, wherever, and however He desires.

The latter part of this command has often been misunderstood. Part of the reason is the literal use of the King James Version of verse 6. God declares that He is a "jealous God," punishing children for the sins of the fathers, to the third and fourth generation of those who hate Him. On the other hand, He shows love to a thousand *generations* (see NIV) of those who love Him and keep His commandments (earlier editions of the NIV may not include the word *generations*).

In this passage the KJV leaves out the word *generations*. While the actual word is not there in the Hebrew, it should be there in English, because it is implied by the context. A contrast clearly exists between punishment lasting three and four generations and love lasting a thousand generations.

If you read the texts suggested in the "Getting Into the Word" section, you will find that this passage is mirrored in three other places in the Pentateuch, not counting Deuteronomy 5. In each of these other texts, the love and mercy of God are stressed, and in one (Deut. 7:9) the word for *generation* is actually in the text. Thus both context and analogy with similar texts support the NIV translation.

This passage thus means that God is both just and loving. There is judgment and blessing/salvation. The predominating characteristics, however, are love and mercy. The results of sin may last three or four generations, but the results of love and righteousness last a thousand generations.

The Third Commandment

Not only must the God of the universe not be captured in images, His name must be respected and cared for.

"You shall not misuse the name of the Lord your God." Popular twentieth-century theology has connected this command to the Western practice of swearing by the use of God's name. This practice has even come to be called in popular vernacular, "taking the Lord's name in vain," which follows the wording of this commandment in the King James Version.

Certainly this practice is a misuse of Yahweh's name. This practice was *not* part of Israel's problems. They would never have done such a thing. In later times the name of God was so sacred it could not be used in even the most sacred of religious practices. To profane or even lightly use God's name would have been crazy and grounds for instant enforcement of the death penalty.

Israel's specific problem was probably swearing *by* God. This involved the use of oaths to support the promises or pledges of people. In business and personal dealings, people would swear by some religious name, person, or symbol to convince people of the truth of their words. The name of God would thus be open to abuse because of the people who used it for personal gain or even deceived others by its use. Use of the name for curses and/or magical formulas may also have been referred to by this commandment.

Thus the commandment prohibited using God's name for personal advantage or gain at the expense of His real character. People who claim to be believers and proceed to conduct shady business practices or to deceive certainly need to hear this commandment.

The key reference here is to the *name of the Lord*. Yahweh cares about His good name. He is not just any God, but the gracious Exodus God, and everything that detracts from who He is, is wrong. This fits with the missionary purpose of Yahweh. If others are to learn of Him through Israel and her dealing with them, all those dealings must guard the good name of Yahweh and properly present Him.

The Fourth Commandment

"Remember the Sabbath day by keeping it holy."

We have now reached the longest of the Ten Commandments. It concludes the section relating to duties toward God.

Although the command does not specifically command worship on Sabbath, the day is to be a special one set apart for God. It is a "set apart" (i.e., holy) day. Such a designation easily led to making it a day of worship.

The command is that the day is to be a *rest* day. God rested during Creation week on the seventh day. He blessed that day then and made it holy, and we are commanded to do the same.

Why is rest so important? To begin with, we can say that physically, emotionally, and socially, people who work hard need it. The Sabbath also symbolizes that God is the One who does the really important things in this world. Our rest shows that all things—especially the things that matter, such as creation and salvation—come from Him. We can't earn them but can simply rest in His good gifts.

The day is *humanitarian*. Not only do Israelites rest, but their children, servants, animals, and visiting aliens all rest as well. All humans and animals are blessed with a day off.

The Sabbath is thus *egalitarian*. Young and old, male and female, slave and free, Israelite and Gentile, rich and poor—all get a rest. God shows no favorites in this beautiful gift of the Sabbath.

The Sabbath commandment as it appears in Deuteronomy 5:12-15 differs somewhat from the Exodus version. Deuteronomy says, "Observe the Sabbath," while Exodus says, "Remember the Sabbath." More important than this, Deuteronomy gives a different rationale for Sabbath observance. Exodus says we keep it because God rested from His work of creation, while Deuteronomy gives the exodus from Egypt as the reason. One need not ask which one is right, because both are. Humans didn't create and neither did they accomplish the Exodus. God did. The only way we can respond is by resting on the day God commanded as a memorial to both creation and redemption. This demonstrates that the commandment did not change, but the rationale and explanation for it could be broadened. The order to rest remains constant, but the reason for resting can grow and be enriched as time passes.

If there is any command hurried and hassled modern people need, it is the Sabbath. We are so busy trying to create meaning in our own life and serving ourselves that we forget that God is the only One who can give meaning to our lives. We show our "resting" in Him by resting on His day.

The Fifth Commandment

"Honor your father and mother."
Our duties and responsibilities to fellow human beings begin with our parents. The family is the key institution in society, and it cannot be strong unless each generation honors those who gave them birth.

Honor means more than obedience. It implies respect, care, affection, and esteem. It suggests a realization that you would not be alive were it not for these two people who brought you into the world. There is never a time when we cease being the children of our parents.

This commandment seems directed at adults. Smaller children by and large can be forced to honor their parents, at least to a certain degree. The challenge comes to adults who need to honor their parents at a time when the parents may need special care and when the adult children have more freedom to neglect their responsibilities.

Strict penalties for flagrant breaking of this law existed in Israel. Attack of father or mother or cursing them was punishable by death (21:15, 17). This demonstrates how seriously God and Israel took this command. The death of family life would be the death of the people of God, so violations needed to be treated as major offenses.

Israel was a patriarchal society. One of the important features of this command and of most of the legislation related to families is that the mother is specifically mentioned. She is to be treated in the same way as the father in these matters and deserves the same honor and respect.

Again Deuteronomy 5:16 is different from the command in Exodus. One difference is insignificant ("as the Lord your God has commanded"), but the other does add something. Instead of one promise for obedience, as Exodus has, the Deuteronomy passage contains two promises. Israel is told that if she honors her parents, it will go well with her in the land of promise. Again, as in the fourth commandment, the basic command does not change, but Moses feels free to add to the promise part of the commandment.

The Sixth Commandment

"You shall not murder."

This NIV translation is more accurate and clearer than the King James's "Thou shalt not kill."

The general word *kill* could be taken by a Buddhist or animal-rights activist to refer to animals as well as humans, but the word is never used in the Bible in connection with the slaughter of animals. *Kill* also raises questions about capital punishment and war. Clearly the Old Testament theocracy did believe in capital punishment, and certainly enemies were killed in battle. The reference to murder comes closer to the core meaning of this commandment. I am neither arguing for capital punishment nor against pacifism, but simply stating the Old Testament facts as I see them. (For an opposing argument, see Fretheim, 233.)

We must be careful, however, not to limit this word too much. The word can at times refer to unintentional killing (Deut. 4:41, 42; 19:3, 4, 6) or the execution of a convicted killer (Num. 35:30).

We can safely say that violence against another person out of hatred, malice, deceit, or a desire for possessions is forbidden. Nothing destroys the community of the people God is creating more than violence against another. God is the author of life, and only He has a right to take it.

This commandment is the first of several that deal with relationships among equals. Parents are special and deserve *honor*. Other fellow humans deserve the right to exist near us with no fear of violence or death at our hands. If they practice violence, they deserve to lose their status in the community of faith.

The Seventh Commandment

"You shall not commit adultery."

In the ancient Near East and in the Old Testament, adultery was called "the great sin." It was used in conjunction with both men and women as subject, though far more frequently of men. By analogy it is a designation for idol worship, which breaks the covenant ("marriage") relationship with Yahweh.

Adultery in the Old Testament was sexual intercourse of a man with the wife or fiancée of another man or sexual intercourse of a wife with a man, probably a married one (see Durham, *Exodus*, 293). As far as sexual infidelity was concerned, the Old Testament treated a man's fiancée the same as it would a wife, which reflects Israel's stronger view of engagement or betrothal (Deut. 22:23-29).

Adultery was taken very seriously. The penalty for this "great sin" was either death by stoning (Deut. 22:24) or by burning (Gen. 38:24; Lev. 20:14; 21:9). Adultery was not only the breach of a human trust that disrupted the family but was also considered a direct sin against God (Gen. 20:9; 39:9). Undoubtedly our society could learn something from this, for often even believers treat adultery as something not too serious.

In the Old Testament, fornication was clearly in a different category than adultery. There are, however, passages that show at least certain kinds of fornication to be wrong conduct (22:16, 17).

Some types of perverted sexual behavior other than adultery were also severely punished, such as bestiality (22:19). For those who want to investigate such matters further, the most extensive treatment occurs in Leviticus 18.

Those who covenanted with Yahweh were expected to keep their marriage covenant faithfully. This was for the sake of family and for God. Any serious violation of either covenant was grounds for death.

The Eighth Commandment

"You shall not steal."

Can you imagine living in a tightly packed tent city with a lot of stealing going on? Nothing is more disruptive of life in such close quarters as thievery. Life in a community demands that stealing be banned. As with all the other commandments, stealing is a sin against humanity, but it also is a sin against God. Covenant keepers must not take the property of others.

Property in Israel was not so much a person's wealth as it was an extension of the person. To be the victim of thievery was more than losing a possession, it was a violation of the self. Stealing was a personal affront.

Many scholars feel that the specific thrust of this commandment had to do with stealing people, i.e., kidnapping others to make them slaves. While such stealing certainly was terrible (and punishable by death—21:16), most students believe that the command applied to any kind of theft. The usual penalty for such general theft was restoration of whatever was stolen. To discourage theft, in many instances people were required to overcompensate—to return more than they had stolen.

The Ninth Commandment

"You shall not give false testimony against your neighbor."

The basic thrust of this command is judicial. It protects the integrity of the court legal system. To give false testimony is to lie in court to the harm of a fellow citizen.

The legal process in Israel was based on the testimony of witnesses. At least two witnesses were required to sustain a charge (Num. 35:30; Deut. 19:15). A lying witness would destroy that process. Guilty people could go free, or innocent people could be condemned. For this reason, the penalties for false accusation were particularly severe (Deut. 19:16-21). People's reputations, status, and even life were at stake. The truth had to be told in court.

Israel perceived God to be a righteous judge who gave honest treatment to all. Israelites had to behave in the same way with each other, so members of the covenant community could receive honest judgment.

By extension the commandment applies to falsehood of any kind. If lying in court could destroy someone, so could lying to them or about them outside of court. The only way to protect human relationships, both in legal situations and in life in general, is to give true testimony.

A slightly broader implication to the commandment is suggested by the way it is given in Deuteronomy 5:20 (Durham, *Exodus*, 296, 297). Although the English translation of the NIV renders the verses in Exodus 20 and Deuteronomy 5 exactly the same way, one Hebrew word is different. The word in Exodus 20 describing testimony refers specifically to lying or false testimony. The word used in Deuteronomy means something vain or worthless or empty. Inconclusive, misleading, or meaningless testimony is thus referred to as well as false testimony.

The reputation and life of fellow human beings depends on our truthfulness. The cohesiveness of the community is based on a legal system of integrity. God has been truthful with us, and He demands that we be truthful with each other. This is part of the covenant.

The Tenth Commandment

"You shall not covet."

The tenth commandment is unique in that it deals with an inner attitude rather than an outward act. In a very real way, it serves as a summary of the commandments, because covetousness can lead us to break the other nine.

In an effort to harmonize this commandment with the others, some have tried to say that *covet* includes not just an attitude but an action as well. This argument is not sustainable when the word for *covet* is studied in the Old Testament, and it is also shown to be false by the context. If coveting your neighbor's wife referred to action, it would already be covered by the seventh commandment.

If coveting your neighbor's property was the action of taking it, this also would be forbidden by the commandment against stealing.

We are back, then, to our original meaning. *Covet* means to want something you have no right to. It signifies wanting with a mind-set that is harmful. The one coveting yearns for, longs for, and lusts over that which is not rightfully his or hers. This need not mean simply desiring the possession or family of another. It can also refer to coveting the religion or religious experience of another, which could lead to idolatry and the breaking of the first four commandments as well as those relating to human relationships.

The Deuteronomy 5 version of this commandment differs somewhat from Exodus 20. The order of house and wife is reversed, and Deuteronomy adds *land* to *house* as a thing not to be coveted. The part that has received the most discussion is the choice of a different Hebrew word for *covet* in the second part of the verse. The NIV signals this difference by its translation of "set your desire" rather than "covet." I do not see any of these differences as significantly altering or changing the meaning of this commandment.

In the first nine commandments, God clearly cares about right actions. Commandment ten makes it clear that He cares about right attitudes and thoughts as well. The breaking of God's inner-attitude commandment is a sin against Him and can easily lead to the breaking of any or all of the other nine.

In conclusion, several key principles should be kept in mind as we think about the commandments.

First, *these commandments can only be truly understood and kept when they are seen in the covenant context following the Exodus deliverance.* The commandments as merely a legal code lose their punch. With the story added, they become the personal words of a delivering, saving Yahweh who establishes a covenant relationship with His people. They are personal and relational, not just legal. Breaking them is not simply a legal violation but a sin against Yahweh and the violation of a relationship. That is what gives the commands power and makes them unique.

Second, *these commandments are truly universal.* I have lived and worked in several cultures. I have studied both ancient and modern history. The applicability of these commandments across time and cultures is amazing. It would be hard to find a culture in which the principles outlined here would not be seen as ideal behavior.

Third, *these commandments need to be heard today.* We are suffering from too much talk of rights and privileges and too little talk of obligations and responsibilities. The wonderful balance in Exodus of the gracious deliverance of Yahweh *and* the corresponding duties that result needs to be heard. The Ten Commandments proclaimed in their Exodus context are strikingly relevant to the needs of society today.

Response of the People

The people are overwhelmed by this whole experience. Perhaps mixed with their fear and trembling is sensory overload. They have seen, heard, and experienced too much. They want Moses to speak to them. They will listen to him. If God speaks to them, they are afraid they will die. Moses responds positively.

"Don't be afraid," Moses says, "for God has come to test you so that the fear of God will be with you to keep you from sinning" (vs. 20). What does Moses mean? How is this all a test, and what would sin mean in this case?

The word translated "test" or "prove" can also mean to "see" or "experience." Durham (*Exodus*, 301; see also 303) translates the phrase, "For it is the purpose of giving you the experience that God has come." God wants the people to experience Him directly. That will bring reverence and awe (words that for us better express the meaning of "fear" in this context), which will help prevent sin, that is, the future breaking of the commandments.

The parallel passage in Deuteronomy 5, and in particular verse 24, seems to support this translation/interpretation. This verse emphasizes the seeing, hearing, and experiencing of God, as does Exodus 20:18. The Samaritan version of the Pentateuch, in fact, inserts Deuteronomy 5:24-27 into Exodus 20:19.

Israel's experience of God on Sinai is not to make them afraid in the sense of being paralyzed by terror, but rather to make them fear in the sense of reverence and holding in awe. This holy awe is seen in many places in the Pentateuch to be a powerful incentive to right behavior.

After this interchange, Moses goes up the mountain, back to God. He seems to have heeded the people's request. God has more to say, so he goes to receive it. We will soon find out what God wants to say.

Israel's Worship

As is normally the case in response to major revelations of God, the issue of worship surfaces. This passage (20:22-26) is no exception. The fireworks on Mt. Sinai lead to a discussion of proper worship.

This section of regulations on worship begins a whole section of laws, perhaps as a prologue to it. This section is often called the covenant code. We will deal with it in detail in the next chapter. What we want to notice here is that this block of laws begins in much the same way as the Ten Commandments—with a statement of God's past merciful interaction with Israel. The Ten Commandments commenced with a recollection of the Exodus, while the covenant code begins with a reminder of God's speaking on Sinai.

There are certain ways that worship should *not* be conducted. These include the making of other gods, particularly those of precious metals of gold and silver. The altar to be used in the worship of Yahweh is not to be made of dressed and shaped stones. Altar stones are defiled if metal tools are used on them. The altars are not to be made with steps going up to them lest the nakedness of the priests be exposed.

The prohibition of idolatry and other gods is clear and harks back to the Ten Commandments. The one difference seems to be the mention of gold and silver. The beautiful idols of other peoples made with precious metals are not to lead Israel astray. Idols made of such things are included in what is forbidden by the Ten Commandments.

The meaning of prohibition against dressed stones is less certain. It probably refers to Canaanite or other heathen practices of using such stones in their altars. Israelite altars are to be different. Many altars of the other nations did include steps, and some priests wore nothing under their robes. The Israelite priests are not to expose themselves in this way as they serve at the altar.

God desires for worship an altar of earth and sacrifices from the flocks and herds of His people. More importantly, *He* is to choose the place of the altar (vs. 24). Wherever He chooses, there He will meet with those who come, and there He will bless them.

God clearly cares about the specifics of worship. Israel is not to worship like the nations around her. She is to worship in the *way* and in the *place* that Yahweh chooses. When she does this, God will be present, and He will bless her.

The powerful Sinai experience of the voice and the presence of God is over. The basis of Israel's responsibilities in her relationship with God has been spelled out. Details need to be worked out, but that is the subject of succeeding chapters.

■ Applying the Word

Exodus 19, 20

1. Try to place yourself at Mt. Sinai and relive with Israel what happened there. What are your thoughts and feelings? What impresses you most? What appeals to you about the experience, and what troubles you? If God were to come and speak with His people today, would He do it in the same way? Why?

2. Has God carried you on eagle's wings and made you a priest? If not, why? If yes, how? Does God want His people today to be special? Why? Are there dangers in being God's treasured possessions? What are they? How

can they be avoided?

3. Do you today have anything like a "holy mountain" that you cannot touch or climb? Is anything in your life so holy that you must be very careful about touching it? Should you have such things? Why? What do you hold in reverence or awe?

4. Go through the Ten Commandments and apply them to your situation. What other gods are you tempted to worship? What idols entice you? How do you misuse God's name, and so on? Now that you know what they *meant*, consider what each *means* to you in your life.

5. How do you view the commandments? Are they a bothersome bunch of regulations, or are they a good gift of God? Do you see them in the context of your deliverance by God or as a requirement for salvation? What part of your story do the commands fit into? Does your history make it hard or easy to obey them? Why?

6. Where does God want His name to be honored today? How does He want it honored? What regulations should govern your worship today? What kind of worship would be false because it mimics those who follow other gods?

■ Researching the Word

1. Using a concordance and looking under words like *Sinai* and *covenant*, look up other places in the Old Testament where the Sinai covenant is referred to. Do the same for the New Testament. Be sure you look at Galatians 4:21-31 and Hebrews 12:18-24. How is that covenant portrayed? Is it good or not so good? Why do you think Galatians and Hebrews talk about Sinai like they do? Are they fair in their reporting? What do you believe on the basis of this study about the nature of the Sinai covenant? How does this affect the way you look at Israel and at God?

2. Use a concordance to look up all the occurrences of the

word *law* in the New Testament (or in a particular book
of the Bible, such as Matthew or Romans). Read enough
of the context that you can be fairly certain what *law*
means in each case. Besides referring to the Ten Commandments, what other ways does the New Testament
use the word *law*? Identify which texts clearly refer to
the Ten Commandments. What place do the Ten Commandments have in the life of Christians since the cross?
Are all passages that talk about the Ten Commandments
equally clear on this? What problems do you encounter? How do you explain them?

∎ Further Study of the Word

1. For a general overview, see Ellen G. White, *Patriarchs
   and Prophets*, 303-310.
2. For an in-depth study of the covenant and its use in Scripture, see Gerhard Hasel, *Covenant in Blood*. See especially chapters 7-9.
3. On the uniqueness of the Israelite Sinai covenant, see
   Nahum M. Sarna, *Exploring Exodus*, 140-144.
4. For an in-depth treatment of the Ten Commandments,
   see John I. Durham, *Exodus*, 284-299.

CHAPTER NINE

God Confirms
the Covenant

Exodus 21:1–24:18

The light-and-sound show of Mt. Sinai is over. The voice of God that spoke His ten words no longer thunders in the ears of the people. The high point of theophany (a vision of God) now moves to the relative calm of daily living.

The Ten Commandments give the foundational principles of life, but for practical use in deciding cases on a day-by-day basis in disputes and court, they must be interpreted. Daily living is too complex, its specific cases too varied, for quick answers. What it means to follow Yahweh in practical terms now needs to be spelled out.

That is what the covenant code is about. How do you live in covenant as the people of God in everyday life? Before Israel can really seal and confirm her "marriage" to Yahweh, she needs to know the details, the "fine print," of her responsibilities. We want to look at that fine print now. I believe it can teach us much about God and our daily lives as His people.

■ Getting Into the Word

Exodus 21:1–23:13

Read Exodus 21:1–23:13 carefully at least twice. As you read, look for answers to the following questions, and write them down. Your study will be much more meaningful if you do.

1. On a sheet of paper, write the numbers 1 through 10, leaving ample space after each number to write down words and references. These numbers represent the Ten Commandments. As you read this section, write the reference for each of the laws that relate to the Ten Commandments beside or under the appropriate number. Do you find any commandments that are not referred to, fleshed out, expanded, or amplified? What new things do you learn about the Ten Commandments from this brief study? Are these laws relating to the commandments to be kept today? Why?

2. Some of these laws deal with people who are not to be mistreated or taken advantage of. Make a list of such people. What are the reasons given for such special attention? What do these reasons teach us about God? Note especially Exodus 22:26, 27.

3. Make a list of all the offenses that are to receive the death penalty. What does this say about the seriousness of these crimes? Would you make the same list? How would your list differ? What principles lie behind these punishments of Israel?

4. Make a list of all the laws that require restitution. What kind of restitution is called for? Why is restitution necessary? What principle can you draw from this?

5. Exodus 23:10-12 deals with the Sabbath. How is the fourth commandment extended in this passage? What is the reason for this extension? See Leviticus 25 for even further extensions of the Sabbath. What additions do you find there? Are any of these extensions valid for us today? Why?

6. See Exodus 21:23-25. This *lex talionis* law has been widely cited as barbaric. What do you think most people believe it means? Read the verse very carefully in *context*. What do you think it means in Exodus? Is it barbaric? Why?

■ Exploring the Word

Israelite Case Law

You may recall the difference between apodictic and casuistic laws that was pointed out in the last chapter. Apodictic laws are broad, general, direct statements of principle, like the Ten Commandments. In this section we meet the casuistic or case laws for the first time. They often have specific punishments connected with them. Exodus 21:2–22:17 is mainly case laws. Exodus 22:18–23:19 contains many apodictic laws, with a few case laws thrown in for good measure.

Having just studied the Ten Commandments, you will be impressed with how many of these laws are closely related to those "ten words." If you did the first exercise, you no doubt found that almost every commandment has at least one case law related to it, and some have numerous cases. The possible exceptions are the second commandment against idolatry and the tenth commandment against covetousness. We should remember, however, that the second commandment was expanded on in the passage just before this one (20:23; 22:20 may also be connected with this commandment), and that the tenth commandment is by nature not an action command. The tenth commandment can actually lie behind many of these commands as the attitude that leads to law breaking.

The first commandment clearly lies behind 23:13. To invoke the names of other gods is related to having other gods and is forbidden. Exodus 22:28, which forbids blaspheming God, is connected with the third commandment. The Sabbath commandment is partially repeated and expanded in Exodus 23:10-12. Exodus 21:15, 17 calls for capital punishment for those who attack their parents or curse them, and thus it expands commandment number five.

The sixth commandment against murder is expanded in 21:12-14, where laws are given that prohibit hurting or attacking another person. Exodus 22:16, 17, 19 is related to the command against adultery. In the first instance, fornication seems not to be classed as adultery but has certain consequences, while the second instance, bestiality, would seem to be classed as adultery. Elaborations in this section on the eighth and ninth commandments against stealing and false testimony are too numerous to mention.

Several factors need to be noted. It is clear that a large number of these laws are directly or indirectly related to the Ten Commandment law. The same is true for the other two major sections of laws in the Pentateuch—Leviticus 17 to 25 and Deuteronomy 12 to 28. If one leaves aside laws having to do with the tabernacle sacrifices, priests, and festival days, *most* laws have some relationship to the Ten Commandments. These laws attempt to put into practice the principles embodied in the Ten Commandments.

The question naturally arises, To what extent are we to keep these case laws today? Are they still valid? My short answer is that *all* of them are to be kept *in principle*. As we have seen, they are by and large applications of divine principles to Israel's specific historical situation. These laws show how God wanted Israel to live in her particular place, time, and culture. Culture and times change. Principles do *not* change, but applications do. To the extent that these laws show divine principle, they are to be kept. To the extent that the application to Israel's setting no longer applies to our culture, we must *re*apply them.

Most of us no longer have oxen that gore, but we may have dogs that bite, or we may drive our cars recklessly. We no longer have slaves, but we have employees and students who deserve to be treated fairly and kindly.

Care for God's Special Ones

The test of any code of laws is largely who gets help and protection. Do the laws protect the interests of those who are privileged and powerful, or do they defend the weak and needy? One would expect God's laws to do the latter, and this section of law amply illustrates the point.

Our world doesn't like the idea of servants, and in particular, it does not like slavery. However, these practices were well nigh universal in the ancient Near East. We today could wish that God had in one great commandment forbidden slavery. He clearly did *not* do this, but He took great pains to make slavery more humane and to point in a direction that would end in freedom for all slaves.

The best way to really understand these laws relating to servants and slaves is to compare them with other law codes in the ancient Near East. If you want more detail, see the references at the end of this chapter. For now, I will just give you the evidence in summary form.

Slaves in Mesopotamia and Israel were by and large domestic. While slaves were members of the household and recognized as human beings, they were also movable property. The Mesopotamian slave was branded and his/her father's (family) home was never recorded. Injury to the slave was recompensed to the slave's master. The slave could be given as pledge on a loan and sold or exchanged.

While Israelite laws are not the ideal, they are considerably more humanitarian. They call for the treatment of slaves more as persons. Exodus 21:20 specifies that if a master beats a slave to death, he is guilty. This provision is unique in ancient Near Eastern law. Also unparalleled is the stipulation that if the slave loses an eye or a tooth at the hand of his/her master, freedom is automatically given.

In Hammurabi's Babylonian law code, the one who helps a slave escape or who harbors a runaway slave will incur the death penalty. In Deuteronomy 23:16, 17, the exact opposite is decreed. Slaves who seek refuge with Israelites are not to be returned, but may choose where they want to live and are not to be ill-treated.

Many of the pentateuchal laws on slavery sound harsh to our ears, but we must remember that they were a big improvement over the laws in the world surrounding Israel. They also point in the right direction and show the right tendencies.

Other groups receive special mention in these laws. Twice, Israelites are specifically forbidden to mistreat or oppress aliens

(22:21; 23:9). The reason given is that Israel was an alien in Egypt. God was merciful to them as aliens, and they must be merciful to those who share their former status. To mistreat such people is to separate the Israelites from their own history.

No advantage is to be taken of widows and orphans. God will hear their cry and severely punish those who abuse them. Their mistreatment makes God angry (22:22-24).

Debtors were often abused in ancient Near Eastern society. Incarceration or slavery could result from an unpaid debt. God is concerned about such people. They are not to be charged interest, and if the cloak that keeps them warm at night is taken in pledge, it must be returned by sunset. They need to be able to sleep in warmth at night (22:25-27).

The poor are not to be denied justice (23:6). Courts must be fair. They are also to get free food (23:11)! This concern for aliens, widows, orphans, debtors, and the poor is unique. Hammurabi's code and other ancient Near Eastern codes have almost no concern for the disadvantaged in society. Non-Israelite laws for the most part safeguard the interests of the upper class—the landowner and slave master. Human life is cheap, and property is highly valued. Many offenses involving only property impose the death penalty on violators. Israel's laws care for the disadvantaged and value human life over possessions.

Besides the treatment of the disadvantaged, law codes can be evaluated on the basis of punishment. By examining the misdeeds that receive the harshest penalties, we can tell what things are most important. Examining where the death penalty is decreed in Israelite law tells us much about what God considers important.

The death penalty is called for ten times in chapter 21. Note that I am assuming that "destroy" in 22:20 means death. This penalty is decreed for murder and intentional killing (21:12, 14), attacks on or cursing of parents (21:15, 17), kidnapping and then keeping or selling a person (21:16), owning a known killer ox that kills again (21:29), sorcery (22:18), bestiality (22:19), sacrifice to other gods (22:20), and mistreatment of widows and orphans (22:24).

These are all sins against *people* or *God*. Property sins are not capital offenses. Thus it is obvious that to God, people are more important than things.

Consider, also, that most of these acts are directly related to the Ten Commandments. If we assume sorcery is a form of worshiping other gods or spirits, the only exception is the treatment of widows and orphans. In this last case, the punishment wording is different. In all other cases, the wording leads us to believe that some person is to execute the judgment, while in this case Yahweh says, "*I* will kill you with the sword." Violators in this case contend not simply with humans but with God.

The idea behind all this is that God cares about these people. He is "compassionate" (22:27). When you care, you make practical provision in laws and everyday life to demonstrate that concern.

The laws that demand restitution or a fine as punishment include those having to do with injury to a human being short of death (21:19), certain violent acts toward slaves (21:26-32), and theft or destruction of property (22:1-15). Perhaps one could also consider the bride price to be restitution in a case in which the seducer of a virgin must pay even if he can't have the woman as his wife (22:16, 17).

Such punishment clearly implies that these sins are less crucial than those calling for the death penalty. In general they are related to human injury and property violations, including theft. This list reinforces what was said earlier: These laws make *things less important* than people and God.

While we may not like the fact that the Hebrews were allowed to have slaves and that maidservants were not treated the same as menservants, we can still learn much from these laws. They are clearly God's adaptation to Israel's culture, which was a slaveholding patriarchal society. The whole tendency of the laws was to lessen abuses and begin pointing Israel in the direction she should go. This nation of slaves was given laws they could live with but that would push them in the right direction. They were pilgrims and people on the way toward a grand ideal.

The Sabbath and Lex Talionis

Before leaving this section, two specific issues are worth think-ing about: the Sabbath and the *lex talionis* rule.

Exodus 23:10-12 restates parts of the fourth commandment and expands it in a significant way. In Exodus 20 all *people* and *animals* are told to rest the seventh *day*. In Exodus 23 Israel is commanded to let the *land* rest as well. Since it doesn't make sense to rest the land every seventh *day*, the land is to rest every seventh *year*. That is, every seventh year the land is to be left unplowed, unplanted, and unused. The same is to be done with vineyards and olive groves. The reason is so that the poor and the wild animals may eat what is left. That implies, I believe, that the owners may also gather food from it.

Remember that this command occurs not only here but in Leviticus 25:1-7 as well, in an expanded form. The Israelites are specifically commanded to let the land "observe a Sabbath to the Lord" (Lev. 25:2). The same idea is mentioned in Deuteronomy 15:1-3 and 31:10, and these passages add the idea that the debts of poor Hebrews are to be forgiven at that time as well. It is a "year of release" from debts.

Immediately following the discussion of the Sabbath year, Leviticus takes the Sabbath idea one more step. Seven Sabbaths of years are to be counted off—that is, forty-nine years. The year following, the fiftieth year, is to be a year of Jubilee in which lib-erty is to be proclaimed. A careful reading of the passage shows what this "liberty" is. It is liberty from the status of alienation through loss of land.

In an agricultural society, land is the primary means people have for achieving status and earning a living. Sometimes, however, a landowner must mortgage or lease his property in order to settle a debt. In Israelite society this was done by the debtor turning his land over to the creditor. However, to keep land within the fam-ily, every fifty years all such leased land reverted to the original owner or his heirs. This helped prevent people from falling into perpetual poverty through loss of their livelihood. In other words, the people were granted rest from a *landless status*.

Since practicing such a Sabbath was not practical every seven years, it came every fifty years. The year before this Jubilee all debts would have been released, and thus the Jubilee year gave everyone a fresh start economically. No wonder Jesus in Luke compares His coming to the fulfillment of the Jubilee (Luke 4:18, 19). This is the ultimate Sabbath rest. One may also recall the Negro spiritual that compares the second advent of our Lord to this Jubilee. The application fits.

Those who cherish the Sabbath find special meaning in the way the Pentateuch expands the meaning of Sabbath. It begins with a *day* of rest for *us* and ends with *years* of rest for *land* and *unfortunate others*. What would happen if our keeping of the weekly Sabbath became the starting point for a powerful proclamation of a modern sabbatical year and Jubilee in which we reached out to feed and to free all those whom Yahweh loves? Perhaps we have only begun to explore what God would have us do as we keep *all* that Sabbath implies.

The law stated in Exodus 21:23-25—an eye for an eye, a tooth for a tooth, etc.—is usually called *lex talionis*, or law of the talion. The law has often been called primitive and barbaric. Ugly stories of putting out an eye in retaliation for putting out an eye have led to the conclusion that in the end, the whole world would be blind. The same law occurs in other places in the Pentateuch (Deut. 19:21; Lev. 24:19). In its context the law is clearly not meant to promote retaliation. Rather, it corrects two miscarriages of justice and is considered a landmark advance. First, the law is meant to make the punishment fit the crime. In the context of Exodus 21:22-25, if there is only minor injury to the fetus, a minor fine is appropriate. If, however, there is serious injury, the punishment should be more severe.

Second, the law is meant to correct a problem I call "the Hatfields and the McCoys"—a feud law calling for retaliation that is both swift and excessive. You take one of ours; we will take three of yours. Opposed to such vengeance is the *lex talionis* principle of *equivalence*. You don't take more; you take something roughly equivalent to what you lost. Thus the punishment is to fit the crime in *type* and *amount*.

In the context of Israelite culture, this law was a step in the right direction—away from retaliation, blood feuds, and overreaction to wrongs. It was meant to promote appropriateness, equivalence, and compensation in order to make the system fair.

When Jesus quoted this principle in Matthew 5:38, He was responding to a distortion of the *lex talionis* in His day, namely, the law of retaliation. What else could He do in a society in which the *lex talionis* had been misunderstood and warped? He urged people to return evil with good—the very direction in which the Pentateuch itself pointed.

In fact, with the exception of the death penalty, nowhere in the Old Testament is physical mutilation called for as punishment for wrong. And even the death penalty is based on the *lex talionis* principle of equivalence. One life equals one life. A murderer cannot buy his way out (Num. 35:31). Thus the *lex talionis* is a general principle that refers to justice through equal compensation. It is not barbaric, but fair.

■ Getting Into the Word

Exodus 23:14–24:18

Read Exodus 23:14–24:18 at least two times. As you read, look for answers to the following questions:

1. **What are the three festivals God asks Israel to celebrate? Who is to appear at these feasts? Does 23:18, 19 have anything to do with the festivals? Use a Bible dictionary to help you find out all you can about each of these festivals.**

2. **As you read 23:20-33, write down the details of how God will lead Israel to take over the land of Canaan. What is the process? Does it sound like Israel needs to do battle? Why? What is Israel's part in this takeover? What is**

God's? In the end, what land will Israel occupy?

3. Make a list of the things God says about Israel's relationship with the present inhabitants of Canaan. In particular, what must Israel avoid? If Israel fails to do this, what will happen?

4. What is Israel to do in response to God's "angel"? What is Israel to do in response to God? If Israel responds properly, what blessings will result for her?

5. Write down in order the procedure followed in the covenant confirmation in Exodus 24. Why is this process needed after what happened at Sinai? What do you think was contained in the "book of the Covenant" (24:7)?

6. Look over and review the whole covenant process from chapters 19 to 24. What steps does God lead Israel through? What does God want from His people? What stands out in your mind from this section?

■ Exploring the Word

Israel's Festivals

This section of Exodus moves on from the laws governing everyday life to special laws dealing with festivals and sacrifices. It concludes with a statement of how God will lead Israel into the Promised Land and the confirmation of the covenant.

The inclusion of the feasts in the Book of the Covenant is significant. Three times in 23:14-17 Israel is commanded to *celebrate*. The command is made in connection with each of Israel's three feasts. This command is as much a part of God's plan as doing justice and avoiding theft. Yahweh not only *wants* His people to celebrate festivals; He *commands* festivals as part of His covenant. This should say something to those of us who see things like joy in worship, potlucks, camp meetings, and church socials as optional sidelines to religion. Celebration is a vital part of God's plan for His people Israel.

Other pentateuchal passages refer to the same three feasts (Exod.

34:18-23; Deut. 16:1-17; Lev. 23:1-44). These feasts are the principal events in Israel's yearly religious calendar, which coincide with the three principal events in their agricultural year: the early barley harvest, the harvest of other grain crops about two months later, and the harvest of fruit and other crops in the fall.

The first of these is the Feast of Unleavened Bread. It took place immediately after the Passover from the 15th to the 21st of Israel's first month on the religious calendar. The time is equivalent to March/April for us. During this feast, the ceremony of first fruits took place, in which a sheaf from the first of the barley harvest was offered to God. In an agricultural sense, the festival praised God for the first of the new harvest, and in a religious sense, it recalled how Israel came out of Egypt so quickly that they had no time to put yeast in their bread.

The second of these feasts is called the Feast of Harvest or of Weeks, or Pentecost. It occurred fifty days after the Feast of Unleavened Bread in Israel's third religious month—our May/June. It was a festival of great joy celebrating the harvest of grains other than barley. During the feast, wheat from the new harvest was presented to God. In a religious sense, it commemorated the giving of the law on Mt. Sinai.

The third feast is called the Feast of Ingathering, Booths, or Tabernacles. Israel's seventh month, from the 15th to the 21st, was the date for this festival—our September/October. It began fifteen days after the Feast of Trumpets and five days after the solemn Day of Atonement. This time of great joy and happiness came at the end of Israel's harvest of fruit. In a religious sense, it recalled the wilderness journey from Egypt to Canaan and God's loving care during that period.

Even though the Exodus passage does not give all this detail, it does fit the picture if you read carefully. The command not to "appear empty-handed" (vs. 15) at the Feast of Unleavened Bread probably refers to bringing an offering from the barley harvest. The Feast of Harvest asks for first fruits from the crops they "sow" (vs. 16), which would be grain, while the Feast of Ingathering asks for crops they "gather," that is, fruit.

Although verse 17 specifically requires only men to appear, these festivals were really *family* festivals. A good example of this is Samuel and Elkanah's family, who celebrated together. The plural *you* (Hebrew) of verse 14 means, I believe, the whole body of Israel.

Exodus 23:18, 19 are probably miscellaneous regulations. The first may relate to the Feast of Unleavened Bread, *but* the next two seem general. The last regulation says that a young goat is not to be cooked in its mother's milk. This regulation is the basis for the Jewish dietary rules against consuming milk and meat together. Some have suggested that the prohibition stems from the fact that this practice was used in Canaanite religious observances. We have no proof for that explanation.

Guidance for the Journey

Before the confirmation of the covenant, God wants to unfold for Israel an outline of what He has in mind for their future. Many undoubtedly were asking, "Where do we go from here, and how do we proceed?" More important, they wanted to know, "What does God have in mind for us?" God graciously answers those questions.

What is the process God will use to bring Israel into Canaan? First, He says, He will send an angel ahead to guard them and bring them to the place He has prepared. Whatever we may say about that angel, it represents Yahweh and does His work. God's messenger—an extension of Himself—will guard and guide them to the place He has for them.

After they come to the land of Palestine, God will wipe out their enemies. He will send His "terror" ahead of them and "throw into confusion" every people they encounter (vs. 27). Some have suggested that this is disease or plague, but it is more likely the total fear and depression that comes on those who realize that *God* is against them and they can't win. This terror will cause people to turn their tails and run.

God will also use hornets to drive some of the people out. If this is literal, as it seems, can you imagine the horror of massive hordes of stinging insects descending on your town? No wonder God said the people of the land would be "terror-stricken"!

All this, however, will not take place overnight, or even in a single year! It will take place over a period of time so that the land will not become vacant and desolate and so that wild animals won't become too numerous to handle. Little by little, as the people grow in numbers, God will drive the former inhabitants out as the Israelites become increasingly capable of taking over.

In the end Yahweh will establish them in the land. Their borders will stretch from the Red Sea (probably the Gulf of Aqaba) on the east (and south) to the "Sea of the Philistines" (the Mediterranean) on the west. They will go from the desert in the south (Sinai Desert) to the "River" (Euphrates) in the north. These boundaries are very generous and were fully reached only during the days of David and Solomon.

The passage makes it clear that this will be the work of Yahweh. He and/or His angel will do it. No specific mention is made of Israel fighting or taking up arms. The only hint that Israel might have to do anything comes in verse 31, where, after God hands the people of the land over to Israel, they are to "drive them out." This could refer to simply making them leave after their defeat or subjugation. This is supported by the following context, which forbids Israel's contact with these people. Thus the real job of defeating Israel's enemies lies with Yahweh. He will do the job!

What is Israel to do, then? Do they have any work or responsibility? Yes! Their part is easy to state, but it was difficult for them to perform. They are to listen to Yahweh and His messenger and follow Him.

The basic response of obedience and loyalty is stated in a variety of ways. In response to Yahweh's angel, Israel is to "pay attention," "listen," "not rebel," "listen carefully," and "do all that I say." In a positive sense, Israel must "worship the Lord" their God.

In a negative sense, Israel must not bow down to Canaanite gods, worship them, or follow their practices. They must demolish foreign Canaanite idols and break down their sacred stones.

The people must be driven out of the land. They cannot live there. No covenant must be made with them or their gods, for they will lead Israel astray. The worship of their gods will be a snare.

If Israel is loyal and obedient, God will not only bring them into the land, but a host of other blessings will be theirs as well. Their food and water will be blessed. Sickness will be taken away. There will be no barrenness or miscarriages, and the people will live a full life span.

The passage can be summarized simply. God will work mightily to lead Israel to a safe home in Canaan. He will fight their battles for them. They must shun all contact with the local inhabitants and their gods. They must be totally loyal and obedient to Yahweh, and He will abundantly bless them in all kinds of practical ways. Sounds good!

There is one catch. You might have read over it in your haste. There is to be *no rebellion*. If they rebel (or I assume, disobey), there is *no* forgiveness (23:21). This is not just the lack of a promise of forgiveness. This is a clear statement that no forgiveness will be given. Why? How can Israel ever live with this? Don't they sin? Why does God seem harsh?

The answer lies, I think, in the context. This is the first basic statement of the covenant. This uncompromising declaration shows how things should be ideally. The seriousness with which God takes this relationship is stressed by this clear statement of what the covenant principles are. God deserves and demands undivided loyalty. Disobedience results in death.

When the Israelites sin the first time in Exodus 32 at the golden calf, God shows that He remembers this statement. Later, of course, He does offer mercy, pardon, and forgiveness (34:7, 9). Only, however, when one genuinely faces death can he or she understand what grace is all about. Grace and forgiveness are *not* required of God by the covenant. They are exactly what the words mean: grace and forgiveness—something God generously offers *beyond* what is required. Only if the first basic statement of the covenant declares the real terms can the true understanding and appreciation of forgiveness take place.

This text, then, serves as a reminder of what the true legal covenant requirements are. Forgiveness is a gracious bonus that is not required.

Did they, and do we, really comprehend what that means?

The Covenant Confirmed

The specific stipulations and laws have been given. God's plans for the future have been clarified. The time is right to confirm the covenant. Chapter 24 outlines for us the procedure.

The first two verses of Exodus 24 contain God's instruction on how Moses is to proceed after the covenant ratification takes place. Exodus 24:3-8 gives an outline of the covenant confirmation ceremony. In verse 9 and onward, Moses and the leaders of Israel follow through on the instructions of verses 1 and 2. The steps of covenant ratification are:

1. *Moses tells the people orally "all the Lord's words and laws"* (24:3). *Words* refers to the Ten Commandments (20:1), and *laws* refers to the other laws just given in chapters 21 to 23 (see 21:1).
2. *The people respond with one voice and declare, "Everything the Lord has said we will do."*
3. *Moses commits to writing everything God has said*, which I assume is all the content of point one.
4. *Moses builds an altar and sets up twelve pillars representing Israel's twelve tribes.*
5. *Moses commands young men to offer sacrifices.*
6. *Moses takes the blood of the sacrifices and divides it into two parts.* One-half goes into bowls, and one-half is sprinkled on the altar.
7. *Moses reads the Book of the Covenant to the people.* I believe this is the writing referred to in point three above.
8. *The people pledge to do everything the Lord has said and to obey.*
9. *Moses takes the blood and sprinkles it on the people.* This is the half of the blood that has been kept in bowls from the sacri-

fice. This is called the blood of the covenant.

10. *Moses and the leaders go up the mountain to see God and eat in His presence.* We can learn much from the covenant ratification sequence.

Let us examine what happened from the standpoint of the three key players—God, Moses, and the people.

God is clearly the stage manager of the covenant. Moses and the people move and respond to His command. He sets the boundaries of closeness, and He gives His words and His laws. In this process God manifests His presence. When Moses and the leaders go up the mountain after the covenant is declared and accepted, they *see* God. They do not seem to see His face, but they describe the clear pavement under His feet as being like sapphire or lapis lazuli. This is God's covenant, and when He makes it, He is active and present.

Moses has a vital role in the covenant process. He is the mediator and go-between. The covenant would not come about without a mediator. The whole process stresses the special status of Moses. He alone can come near to God (24:2).

The response of the people is vital to the covenant. As a body they must understand and react to what God is saying and doing. What especially stands out in the covenant process is the great pains that are taken to make sure the people understand. The specific terms of the covenant are spoken to the people, and then, after being written, they are read aloud to the people. The book is written so that there is a clear record of God's words and so that the words can be read over and over as needed. God desires an informed, intelligent response. The people agree to obey, not once, but twice.

The people and God seal the covenant with vivid ceremonies to make the commitment more sure. Sacrifices are made. An altar and twelve pillars are erected. Blood is thrown on altar and people. Most of us would not forget if blood were sprinkled on us! This is the only instance in the Old Testament where blood is directly sprinkled on the whole group of people.

Later the leaders see God and eat and drink in His presence. Thus through erected places of worship, sacrifice, blood, and ceremonial holy meal, the great "marriage" of God and Israel is completed.

Christians cannot help but see these things through the eyes of believers in Jesus and compare the sacrifices and the meal in God's presence with the Lord's Supper. The early Christians from a Jewish background could not have helped seeing Communion through the lens of this covenant ratification. Having just lived through this story again, I believe they looked at it through the eyes of covenant fellowship and relationship.

The sacrifice and the meal sealed the relationship. The sacrificial blood was sprinkled on the altar (representing God) *and* on the people. The sacrificial blood tied the two parties together and made them one. In Semitic culture, a meal together is not simply a physical taking of nourishment. It is social bonding. Those who have eaten together cannot remain enemies but are made friends by the shared food. On the mountain the leaders of Israel have a Communion meal with God. They are in a new relationship because they have eaten together.

Present-day Christians often see the Lord's Supper primarily as a means of remembering and cleansing. Through the bread and wine, we recall what Jesus did for us, and we are cleansed anew by His death for us. But important as these elements are, they don't tell the whole story. The Lord's Supper is a celebration and reestablishment of friendship. In God's presence we eat and drink and cement anew our bonds of community. In a sense the Communion service is a wedding reception where we celebrate socially what has just been done legally. We rejoice in the new bonds that have been created. We have by sacrifice been made one, and now we eat in the presence of God.

After Israel and God have made firm their relationship, God summons Moses to the mountain again. What Moses has written in a book, God wants to summarize on tables of stone. What started as spoken words has been recorded in a book, and now God wants to make the Ten Commandments even more permanent by engraving them on tables of stone. This relationship is meant to be permanent and enduring. It is to be memorialized on the medium that lasts the longest—stone.

Conclusion

It is easy to get bogged down in details as we read through the various elements of Exodus 19 to 24. As we come to the end of this crucial passage, we need to recall the general outline of what has happened in this section so we can see clearly the principles both explicit and implicit in the material.

The commandments, laws, and covenant can be properly understood only in light of Israel's story. If any element is isolated and examined alone, it leads to confusion. Only a people delivered and led by God can receive commandments and enter into covenant. Law without covenant is legalistic, and covenant without law is empty. Either one without Exodus deliverance is baseless. *All* elements must work together in balance and unity.

Relationships are at the core of the whole section. God is at work to reveal Himself to Israel and draw them into relationship with Him. The whole process of deliverance is designed to lead to covenant, which is a mutually binding relationship. Law governs the relationship, but wrongdoing is not so much law breaking as it is covenant or relationship breaking. Sin is not so much against law as it is against Yahweh, a person.

Important events and relationships need to be memorialized in extravagant ways. This section has a lot of sound, light, thunder, and show. From the performance in chapter 19 on the mountain to the vivid ritual in chapter 24, God is calling attention to how crucial this covenant is. It deserves to be trumpeted and written and engraved. Thundering, sprinkling blood on people, and erecting pillars help us remember. The idea seems to be that if something is important, make it important in as many ways as you can.

The importance of these events as models or patterns for future events cannot be overemphasized. The rest of the Old Testament and the entire New Testament see the events of these chapters as foundational. There is constant reference and allusion to them. Particularly in the New Testament, there is often reinterpretation, but this is still proof of the centrality of what happened here. If we know what happened, we will be better prepared to understand those passages that point back to this part of Scripture.

■ Applying the Word

Exodus 21:1–24:18

1. We have groups of mistreated people in our society. Do the laws in Exodus against taking advantage of the poor and handicapped still apply to us, either in whole or in part? If God were to give us specific laws against mistreating people as He did Israel, what laws do you think He would give us? What penalties do you think He would attach to these laws?

2. Exodus requires the death penalty for a number of offenses. Does this mean that we as Christians should advocate the death penalty? Why? Which of the laws suggesting the death penalty do you agree with? Do you disagree with any? Why? On what basis did you decide? What can we learn from the death-penalty laws of Israel?

3. Should we require restitution for theft and damage to property? Do the penalties for "sin" against property still apply? Why? What about injury to people? Should we pay fines and compensation? What principles from these laws should apply today?

4. Do we have festivals of celebration? What are they? Should we celebrate the acts of God for us? How should we do it? Would it be wrong to celebrate the Jewish festivals? Can we set up our own? What do the festival laws teach us today?

5. Do the Christians you know see the laws and command-

ments of the Pentateuch in the context of God's story of deliverance and relationship with Him? Why do some separate the laws from God and His love? What happens if a separation takes place? What can we do so we and others never forget the total context of law and covenant?

6. What events and relationships in your life do you make a "big thing" over? What about your church—what do you memorialize in extravagant ways? Are you emphasizing anything, or are you emphasizing the wrong things? Should you have more celebration in your life and in the church? What things are most important and deserve recognition and memorializing?

■ Researching the Word

1. In the Old Testament, God takes special interest in the poor. Using a concordance look up the references made to the "poor." You will find many, especially in the Pentateuch and in Psalms. Who are the poor? As you read, does it mean more than just having little money? How does God say we are to relate to the poor? What rewards and punishments are connected with our treatment of the poor? To what extent does this instruction apply to us?

2. Check the *SDA Bible Dictionary*, 4:18, for a list of the Old Testament prophets who lived before the exile of the Jews to Babylon. Then, with the aid of a concordance, look up all the references in the books by these prophets to *poor, widow, alien* (KJV concordance: *stranger* and *fatherless*). Also look up all verses in these books that talk about *interest* (KJV concordance: *usury*). Note especially those passages that apply the instruction in Exodus 22:21-27 to the times of the prophets. What conclusions can you draw about the cause of the Babylonian exile? Do similar circumstances exist today? What are

you personally doing to help unfortunate people? What is your church doing? What is your government (city, county, state or provincial, and national) doing? What should they do?

■ Further Study of the Word

1. For a general overview of the section, see Ellen G. White, *Patriarchs and Prophets*, 310-313.
2. For a description of the distinctive Israelite laws in context of the ancient Near East, see Nahum M. Sarna, *Exploring Exodus*, 171-182.
3. For a detailed description of "an eye for an eye" in Scripture and the ancient Near East, see Nahum M. Sarna, *Exploring Exodus*, 182-189.
4. For a detailed Adventist description of law, see Alden Thompson, *Inspiration*, 110-136. For a critique of Thompson's view, see Gerhard Hasel, "Reflections on Alden Thompson's 'Law Pyramid' within a Casebook/Codebook Dichotomy," in *Issues in Revelation and Inspiration*, 137-171.

PART FOUR

God Lives Among His People

Exodus 25–40

CHAPTER TEN

God Establishes a Sanctuary and Priests

Exodus 25–31

In this chapter we move into the fourth and final major section of Exodus. In part 1 we saw God's concern for Israel's desperate situation of slavery and oppression. God acted powerfully to deliver Israel in part 2. Part 3 has God initiating and making a covenant agreement with Israel that bound them together with strong ties of relationship based on love and responsibility. In part 4 we will find God establishing a system of worship for His people. That system will include a place of worship, the tabernacle—and the necessary personnel to facilitate worship—the priests.

In Exodus worship has at least two major functions. The first is a response to all that God has done. The gracious acts of God call forth worship from His people. By their offerings, sacrifices, praise, and other acts of worship, God's people recognize His graciousness to them. Worship naturally follows in logical and theological sequence from salvation and covenant.

Second, worship maintains God's presence in the midst of His people. The tabernacle must be built because Yahweh says that "I will dwell among them" (29:8). In Exodus God has manifested His presence in many ways and in a variety of places. That presence is always desired. Now that God has made a covenant with His people, the question arises, How can the divine presence be maintained among His people? God's answer is the tabernacle, where Yahweh can live and always be met by His people.

■ Getting Into the Word

Exodus 25–27

Read Exodus 25 to 27 through carefully at least twice. In your reading, please answer the following questions:

1. Exodus 25:1-9 is crucial, for it introduces the whole next section of Exodus. What are the Israelites to bring to God? Who is to give? What kinds of gifts are to be brought? How are the gifts to be used? What is the purpose of a sanctuary, and where does its pattern come from? Why and how are these facts significant for what follows? What is Israel's incentive to follow these instructions?

2. If a cubit is eighteen inches, how big is the ark? What is to go inside the ark? Using a Bible dictionary, try to discover what "the testimony" (25:16, 21) and the "atonement cover" (25:17—KJV: "mercy seat") mean. What significant things happen just above this atonement cover (25:22)? What does all this tell us about the importance of the ark? Do you think some people might think the cherubim were idols? In what way are they different from idols?

3. Besides the ark, three other articles of furniture for the sanctuary are described—a table (25:23-30), a lampstand (25:31-40), and an altar of burnt offering (27:1-8). Describe the size of each of these. List the other items that go with each piece of furniture. What is each of these articles made of? What does the Bible say about the use or function of each of these pieces of sacred furniture? Where is each one to be placed (26:34, 35)? As you read about these things, what impresses you most? Do you think God cared about detail and about making things nice? Why?

4. Describe in general how the tabernacle was made. What

is the most common material used? What are the colors used? What do you think it looked like from the inside and the outside? How big is the tabernacle? How does it compare in size to your house? What impresses you most about the tabernacle? Why?

5. How big is the tabernacle courtyard? What is it "fenced" with? How many entrances are there? Why? Which direction is the entrance? Why? Does the layout of the courtyard enhance worship? How?

6. After studying all of this, either draw a diagram of the tabernacle and courtyard, or, if the weather permits, measure off its size outdoors, and picture yourself as a worshiper. Enter the tabernacle grounds with a sacrifice. How does the whole experience strike you? What can we learn by identifying with the Israelites?

■ Exploring the Word

Reasons for the Sanctuary

The instructions for building the place of worship begin with a call for an offering (25:1, 2). God asks Israel to bring an offering as their hearts prompt each to give. The offering called for is of the most precious things the people have: the best of their metals—gold, silver, and bronze; and the best of their cloth—blue and purple. Today's experts tell us that twelve thousand murex snails were needed to make 1.4 ounces of blue dye (Durham, *Exodus*, 354). Any cloth colored by that dye is precious! God wants top-notch leather, wood, spices, and gems.

All this material is to be used in making a sanctuary—literally, "a holy place." The purpose of this holy place is so that God can dwell among them, that is, "in their midst." This dwelling place for God and all its furnishings are to be made exactly like the pattern God will give (vs. 9).

The above facts are extremely significant because they are the background and basis for the sanctuary construction. They give the very reason the sanctuary was built. Considering the fact that almost one-third of the book of Exodus—13 chapters—deals with the sanctuary, it is clear this structure is a vital part of the book. Worship is a major issue for the creation of a people belonging to God.

These facts tell us something about what God desires from people. He wants a *freewill response*. As slaves, Israel had built things for Pharaoh by forced labor. They are now free to build a place of worship for God as their hearts prompt them. God wants His people to build for Him in loving response.

The response God wants is a gift of the very best materials. Cast-off and second best won't do. God desires that which is precious. This call for an offering turns our minds back to all the things Israel got free from their Egyptian overlords just before the Exodus. Those things that once served the gods of Egypt will now serve the worship of Yahweh.

God initiates this system of worship. Everything—even the details—come from Him. There is no place here for human invention or plans. God will use human beings to construct the sanctuary and serve as priests, but they are to operate according to His instructions. He must be the source of all true worship.

The sanctuary will be the means of God's dwelling in the midst of Israel. This is a major shift. In Exodus 19 and on, God's presence has been on the mountain. Moses could ascend and be with God, but the people were not permitted to go beyond the foot of the mountain. The mountain was the typical dwelling place for gods in the ancient Near East, but Yahweh is different. He starts on the mountain, but when He has established a covenant with His people, He comes down to live in their midst. No longer are Moses and the people called to "come up," because *God* wants to "come down."

He is not aloof and distant but comes into the middle of life's struggles and needs and tabernacles right at the center of His people. This should allay any fears the people may have that God will abandon them or cease to work for them. The distant God is now the near God.

Building Laws and Execution

With that understanding in place, we move on to the plans for the tabernacle itself. We should remember that Exodus describes the tabernacle in much detail two times. The first time is in this section—25 to 31. Yahweh's plans for the tabernacle and its priesthood are laid out. Then in 35 to 40 the actual building is described. These sections are the same, with minor variations in order and detail. Specific reasons exist for the twofold description, which we will discuss when we come to our discussion of 35 to 40. However, our major treatment of the tabernacle and its furnishings will be in this chapter.

The description of the sanctuary itself moves in three steps from the holiest of all to the area of preparation or least holy. Step one is the description of the ark, the core of the Most Holy, and the other two furniture symbols of God's provisions and light—the table and candlestick.

Step two is the tabernacle itself, which covers and shelters the special furniture of God's presence. Step three is the altar and the courtyard, which are the areas of preparation for entry into God's presence.

The Ark

The ark (25:1-22) is the most sacred of the sanctuary articles. It is the place of Yahweh's very presence, and for this reason, it is the first part of the sanctuary to be described.

The ark is a chest or box measuring about 45 inches long and 27 inches wide and deep. Some suggest that the longer 20.6-inch royal cubit may have been meant rather than the shorter 18-inch cubit. If this is true, the ark would be about 52 inches long and 31 inches wide and deep. Either way it is fairly small.

The ark, as with much of the tabernacle furniture, is made of acacia wood. This tree survives well in arid areas. The wood is hard, close grained, and durable and is good for cabinetwork and furniture. The wood is overlaid with pure gold.

Inside this ark-chest is to be placed the "testimony" (25:16). This testimony is so closely connected with the ark that the ark itself at times is called the "ark of the Testimony" (25:21, 22; see also Num. 7:89). The term is synonymous with the more common expression "ark of the covenant" (Num. 10:33). The word *testimony* is related linguistically to a word meaning "covenant stipulations." This "testimony" actually consists of the two tablets of stone that were inscribed by God's hand with the Ten Commandments or "words" given on Mt. Sinai (31:18). These commandments are literally the covenant stipulations or responsibilities of Israel. They represent in a graphic way the whole covenant relationship of Israel with God. They are shorthand for all that has taken place in Exodus up to this time.

The top of the ark-chest is not made of wood but has a special cover made of gold. The NIV calls this an "atonement cover" (25:17). The traditional translation for this cover is "mercy seat." The exact meaning of the word in Hebrew has long been debated by scholars. The root word means "cover," but forms of it are also the main words that are usually translated "propitiation," "atonement," or "cleansing."

My opinion is that we have here not an "either-or" situation but a "both-and." Clearly this is a literal cover over the "testimony" on top of the ark-chest. It is also a very special symbolic "cover," since under it is the law, and above it is the very presence of Yahweh. It is also the place where, according to Leviticus 16, atonement on the Day of Atonement takes place. The word thus has the double meaning of "covering" the ark and of a place for "covering" sin.

Above this "atonement cover" and actually attached to it are two cherubim. We have no actual example of what these looked like, but most scholars believe they were winged angel-like beings similar to those that adorned the armrests of royal thrones in many parts of the ancient Near East. This fits well with other parts of the Old Testament, which see cherubim connected with God's throne in heaven (1 Sam. 4:4; 2 Sam. 6:2; 2 Kings 19:15; and Ps. 99:1).

This picture would also fit well with 25:22, where the very presence of God is over the ark between the cherubim. The cherubim would represent the watching guardian angels that form the sides and/or armrests of the throne. The mercy seat and ark would be the base or footstool of the throne (1 Chron. 28:2; Ps. 99:5, 132:7). The cherubim look down, because even they cannot gaze on the face of Yahweh.

These cherubim are not to be mistaken for idols. They are attendants to God, not God Himself. In fact, they themselves are in an attitude of worship, humility, and service. We have no records of worship being accorded the cherubim. They are not gods.

The whole imagery of the ark is very powerful. Clearly it symbolizes the entire covenant relationship between God and Israel, both by its name and by the fact that it contains the Ten Commandments. It also speaks to the very presence of God. God is enthroned in Israel's midst. There He can be met; there He gives instruction. The ark is also the supreme place where Israel's relationship with God is restored and maintained through the Day of Atonement ceremonies. No wonder Israel is so eager to use and abuse it.

The fact remains that God's presence is *not* naturally inherent in this furniture or any part of the tabernacle. He meets Moses *above* the mercy seat. There is nothing magical about the ark itself. God is not *in* any part but above and beyond and present only by grace and choice. The clear implication is, ruin your covenant relationship with God, and the ark does you no good. Would that Israel—and we—remembered that fact!

The Other Furniture

The next article of furniture described is the table (25:23-30). Other names for it are "the table of the Presence" (Num. 4:7), "the pure table" (Lev. 24:6; 2 Chron. 13:11, KJV), "the table of the row arrangement" (2 Chron. 29:18), and "the golden table on which was the bread of the Presence" (1 Kings 7:48; see also Durham, *Exodus*, 361).

The table is three feet long, eighteen inches wide, and twenty-seven inches high. It is made of acacia wood covered with gold and with gold decorative molding or trim.

In connection with the table, there are to be gold plates, dishes, pitchers, and bowls for pouring out offerings. The plates seem to be used for holding the bread. The "dish" is probably a small pan for incense (Durham, *Exodus*, 361). The pitcher is for the drink offering, while the bowl is what the drink offering is poured into. The table is placed on the north side of the Holy Place ("outside the curtain"), opposite the candlestick (25:34, 35).

"The bread of the Presence" (vs. 30) is to be on this table before God at all times. This special bread is to be placed on the table each Sabbath with incense. The bread of the previous week is eaten by the priests, and incense is burned (Lev. 24:5-9). The bread is arranged in two rows of six loaves each with frankincense beside it.

The exact meaning of this bread is never spelled out in detail in Scripture. Certainly it symbolizes God's presence with His people. Most likely it symbolizes God's presence through His care in giving food and drink to His children. By placing this bread gift before Yahweh, Israel demonstrates their thanks to God for providing for their needs. In the New Testament, Jesus undoubtedly recalls this bread that God provides when He calls Himself "bread of life" (John 6:35).

The lampstand (25:31-40—KJV: "candlestick") is to stand on the south side of the Holy Place—on the priest's left as he enters. No size dimensions are given for this piece of golden furniture.

The lampstand is to have a place for seven lamps—a center lamp with three branches on each side. These branches each have a cup (a place for a lamp) shaped like an almond flower.

With the lampstand are seven lamps. Other articles include wick trimmers and (wick) trays. The lamps are placed so that the light shines in front of the lampstand.

The almond tree is the first tree to bloom in the spring, and the lamps are so placed that the lampstand will look like a tree bursting into bloom. The continually burning lamps have a multitude of meanings. The presence of Yahweh in light and fire recalls the fire and light of the burning bush, of Mt. Sinai, and of the pillar of fire that led them by night. The ever-burning light on the almond tree shows God's perpetual wakefulness and watchfulness over His people. Those who walk with Yahweh are never in darkness.

For a description of the altar of burnt offering, we must skip over to 27:1-8. Since the altar is in the courtyard and not as direct a symbol of the presence of God as are the ark, table, and lampstand, it is treated at a later time.

The altar is built of acacia wood overlaid with copper. It measures about 7.5 feet square and is about 4.5 feet tall. The square, boxlike altar has no top or bottom but contains a bronze grate affixed at the midpoint of the altar. Coals, fat, ash, etc., can fall through the grate onto the ground below.

The utensils that accompany the altar are: ash pots, shovels, sprinkling bowls, meat forks, and fire pans. The pots and shovels are necessary to remove ashes. The basins are for dashing liquids. The pronged forks are for the manipulation of meat and fat, while the pans are for keeping and transferring coals (Durham, *Exodus*, 375). All these are to be made of bronze.

The furniture inside the tabernacle uses the precious metal gold, while the altar and other outside articles are mainly made of bronze. The closer one comes to God, the more extensive the use of the most precious metals. All of the articles of furniture are mobile, and all except the lampstand have rings where rods can be inserted to carry them. The ark is unique in that the poles are never to be removed. All other articles of furniture have the poles removed when they are not being carried.

The Tabernacle

The tabernacle (chap. 26) is a tentlike structure measuring 30 by 10 cubits by 10 cubits (45 ft. x 15 ft. x 15 ft.). It is divided by a curtain between the Holy Place (30 ft. x 15 ft. x 15 ft.) and the Most Holy Place (15 ft. x 15 ft. x 15 ft.). The total area of the tabernacle is thus about 810 square feet. The frame of the tent is made with acacia-wood pillars set in silver sockets that are bound together by wooden crossbeams. Over this frame is spread a four-layered set of curtains.

From the inside out, these layers consist of the following: First is an inner set of tent curtains woven from linen and yarn. It is colored blue, purple, and scarlet and has cherubim pictures woven into it. Covering the linen are curtains of cured goatskin that are bigger than the linen curtains to ensure that the inner curtains are covered. Third, on top of the goatskin are tanned cows' hide, and last but not least is an outer layer of sea cow or dugong skin. Presumably this outer layer is waterproof.

The open east end of the tabernacle is covered by a screen made of the same material as the inner curtains and the veil. It is embroidered with multicolored patterns rather than cherubs. This curtain is not shielded from view by the rams' hide and sea cow–hide covers as is the rest of the tabernacle. Since this curtain is farther from the Holy of Holies, its pillar sockets are constructed of less valuable bronze rather than silver or gold. Again we see the material gradation from more precious to less precious materials as one moves away from the Holy of Holies.

The courtyard (27:9-19) measures 150 feet by 75 feet. It is curtained or fenced off by linen curtains that are held up by wood posts set in bronze sockets and frames. The fence is 7.5 feet high. Since the tabernacle is 15 feet high, it will be partially visible from outside, although events at ground level will be hard to see.

The east end or entrance side of the courtyard is covered by the same linen as the other three sides. The distance from each corner to the entrance is 22.5 feet. The entrance itself is 30 feet. It is covered by a screen made of the same materials as the outer screen of the Holy Place.

The orientation of the courtyard is interesting. Morning worshipers at the tabernacle will enter with the morning sun at their backs. To worship a rising sun, as sun worshipers did, they would have to turn their backs to the tabernacle—not a likely occurrence.

Conclusion

Looking back on this very detailed description of the tabernacle, certain things stand out:

1. *The entire complex is small.* Even if the courtyard is included, the tabernacle is about the size of an average suburban lot, and the tabernacle itself is smaller than the average house. If large numbers are to worship here at one time, they must clearly stand or kneel outside the tabernacle area.
2. *Everything is portable.* The entire structure and all of its furnishings are designed to be portable so the tabernacle—and God—can move with the people.
3. *There is great attention to detail.* We may feel bored with all the details, but Exodus seems to savor them and delight in them. God is interested in fine details, pretty things, and good craftsmanship.
4. *Precious, costly, and colorful materials predominate.* Everything is first-class. The closer we get to the actual presence of God, the better things get. Nearest God, gold predominates. Bright colors pervade the interior of the tabernacle. It is clearly not drab.
5. *Few, if any, details are given about the meaning of the individual parts.* We know clearly from the introduction what the basic significance of the sanctuary is, and we can glean some knowledge from other sources. But the text gives little information about the symbolic meaning of the furnishings. We must either assume that everyone knew (thus the point didn't need to be spelled out in Exodus), or else it was not important to God for the people to understand the symbolic meaning of every detail. I favor the latter view. God's primary purpose is to initiate a worship system.
6. *The whole sanctuary seems based on a pattern given to Moses in the mountain* (25:9, 40; 27:8). Moses appears to have been given a pattern or mental picture of the sanctuary. The Hebrew word for *pattern* usually refers to the imitative repro-

duction of a material entity existing in reality (Sarna, 200-203). Exodus wants to tell us that God gave a detailed mental view of the sanctuary, which Moses used in his instruction to Israel. Divine origin is thus stressed.

■ Getting Into the Word

Exodus 28–31

Read carefully Exodus 28–31 at least twice. As you read, answer the following questions:

1. Name all those who are to be priests. What qualifies them? Why do they wear special clothes? Describe briefly the ephod, breastpiece, robe, turban, and underwear of the priests. What are the reasons for all of these articles of clothing? What should we learn from this?

2. List the things that Aaron and his sons are to do or have done to them in the consecration service in Exodus 29. What do these things mean? On the basis of what happens in this passage, try to define *consecration* as best you can. What does consecration lead to? Why is it important (29:44-46)?

3. Read about anointing in Exodus 30:22-32. Using a Bible dictionary to find out what shekels and hin are, calculate how much perfumed oil we have here. List all the people and things that are to be anointed. Who and/or what are *not* to be anointed with this perfume? Why? What does anointing do for people and things? Why is it important? Could this anointing have anything to do with the practical work of the priests in manipulating meat and blood?

4. Who is actually going to do the work of building the tabernacle and all of its furniture? What are their qualifications? Who oversees the work? Do you think there are other qualified people in Israel? Why did God choose

these two and not someone else?

5. **This whole section closes with a command to keep the Sabbath (31:12-17). What is the practical relevance of this reminder here? Could it be related to tabernacle building? What is the meaning and function of the Sabbath? What about this meaning fits well in the context? What elements do we have here that are not in the fourth commandment? How much of this applies to us?**

■ Exploring the Word

Priests and Their Dress

Now that Israel has a tabernacle, or place of worship, they need people to serve and minister there. The people naturally question, "Who will serve in the tabernacle God has just described?" This section of Exodus answers that question. It not only describes who serves, but it outlines their clothes, some of their duties, and the consecration service that fits them for the task.

Aaron is chosen for the position of high priest. Along with him are his four sons: Nadab, Abihu, Eleazar, and Ithamar. The first two sinned against God and came to an early death (Lev. 10:1, 2). Nothing is known of Ithamar personally after the death of Nadab and Abihu. He did, however, found a priestly family, and Eli was his descendant (1 Sam. 1:9). Eleazar eventually succeeded his father as high priest.

Moses has served as priest as well as leader up to this time. He cannot, however, do everything, considering the increased work load. He willingly follows God's command and makes his brother and his descendants after him priests. Most of this first section describes the clothes of Aaron the high priest, rather than priests in general (28:1, 4, 40-43).

Sacred garments are to be made for Aaron so that he may receive "dignity and honor" (vs. 2). And the special dress associated with the high-priestly office honors not so much the person but the position that God has graciously given to His people. Just as the temple is beautifully adorned, so should the priests be well clothed. A careful reading shows that their clothes are made of the same material (linen) and contain exactly the same colors as the interior curtains of the tabernacle (compare 28:5, 6, 8, 15, 33 with 25: 1, 31, 36). Priestly clothes match tabernacle curtains. God even makes priests color coordinated with the tabernacle.

The first article of clothing described is the ephod. If the order in which the priestly garments are described follows the pattern of the sanctuary furniture, we can assume that the ephod is considered the most important part of the high priest's clothing.

In spite of the fact that we are told in detail what the ephod is made of, the passage does not make it clear exactly how it is to be worn or the way it is to fit Aaron's body. Most likely it is like a long vest or shift, with front and back parts held together at the top by two shoulder pieces and with an ornate waistband or belt.

What seems most important about the ephod is the two onyx stones attached to the shoulder pieces. On each stone are engraved six names of the sons of Israel in their birth order. Aaron is to bear these names on his shoulders as a memorial before the Lord. The idea seems to be that this reminds both Aaron and perhaps God about all Israel. Whenever Aaron wears the ephod, he visibly shows that he represents not just himself but his people as a whole, and he must serve them.

Next in order, and most likely in importance as well, is the breastpiece (KVJ: "breastplate"). This item of clothing is a square piece of cloth attached to the front of the ephod over the chest ("heart"—28:9). It contains twelve different gem stones, each one representing one of the twelve tribes of Israel. This, too—like the ephod's onyx stones—is to serve as a continuing memorial of all the people before the Lord. How this functions differently from the ephod's onyx stones is not made clear, but perhaps their position over his heart gives a new nuance and suggests the priest's care and affection for the people.

Also a part of this breastpiece are the urim and thummim. While it is not clear exactly how these are to be used, the passage clearly points to them as having a part in making decisions (vss. 15, 30).

Evidently God will make His will manifest in some way through the urim and thummim (see, for example, Num. 27:21; Deut. 33:8; and 1 Sam. 28:6).

Next comes the robe of the ephod. This robe seems to have been worn under the ephod and breastpiece. No mention is made of sleeves. The skirt of the priest's robe is to be decorated with alternating pomegranates made of yarn and golden bells. The pomegranates probably symbolize the fruitfulness of Yahweh's provision for His people (Deut. 8:8; Num. 13:23). The bells are required by God, on penalty of death, to signal the movements of Aaron in and out of the Holy Place.

The high priest is also to wear a turban. Attached to its front is a pure gold plate or medallion engraved with the words *Holy to the Lord*, or *Set apart for Yahweh* (Durham, *Exodus*, 388). Verse 38 points to the fact that this medallion does not refer primarily to Aaron or the priests, but to Israel—the entire nation. Aaron in God's presence will represent Israel in God's presence. He will both bear Israel's guilt and receive her acceptance as each specific case may indicate, for he is her representative.

Last on the list of clothes is linen underwear. It must cover from waist to thigh. Whenever a priest enters the tabernacle or approaches the altar, these undergarments must be worn. Disobedience brings guilt and death. This is required so the priests do not violate the prohibition of Exodus 20:26. There is to be no exposure of genitalia in Yahweh's tabernacle area. This probably shows that Israelite worship is to be different from the worship of the nations around, where fertility symbolism and sexual practices were part of the cult.

These descriptions of clothing show us several things. First, at the most basic level, they portray the status and the authority of the priests. Israel's relationship with God is crucial. The priests are mediators of that relationship, and their clothes must fit the sacred office. Second, the clothes are a confession that *God* is the source of the priests' authority. He chooses them, and He commands what clothes they are to wear. Punishment comes from breaking these rules because God is the only one who can declare how He is to be met and worshiped.

The priestly clothes fit the tabernacle. They use the same material and the same colors and metal. They are both precious and carefully done. The vestments and sanctuary mesh perfectly.

Many symbols portray the fact that Aaron represents the whole people. When he enters, they enter. From the onyx stones on the ephod to the twelve gems on the breastpiece to the medallion on the turban, we have constant reminders that Aaron (and the other priests) and Israel are not two separate entities but one.

The Consecration

Near the end of the description of the priestly clothes, Yahweh says that after the priests are clothed they must be "anointed," "ordained," and "consecrated" (28:41). The very complicated service by which the priests are consecrated is described in Exodus 29. We will concentrate specifically on what happens to Aaron and his sons.

In preparation, Aaron and his sons are brought to the entrance of the tent tabernacle. They are to bathe and then put on their priestly clothes (vs. 4). Anointing with oil follows (vs. 7).

Aaron and his sons are to lay their hands on the head of a bull brought for a sin offering. They are also to lay their hands on the heads of two rams. All of these animals are to be slain. The blood of the bull is to be placed on the horns of the altar; the blood of one of the rams is to be sprinkled against the side of the altar; and the blood of the third ram is to be placed on the lobes of the right ears of Aaron and his sons, on their right thumbs, and on the big toes of their right feet. Blood is also to be sprinkled on all sides of the altar, and blood and anointing oil are to be sprinkled on the garments of Aaron and his sons. When this ritual has been completed, they are consecrated (vs. 21).

Then unleavened bread, cakes, and a wafer are to be put in the priests' hands, and they are to wave them before the Lord as a wave offering. These things are then burned on the altar.

Later, at the entrance to the Tent of Meeting, Aaron and his sons eat the meat of the ram whose blood was sprinkled on them, and they eat the bread. They also eat the offerings by which atonement was made for their ordination and consecration (vss. 32, 33).

This whole ordination process is to take *seven days*. Each day, a bull is to be sacrificed besides the regular morning and evening lamb.

Most people today would find the length and intricacies of such a ritual to be very boring. However, apparently Moses, the five priests, and the people of Israel like it. They savor it. Why else would they spend so much time explaining it? By extension we can also assume that God likes it!

But what did He and they see in it?

Certainly it has elements of pageant and drama. One can see in it an acted, visual story of the way God deals with people. We can also assume that it gives the priests and the people a vivid sense of the place, work, and importance of the priesthood.

In the end the essential thing is God's presence. God and Israel want to be near each other. This nearness can happen after proper consecration has taken place (vss. 44-46). If these ceremonies lead to the blessed saving, helping presence of God, then they deserve close attention. What, then, are the key elements in this service of consecration?

First, there are strong elements of cleansing and purification. People who want to be priests need to be cleansed, and this cleansing is symbolized by the initial washing of the priest (vs. 4). It is also shown in the fact that a sin offering is sacrificed for the priests (vss. 10-14). Priests are sinners and need their wrongdoing taken care of as well.

Second, there are important elements of anointing or blessing. First, the head of Aaron is anointed (vs. 7), and later the priests and their garments are sprinkled with the oil of anointing. Anointing is typically associated with an endowment by Yahweh (or His Spirit) of special spiritual power (see, for example, Isa. 61:1). Typically, prophets, priests, and kings were anointed as part of their setting apart for service to God.

Third, there is a strong element of dedication or setting apart. Special clothes are put on. Special food, which only priests can eat, is consumed. While the meaning of blood on the ear lobes, thumbs, and big toes is not clear, it is obviously something special for priests—a part of being a priest. All these things speak of special work as well as special responsibility. In a very real way, this whole complicated service makes the priests different.

Exodus 29:44-46 makes it clear that *everything* connected with the tabernacle must be consecrated, including tent/tabernacle and altar as well as priests. Only then can the coveted presence of Yahweh dwell with His people.

On Anointing, Craftsmen, and Sabbath

This major section concludes in chapters 30 and 31 with an assortment of issues. After the lengthy connected descriptions of tabernacle and priesthood, a variety of topics are briefly dealt with. We will consider several of them.

Exodus 30:22-32 discusses the anointing oil. Chapter 29 covers the anointing of the priests and their garments, while this section gives the recipe for the oil of anointing and clarifies where and how it is to be used.

This anointing oil is clearly not just oil. The base is a hin (about a gallon) of olive oil, and large amounts of spices are added, including eleven pounds each of myrrh and cassia, both of which are aromatic. The trees and probably their gum resin are used. Five and a half pounds each of cinnamon and fragrant cane (cane spices) are also added to the mixture. Fragrant cane (also called calamus or sweet cane) is derived from a reed whose leaves, stem, and roots give off a fragrance like ginger.

This is clearly no ordinary mixture. To add thirty-three pounds of perfume and spice essence to one gallon of oil is to make something more like perfume than oil. This is undoubtedly why this "fragrant blend" has to be the work of a "perfumer" (30:27). This powerfully perfumed oil is as much an expensive work of art as is the tabernacle itself.

Literally everything in the tabernacle is to be anointed with this essence (vss. 26-28). The priests also are to be anointed with it. The fragrance consecrates or sets apart everything it touches for God. It makes them "most holy." Whatever touches these anointed things will then be holy as well (vs. 29).

Because it is so special, this perfume cannot be used by regular people. The formula is not to be used by any Israelite making perfume. Anyone making perfume like this and putting it on ordinary people will bring on himself the dire punishment of isolation from God's people (vs. 33).

This perfume is thus literally the *smell* or *scent* of holiness. The odor has to be distinctive and easily identifiable. The people can literally tell with their noses that something is holy. The presence of Yahweh is recognizable by smell.

We are not sure that the same formula was used for later prophets and kings who were anointed by priests, but it well could have been. For priests who worked so much with blood and sacrifices, with their accompanying odor, this holy smell must have been sweet relief to their nostrils.

Making the Sanctuary

The tabernacle and all of the wonderful things connected with it and the priesthood have to be made. The raw materials are available through the freewill gifts of the people, but who has the skills to make them? In Exodus 31:1-11, God answered that question. This is a fitting conclusion to the description of all these articles.

God chose Bezalel and filled him with His spirit. This gave him skill, ability, and knowledge to do the work of overseeing the construction of the tabernacle. He was the grandson of Hur, who helped hold up Moses' hands (17:10). If our earlier supposition that Hur was Miriam's husband is correct, then Bezalel was a grandnephew of Moses and Aaron.

Oholiab is to be Bezalel's assistant. It is clear these two men are to oversee the work, because God says, "I have given skill to all the craftsmen to make everything I have commanded you" (31:6).

God has blessed and given special skills to two leaders, and He has also blessed a large group of others as well. This guild of crafts-men are to make everything needed for the tabernacle and the priestly items, including clothes, anointing perfumes, and incense.

This is an important point. Some people with crafting skills see themselves as inferior, with only natural, as opposed to special God-given, abilities. This passage makes it clear that artistic, con-struction, and crafting skills of all kinds are gifts of God—spir-itual gifts—which have a key place in God's plan. Without them, no tabernacle or priesthood can exist.

This section concludes with a renewed reminder about the Sab-bath (vss. 12-17). This is appropriate in a very practical way, because Israel must remember that even though they will be build-ing something special for God, they still need to observe the Sab-bath rest. The tabernacle and the priesthood are holy, but so is the Sabbath, and it must always be kept.

Some things are said here about the Sabbath for the first time. The Sabbath is for the first time called a "sign" (vss. 12, 17), that is, a special mark or symbol. This sign means two things. First, it is a sign of the *covenant*—the special relationship between Yahweh and Israel. It helps Israel remember God, who made them special and holy. Second, it is a sign of *creation*. By it they show that they believe in the Lord, who made the earth in six days and rested the seventh. What a powerful "sign" the Sabbath is!

These powerful meanings make the Sabbath a perpetual and lasting covenant. These meanings are so crucial that those who violate the sign destroy its meaning and deserve severe punish-ment. Thus for the first time the Sabbath is said to be always valid, and Sabbath breakers are to be put to death.

Also, for the first time, Israel is told to celebrate the Sabbath (vs. 16). It is more than simply a day of rest. It is to be a celebra-tion of their relationship with the God of the covenant. Joy is to accompany its observance.

The mention of the Sabbath here is fitting because it comes at the end of the section on Israel's worship system. To worship is to enter Yahweh's presence, and the Sabbath is a time to enter

Yahweh's presence. The *tabernacle* is holy in space, while the *Sabbath* is holy in *time*. The two go hand in hand as ways to experience the presence of God in space and time.

Other interesting facts can be mentioned about the Sabbath in this passage. This whole section on Israel's worship system (chaps. 25–31) includes seven speeches, the seventh of which is about the Sabbath. Creation week has seven days and concludes with the Sabbath in Genesis 2:1-3. Exodus seems to be saying that the creation of Israel's worship system is a unique work of God in seven phases, just as the creation of the world was a unique work of God in seven phases (Fretheim, 270).

The Sabbath concludes this section of Exodus. Next come the golden calf and the covenant renewal, followed by the final section of Exodus, which describes the actual building of the tabernacle. The Sabbath is mentioned at the very beginning of this section (35:1-3). Thus the Sabbath is both the *end* and the *beginning* of worship.

Conclusion

Lest we forget, everything in this section (chaps. 25–31) has been God's private conversations with Moses on the mountain. That now ends. God gives Moses the two tablets of stone with the Ten Commandments inscribed by His own finger. Moses must now descend the mountain and give this instruction to Israel. What he finds will greatly distress, but that is the subject of our next chapter.

■ Applying the Word

Exodus 25–31

1. **Do I consider the presence of God important? Where does He dwell now for me? Where are my "ark" and "cherubim"? If I want to meet God, where do I go? What do I do? How can Israel's tabernacle help me experience God?**

2. How elaborate and "rich" should our worship be? Should we use the most expensive and beautiful things we have for God and places of worship, or should we give them to those in need or to missions? Why? What do the beauty, care, and expense we see in Israel's tabernacle teach us?

3. How much should our worship appeal to the senses? Israel's had gorgeous colors, precious metals and stones, pleasant sounds, and lovely scents. Should our worship appeal to the eye, ear, and nose? Why? What about the use of art and craftsmanship? Should our worship appeal to cultured people? Why?

4. How should we dedicate special people to God's service? Are ministers like priests? Should the consecration of priests and the tabernacle teach us anything about how we should ordain or consecrate people, places, and things today? Can you think of anything in the New Testament that would negate the Exodus ordination practices? Do the same principles apply today?

5. Would I rather be an Aaron or a Bezalel? Has God anointed me to specifically religious duties, or have I been given practical skills by God? Which are more important? Why? What kind of people does God most need today?

6. What does the Sabbath mean to me? Is it a law, a sign, an obligation, a privilege, or something else? What should the Sabbath as it is described in Exodus 31:12-17 mean to me? Is the Sabbath to be a day of celebration for us, as it was for Israel? Why? What could we do to make the Sabbath more what it should be?

■ Researching the Word

1. Exodus 29:1-37 and Leviticus 8:1-36 describe the ordination of priests. Compare these two accounts carefully. List the ways they are the same and the ways they differ.

Look carefully at the context of both passages. How might this context help explain the differences? Why do we have two accounts? What can we learn from having both that we would miss with only one? What does all of this teach us about the priesthood? Should this tell us anything about ordination today? What?

2. The sanctuary was the "workplace" for the priests. Use a concordance to find the places in Exodus, Leviticus, Numbers, and Deuteronomy where the words *priest* and *priests* are used. (Be sure you read before and after each verse to get the context.) Next, make a list of the duties of the priests. Reflect on how the priests' activities helped the people to be saved and to feel that they were saved. What similarities do you find between the ministry of these earthly priests and Christ's ministry as our heavenly High Priest? For answers to this question, refer especially to the book of Hebrews in the New Testament.

■ Further Study of the Word

1. For a general overview of the material, see Ellen G. White, *Patriarchs and Prophets*, 343-358.
2. For a modern Jewish explanation of the tabernacle, see Nahum M. Sarna, *Exploring Exodus*, 190-215.
3. For a scholarly, in-depth treatment of the Sabbath, see Niels-Erik Andreason, *The Old Testament Sabbath*.
4. For a scholarly, in-depth treatment of the sanctuary by an Adventist, see Frank B. Holbook, "The Israelite Sanctuary," in *The Sanctuary and the Atonement*, 1-26.

CHAPTER ELEVEN

God Responds
to Sin

Exodus 32–34

We move from the mountaintop of communion with God to the valley of idolatrous revelry. We pass from Moses and Yahweh to Aaron, Israel, and the golden calf. We see how soon people can lose the joy of communion with God and move to the debauchery of doubt and unbelief. The story is disgusting in many ways, but the Bible would not be true to the story of the Exodus or to human experience if it were passed by.

The story challenges our beliefs about Yahweh and amazes us when it comes to Moses. We see Aaron and the people at their worst and a supposedly meek and mild Moses giving vigorous leadership. We see a covenant dramatically broken and then graciously restored. We see bodies pulsating in the dance and faces shining with the glory of God. In this short three-chapter story, we move from the highest point of human experience to the lowest and back again, and we experience a whole range of emotions.

This shocking story is recalled by other Old Testament writers. Psalm 106:20 says, "They exchanged their Glory for an image of a bull, which eats grass." Ezekiel 20:8 says, "They rebelled against me and would not listen to me" (see also Neh. 9:16-19). We must now examine this story for ourselves.

While the core of this incident starkly portrays human weakness and sin, our gaze must not rest solely on the shame. Notice where God is in the story. How does He respond to the people and to His designated leader, Moses? Yahweh's response should give hope to all whose memories recall all too clearly their personal golden calves.

244

■ Getting Into the Word

Exodus 32:1–33:6

Read Exodus 32:1–33:6 through two times. Then think about and find your answers to the following questions:

1. What is the nature of the people's sin? Why do they ask for gods? Is the calf another god or an image of Yahweh (note 33:4, 5)? What does Aaron build in front of the calf? List all the specific things people do in connection with the calf (be sure to notice 32:25 also). Do you see any progression? What does this teach us about sin?

2. Note carefully 32:9-14 and 33:4, 5. These verses seem to portray a God who either changes His mind or is not exactly sure what He will decide. Is this true? How do you explain this? Using a Bible concordance, look up other references that refer to God's "relenting" (NIV) or "repenting" (KJV). (Be sure to check which version your concordance is based on so you look up the right word.) Is "relenting" or "repenting" good news or bad news about God? Why?

3. In this chapter Moses is a powerful intercessor. Read and study carefully 32:11-14, 30-33, and list the techniques of intercession (intercessory prayer) that Moses uses. Can we still use these? What can we learn from Moses' acts of intercession?

4. In this section two threatened punishments (32:10; 33:1-5) and three actual punishments (32:20, 27, 28, 34, 35) are mentioned. List what things are threatened and what actually takes place. Do you think these punishments are fair? Why? What can we learn about punishment from this chapter?

5. Many have compared and contrasted the golden calf with the tabernacle—true worship with false worship. List as many comparisons and contrasts as you can think of as

246 BIBLE AMPLIFIER—EXODUS ■

**you compare this passage with what we studied in the
previous section of Exodus. How does this contrast help
us understand true worship?**

■ Exploring the Word

The Golden Calf

What exactly is the problem with the golden calf? Why is this
such a terrible sin? The story must begin with the long absence of
Moses. He is their leader and the people's main point of contact
with God. The people are clearly disturbed by his absence. Maybe
Moses is never coming back, or perhaps something tragic has be-
fallen him. As a group they came to Aaron, who is Moses' stand-in.

They ask him to make them "gods who will go before us" (32:1).
Aaron orders them to take off their gold earrings and bring them
to him. From the story it appears that women and children of
both sexes wore such things. From these gold earrings, Aaron made
the golden calf.

This calf was not a representation of a false god. The people's
request for "gods" (vs. 1) is a request for an idol (idols), a representation of God. This calf was a representation of Yahweh, who
was to go before them in Moses' absence. This is plain from several facts in the story. First, the calf is viewed by the people themselves as the one who "brought you up out of Egypt" (vs. 4). Yahweh
was known as the one behind the Exodus. Second, the reaction of
Aaron to the people's acceptance of the calf is to declare a feast "*to
the Lord,*" that is, Yahweh (vs. 5). Third, Aaron builds an altar
before the calf, and the very next morning the people bring offerings that Yahweh has specified for Himself (vss. 5, 6).

Calves, and in particular, bulls, were commonly used by many
peoples in the Near East as images of their gods. Memphis and
Heliopolis in Egypt were centers of bull-god cults. Israel has simply taken a familiar god symbol and used it for Yahweh. The people
have not abandoned the Lord. They simply want Him on *their*
terms, not *His.* They want to worship Him through an image.

This is a direct violation of the *second* commandment.

The people sacrifice to this idol, eat and drink before it (compare with 24:11), and then "indulge in revelry" (32:6). This final act has the connotation of sexual play (see Gen. 26:6-11). They shout (32:17), sing (vs. 18), and dance (vs. 19). Later they are said to be "running wild" and "out of control" (vs. 25). The whole story suggests wild celebration that includes sexual immorality. In short, an orgy is going on. We know similar things regularly took place in Canaanite worship.

The sin of idolatry has led to all kinds of attendant sins and problems. It is a slippery slope. When Israel starts to worship like idolaters, they fall into many other sins as well. This story is a paradigm for what will happen time and time again in Israel's history. One very prominent episode, with obvious ties to this one, is the story of Jeroboam in 1 Kings 12:25-33.

God Relents

This whole story has posed major questions for sensitive believers and theologians. The portrayal of God in this passage certainly gives us something to think about.

First, there is His burning anger and severe punishment that follows. God sees the sin, calls Israel a stiff-necked people, and tells Moses to leave Him alone so His anger can burn against the people and He can destroy them. Then He will make Moses and his descendants a new nation. God orders the true believers to strap on swords and kill three thousand of their fellows, and when the Levites obey, He blesses them (32:27-29). Later He strikes Israel with a plague (vs. 35).

Those who believe God never gets angry and/or never punishes have difficulty with this passage. Even those who believe God punishes and shows anger must pause to think about His seemingly vindictive behavior in this story.

The second problem in this passage is God's "relenting" or "repenting" (vs. 14). Later He seems to be undecided about what He will do (33:5). All that we have believed about an all-knowing, changeless, and all-powerful God is called into question. Does God change? If so, how? Does He know what He is doing, or is Exodus showing us Moses' misunderstanding of God? How should we relate to all these questions?

Several things about the text can help us. The phrase *Leave me alone* (vs. 10) may not mean "leave so I can execute My wrath," but rather, "leave so I can grieve over what has happened." At least we have here a sign that God has not yet made the final decision to bring destruction on the people. Some have even seen the whole Moses/God dialogue as a test of Moses. Will he take God's offer to make him a great nation and run with it, or does he really care about the people?

Even though some or all of the above readings may be correct, I believe the basic answer lies elsewhere. Given what has happened between God and Israel, is there any other way for God to react? God and Israel have just made a solemn covenant, which is like a marriage. The conditions have been clearly laid down. Idolatry has been forbidden. Yahweh has said He will not forgive rebellion (23:21). Now the people directly rebel and sin. They have broken their marriage vow—and so early in the marriage! To be true to Himself, how else can God react except feel outraged? The outrage is an evidence of care about the relationship and His fidelity to the covenant. In a story like this, how else can God say, "This is horrible!" than to react as if it is?

Although this first section of our reading does not take us to the end of the story, let's peek. In the end God does forgive, and the covenant is restored. But restoration is cheap unless there has been a real problem and a real threat. Forgiveness for little or nothing means little or nothing. Forgiveness for much means much. Forgiveness in this story is costly and real!

As for the punishments, we also need a closer look. We see two threatened punishments: destruction of the people (32:10) and an unwillingness to accompany them on their journey to Canaan. The first of these the people do not know about. Moses hears the threat and intercedes successfully for God to withdraw it. The second threat moves the people to distress, mourning, and the stripping off of their ornaments. The people are deeply moved to grief and sorrow. To lose the presence of God is horrible. That is exactly what they wanted to avoid by making the golden calf! That presence is what has brought them thus far. This is the first time they show any sorrow for what they have done.

Up to this point, they have suffered three actual punishments. They have been forced to drink the ground-up gold dust of their calf (vs. 20); three thousand people have been slain (vs. 28); and God has sent a plague (vs. 35). All of these punishments or judgments have come with no sign of a change of heart! Only the final threat of abandonment by Yahweh leads to change. The prospect of losing God's presence brings repentance.

Israel clearly deserves these punishments. They are outlined in the law we have studied. Before even one person loses his life, the people are given a chance to change, because Moses says, "Whoever is for the Lord, come to me" (vs. 26). Those destroyed have been warned and even given another chance. Punishment is justified and necessary. No one takes judgment seriously unless it is executed. No governing is possible if flagrant sin receives no response.

However, when people are sorry for their wrongdoing, threatened judgment may be averted, as is the eventual case with the threat of 33:1-5. Thus punishment and judgment are not only necessary for fairness and governance; they also must take place to lead to sorrow, repentance, and change. God's response and punishments are not simply explainable; they are *necessary* in this circumstance. God can in essence do no other and remain God.

This leads us to the second question, about God's "repentance" or "relenting." This is not the only place in Scripture where God is said to "repent." Two classic examples that you may like to study are found in Jeremiah 18:7-10 and 26:3, 9.

In Scripture, God never repents of *sin*. He is sinless. He does, however, repent of what some Bible translators call "evil," which means judgment or punishment. The picture of God is of justice and fairness. He knows what should be done, but in His heart He finds it hard to do. He looks for reasons to "repent of evil" because of His very nature, which we will discuss in more detail in the next section.

This means that God is *open to change*. This change is never opposed to His basic purposes but rather takes place on issues that are negotiable. This change takes place in ongoing dialogue and interaction with those who are affected by His actions. In this case it is Moses who is treated like someone who really is valuable. He can dialogue with God and change Him. God takes human relationships so seriously that He is truly *affected* by them. God reverses preliminary decisions for punishment in response to people in relationship with Him.

Moses first of all intercedes to have God renounce His decision to destroy Israel. Later he continues his intercession to ask God for their forgiveness (32:30-34; 34:9). Although the latter takes some time, he is successful in both endeavors. The Old Testament here and elsewhere clearly shows us a God with some openness to the future. I find that to be good news. What power and dignity God has given His people!

This story leads naturally to a discussion of intercession and intercessory prayer. I find this "repenting" of God to be the very basis of prayer for others. Hope is always there if God really listens and interacts when His servants come to Him with requests.

Moses does not take God's initial response to Israel's sin as final. With no excuse for their sin, he boldly confronts God with reasonable arguments to convince Him to change. He begins with two questions and ends with three imperatives. Read 32:11-14 carefully again, and note what Moses' intercessory techniques are.

1. *Why should Your anger burn against those You just brought out of Egypt?* This is an appeal to *reason*. Does it make sense to destroy what You just saved? Moses actually uses logic on God and expects results!

2. *What would the Egyptians say?* This appeals to God's *reputation* and *mission*. What the neighbors think is important, because God wants them to believe also. Destruction of Israel would be counterproductive in both of these areas.

3. *Turn*! This is an imperative—a command—as are the next two appeals. The word used here is commonly used for and translated as "repent." Moses literally tells God to repent of His anger by turning from it.

4. *Relent*! This imperative word is the exact one used in verse 14 to say what God actually did do. His relenting is in direct response to Moses' command to do so.

5. *Remember*! Remember what? The covenant! The one made with Abraham, Isaac, and Jacob, and, by implication, its continuation on Mt. Sinai. You made promises, Lord. Israel may have broken her side, but don't forget Yours! If You destroy Israel, what will happen to *Your* promises? God responds positively to this.

In his second intercession, Moses changes tactics because his *aim* is different. The above intercession was to avoid punishment. The one in Exodus 32:30-35 is to secure forgiveness.

In his second intercession, Moses acknowledges the sin of the people and then asks for forgiveness. If God is unwilling to forgive them, then Moses wants his own name blotted out of the book of life. In this second intercession, Moses seems to have been only partially successful. Some punishment comes (vs. 35), but later God does respond in forgiveness. This intercession continues on into the next section, where we will discuss it further.

If we take this story seriously, we can learn much about intercession. Certainly it should make us *bolder* in our approach to God (Heb. 4:16). It should give us *hope*, because God does interact and truly hears His people. We can also benefit from some of Moses' *methods* and *techniques*.

Just recently, with a group of others, I prayed for one who was sick. In our group was an African pastor. As I listened to him pray, there was a whole different tenor to the prayer—confidence, a sense of real interchange, and actual entry into God's presence. I was taken back in my mind to Moses and his intercession, and I wondered what my prayers might have been like if my culture had been more Mosaic in its intercession for others!

Tabernacle and Calf

Many students of Exodus have seen a contrast between the description of the tabernacle and its furnishings in Exodus 24 to 31 on the one hand and the story of the golden calf in chapters 32 to 34 on the other. The contrast is between true and false worship. I cannot help but think that this was in the mind of Moses when this passage was written. The positioning of the two accounts next to each other is so appropriate. The contrast is most easily seen if we look at it in chart form (see Fretheim, 267, for a basic chart to which I have added).

	Tabernacle	**Golden Calf**
Initiative for building	God	People
Offering	Freewill request	Aaron commands
Planning	Detailed, careful plans	No plans
Workmen	Many—gifted by God	One man, no gifts
Divine presence	Carefully guarded	Assumed direct
God	Invisible—cloud	Visible—idol
Covenant/ commandments	Carefully guarded/ in ark	Broken/forgotten
Results	Presence/blessing	Sin/punishment

Israel sought the presence of God *in their own way*, and the result was disaster. When they sought the presence of God in *God's way*, He came and blessed. God's presence is vital to His people. Worship is central to covenant and faith, but these things must be sought and done in *God's own way*.

■ Getting Into the Word

Exodus 33:7–34:35

Read carefully Exodus 33:7–34:35 at least twice. As you read, ponder and answer the following questions:

1. Exodus 33:7-11 concerns the tent of meeting. Is this tent the same as the tabernacle described in earlier and later chapters? Give reasons from the text. Check a concordance and Bible dictionary for discussion. What seems to have been the purpose of this tent? Why does this passage occur here? It seems to break the flow but must have some relevance. What is it?

2. In this section Moses again spends time interceding with God. (Note especially 33:12–34:9.) Carefully analyze and then *list* the techniques he uses and their final result. How does this build our knowledge of intercession that we began to see in the first part of this section? What do we learn about Moses from this?

3. In contrast to what seem like harsh statements in the first part of this story, we now find some of the most loving and gracious statements about God. Note especially 33:19-23 and 34:6, 7. Make a list of all the qualities of God mentioned here. What general impression do you get? How does all this fit into the story of what is happening here?

4. Exodus 34:10-28 performs roughly the same function in this new covenant as does Exodus 20 to 23 in the Sinai covenant. Compare the two for general and specific content. Make a list of the major differences you see in content and emphasis. Why are there these differences? How does the context affect the content? What can we learn from this?

5. What is the reason for Moses' radiant face in Exodus 34:29-35? Read the passage carefully, and decide when

the veil is on and when it is off. Why is this passage here? What is it trying to teach us in conclusion to this whole story?

■ Exploring the Word

We must be sure to see this all as a continued story. What happens here follows directly and closely on what we have studied in the first part of our chapter. At least two of the questions in the section just preceding are really follow-up, continuing questions to the first section of the chapter.

Tent of Meeting

The section opens with a discussion of the tent of meeting in 33:7-11. Although the tabernacle/sanctuary described in 25 to 31 is in some places called "the Tent of Meeting," the context makes it clear that what is spoken of here is something different. The tabernacle is in the midst of the camp, and this "tent of meeting" is outside the camp, some distance away.

Some have even suggested that there are really *three* "tents" in Exodus (see Ramm, 187, and Durham, *Exodus*, 440). The first one is a sacred tent that was used as a preliminary sanctuary before the building of the tabernacle proper, which constitutes the second tent. The third tent is, of course, the tent of meeting described here. It is a special place for communion and communication with God.

When Moses went to this tent, the pillar of cloud descended to the entrance of the tent while God communed with Moses, or perhaps with others who went there to inquire (see 33:7—"*anyone* inquiring of the Lord would go"). When this took place, people in the camp worshiped while the cloud was present. When Moses was finished, he returned to the camp, leaving Joshua, perhaps as a guard or *keeper* of the tent.

The question arises, What is this section doing in the passage? At first glance it seems to interrupt the flow. Just preceding this section, we have Israel mourning because of God's absence and their possible destruction (33:1-6). Just following these verses is Moses' ongoing discussion with God on the problem. What is the reason for this interlude?

I suggest that it is showing the *contrast* between the *past* of God's communion with Moses and the threatened *future* of God's absence. Because of Israel's sin, God has just said, "I will not go with you" (vs. 3) on your journey into Canaan. This is in direct contrast to what "used to" (vs. 7) happen with Moses and the people at the tent of meeting. Whereas before God was visibly available at the tent of meeting for direct contact with Moses and other inquirers, He will now be absent. The tragedy of His absence is heightened by realizing how wonderful that presence was. This makes all the more urgent Moses' diligent intercession and efforts to have that presence restored.

One cannot help ask, Do you and I today have a "tent of meeting"? Where do we meet God? Or has He been absent so long we do not even know what it is like to have Him near? Does the presence of God mean as much to us as it did to Israel?

Continuing Intercession

Our discussion about Moses' intercession for Israel can now continue. Moses' earlier intercession resolved the first issue of Israel's threatened destruction. God relented from His plans to destroy Israel. The second issue having to do with atonement and God's forgiveness remains unresolved. God has made some concessions (vss. 1-3). He will send His angel before Israel and drive out their enemies. He will bring them to Canaan, the land of milk and honey. *But*, He will *not* go with them.

The reasons given for this are twofold (vss. 3, 5). First, they are a sinful, stiff-necked people. Sin separates them from communion. Second, if He were near, He might destroy them. For *their good* it is better for Him not to be there, because their sin may lead to His judgment on them. God does not want to be confronted with an occasion to exercise divine judgment and wrath.

Thus for both the good of God and Israel, Yahweh is reluctant to go with Israel. He will send *His angel*, but He Himself will not be in their midst through His tabernacle or through the tent of meeting, as He had planned.

Into this situation steps Moses, the crucial intercessor. Exodus 33:12–34:9 is a wonderful passage, which builds on our earlier picture of Moses and also provides excellent insights into God's character and nature. This passage deserves a careful, detailed study.

Moses uses the best methods he knows to seek a reversal of God's decision not to be present with Israel. His initial tactic is to make two statements about himself and then two requests (vss. 12, 13):

1. *You told me to lead; now tell me who will be with me.* Moses argues from his own relationship with God. Yahweh has called him to leadership. Is God not going to be with him? Will it be only His angel? If Yahweh has asked him to lead, shouldn't He be with him?

2. *You say that You know me by name, and I have found favor with You.* Though Exodus nowhere directly tells us this, we assume that. Moses is saying, in effect, "Lord, You said all these good things about our relationship—did You mean it?" If these first two points really are true and You are pleased with me, then:

3. *Teach* me Your ways. Show me what You are really going to do so I can continue to work with You, and

4. *Remember* that this nation is *Your* people.

Moses intercedes on the basis of *his relationship* with Yahweh. He has *not* sinned. He's in Yahweh's favor, and thus he can make requests. These requests have to do with himself and the people. If he is expected to lead, God had better go with him, and the people do belong with him also.

Yahweh replies, "My presence will go with *you* [singular] and I will give *you* [singular] rest." God promises to be *with Moses*. But what about the people? Will God's presence be with them as well?

Moses pressed on. "If Your presence will not go with *us*, don't send *us* out." Moses wants to make sure the presence includes the people.

Unless God goes with the *whole nation*—Moses and people—His pleasure with Moses and the people will not be manifest. Israel's very existence as a unique people of God will be jeopardized. To fulfill His word to Moses and to keep His covenant, God must go along.

The wonderful reply comes, "I will do the very thing you asked" (vs. 17). The reason, God says, is that "I am pleased with *you* and I *know you* by name" (vs. 17). God will go with His people because of His relationship with their intercessor.

Moses has succeeded! Intercession has borne fruit. He has used reason as before, but a new element has been added. He has used his own relationship and standing with God on behalf of the people. God's promises to him are shown to be connected to the people. God can only do what He has promised Moses if He goes with the entire nation. Moses has put his own ties with God on the line on behalf of the people. What an intercessor!

Moses has one last request. He wants all this confirmed by a special theophany, or appearance, of God. If he could just see God again, that would confirm what has transpired between them and enable Moses to go on. God obliges by giving a gracious glimpse of Himself—as much as a human can stand. That glimpse we now turn to.

God Passes By

Moses asks to see God's glory. God will show His goodness and proclaim His name, Yahweh. He will not, however, show His face, because no one can see Him and live. Moses will see only the back of God.

In this initial statement, God says, "I will have mercy on whom I will have mercy, and I will have compassion on whom I will have compassion" (vs. 19). This is the essence of His goodness—that is, His mercy and compassion. This is why He is even willing to show Himself to Moses. He, the Lord, is *sovereign and good*. He can show mercy as He *pleases*. His mercy is thus not bound by outside constraints. His mercy is *His* mercy.

God instructs Moses to chisel out two stone tablets like the first ones. How Moses' heart must have leapt. God was going to renew the covenant! The earlier "broken" words will be restored. In the morning Moses is to go back up the mountain.

Early morning on the mountain finds Moses standing before God, tablets in hand. The Lord passes by before Moses and expands on His earlier summary statements of who He, Yahweh, is. This statement of the attributes of Yahweh is really an expansion of what His name means. Notice the double statement of the name at the very beginning of the list. This is what Israel is to call to mind when the name is invoked.

Here is a list of God's character traits:

Compassionate
    Gracious
        Slow to anger
            Abounding in love
                Abounding in faithfulness
Maintaining love to thousands (of generations)
            Forgiving wickedness
                Forgiving rebellion
                    Forgiving sin
Does not leave the guilty unpunished.

This wonderful confession of the name of Yahweh with its meaning is clearly reflected in eight other Old Testament passages (see Num. 14:18; Neh. 9:17; Ps. 86:15; 103:8; 145:8; Joel 2:13; Jonah 4:2; Nahum 1:3). Earlier, we also looked briefly at Exodus 20:5, which contains a portion of this confession.

This is the most basic, direct statement of the nature of Yahweh that we find in the Old Testament. Much could be written about it. We will mention a few basic points.

1. *The revelation is given in the context of Israel's sin.* The occasion
   for this wonderful list is the horrible sin of the people at the
   golden calf. The essence of the character of Yahweh is given
   in the midst of dealing with sin. The irony of this fits the
   God who reveals Himself later on a cross. Where sin abounds,
   mercy and grace abound even more!
2. *The emphasis is clearly on grace and forgiveness.* Forgiveness itself is mentioned three times. Each time it is used with one
   of the three main Hebrew words for sin. The clear idea is
   that forgiveness is there for all kinds of sin and wrong. Love
   lasts for a thousand generations, while the results of punishment continue only three or four generations.
3. *A balance is maintained between mercy and justice.* While grace
   and forgiveness are emphasized, God does not leave the per-
   sistent sinner unpunished. This justice statement, however,
   comes at the *end* of the list and is stated as an act of God
   rather than as a general attribute (vss. 6, 7). Grace cannot be
   grace without justice.
4. *The revelation of God leads to worship.* In the face of this glorious revelation of God, all Moses can do is prostrate himself
   in worship. Time and again in Exodus we see the worship
   response. When God really shows Himself, the only valid
   response is worship. Moses is no exception.

The importance of this revelation of God and the forgiveness
He offers cannot be overemphasized in the story. Israel desired
God's presence. Unless there is forgiveness, even that presence, if
granted, could be dangerous and destroying. If God's presence is
to come, it must come along with forgiveness to be helpful.

Remember that at the earlier covenant, *no* forgiveness was promised. The statement was even made that there was no forgiveness
(23:21). *Both* sides of the equation must be maintained. Techni-
cally, no forgiveness needs to be given. For forgiveness and mercy
to be genuine, they must come about in a plan or system that does
not require them. If they were part of the system, they would be
just that and not mercy. Thus to understand the sinfulness of apos-

tasy and the character of true grace, the story has to take place like this. Only then can sin be sin and grace be grace.

The extensive dialogue between Moses and God is necessary to teach the same lesson. God is not grudging in His mercy, but it must be clear that mercy is what it is, and not just cheap indulgence built into the system. God is not an easy mark or an indulgent grandpa. He is not obligated to give grace.

The dialogue also teaches what I call the "relationalness" of God. He operates in relationship and dialogue with people and situations. He does not sit aloofly apart from everything, unilaterally deciding things on some abstract basis. He is open and acting and reacting. While the basic character of God is not negotiable, much of what goes on does seem to be. Humans play, according to Exodus, a major role in what takes place. What a serious responsibility God gives to His people.

The New Covenant

In Exodus 34:10-28 God proclaims the renewed covenant. Many of the same statements and laws occur here that we first find in chapters 20 to 23, but there are major differences as well.

The initial verse of the proclamation of this covenant is significant (vs. 10). God declares in an almost *exuberant fashion* that He is making a covenant. He is making it in a sense before the other nations, who will see how awesome a God He is. This covenant is to be a demonstration with a *missionary purpose*.

The Hebrew word used to describe what God is "doing" for them (vs. 10b) is powerful. It comes from the word translated "create" in the creation story of Genesis. God is going to literally *create* a new people—a new act, a new covenant. The making of this covenant is literally a new creation, like the creation of the world. God is excited and evangelistic about what He is doing.

Although Israel is given many laws and commands and is specifically told to "obey" (vs. 11), there is no specific call for the *people to promise* that they will keep this covenant, as was the case earlier (19:8; 24:3, 7). Israel has sinned. They have *not* kept their promise. In chapter 34 God does not ask for a promise. He asks the people to obey, but experience has shown that their promises mean little. God still wants to marry His people. He loves them dearly and wants their obedience, but extracting a promise from them will not do the trick!

Exodus 34:11-26 in many ways summarizes in shorter form the laws of chapters 20 to 23. There are also some significant differences. There is not enough space to describe these differences in detail, but several major ones should be noted.

1. *Laws concerning worship seem to be emphasized in Exodus 34.* This makes sense because Israel has just gone through a crisis related to worship. She needs special instruction in this area, so a higher percentage of laws apply to that crucial area. Numerous laws call for destruction of pagan worship devices and avoidance of relationships with Canaanites for the very reason that these ties may lead to false worship. Proper sacrifice is also a part of proper worship.

2. *Conditional elements like Exodus 23:21, 22 are missing from Exodus 34.* The "if" clauses are not there. The standards have not changed, but the golden calf has ushered in a new era. God wants obedience, but now is not the time to make His presence totally dependent on it. Better not to make statements that later must be lived with!

3. *Exodus 34 does not contain a statement of the Ten Commandments.* While the list of the Ten Commandments is not given, verse 34:28 makes it plain that they are on the tables of stone and are part of the covenant. Several of the commandments are also specifically referred to individually. For example, the first (vs. 14), second (vs. 17), and the fourth (vs. 21). Moses assumes all are familiar with the ten and mentions only three—interestingly, three specifically related to worship.

   Law in the Old Testament is always *relevant* law preached in a certain situation. All statements of law are meant to fit with the context in which they are given. Exodus 34 certainly illustrates this point.

The Radiant Face

This whole golden calf episode closes with Moses' descent from Sinai with the two tables of the covenant in his hands. The same commandments are on the second tablets that were on the first, but much has changed. The second descent is not like the first. Instead of anger there is radiance.

When Moses descends from the mountain, his face is radiant from God's presence. The people are initially afraid to go near, but after he reassures them, they approach, and Moses can give them the commands of God.

When Moses finishes speaking, he veils his face. He only unveils it when he comes into God's presence and when he delivers his message from God to the people. The rest of the time his face is veiled.

This passage has given rise to many visual portrayals of Moses as a man with horns. Michelangelo's famous statue of Moses, for example, has two horns coming out of Moses' head. The Hebrew words for *radiance* and *horn* are very closely related, and some early translators and interpreters taught that Moses' symbol of being in God's presence was the horns. If you see a picture or statue of Moses with horns, remember that he's not being portrayed as a devil but as one coming from God's presence!

This story is a fitting conclusion to this section for several reasons. First, it restores Moses to his rightful place of leadership. The golden calf rebellion was not only against God but was in a sense the questioning of Moses as well. Moses needed to take drastic steps to solve the sinful situation. This time the people are able to wait forty days for Moses to return. When he does, he shines with the glory of God. He has not been inactive but has been in divine communion. His role of leader and mediator, which was questioned, is now restored, and Aaron and the people clearly recognize his true position.

The story also confirms that the renewed blessing and presence of God are still with His leader and thus with His people. The people see the new tablets of stone and hear the commandments read. God has indeed made a new covenant with them, and their future is secure. What was lost through their sin has been restored.

Conclusion

What has been a horrible breach in the Israel-God relationship is now restored. Although the whole thing has been wrenching, God has worked in marvelous ways to teach His people new things about Himself. The true graciousness of God has been revealed in a way that had never been known before. Out of tragedy has come new life with new blessings and revelations. The story line can now go back to where it left off in Exodus 31. The tabernacle can immediately be built. That which symbolizes God's presence with His people can now be safely constructed, because the people know that Yahweh *forgives* as well as *delivers*. That is an even greater reason to desire to have His presence near.

■ Applying the Word

Exodus 32–34

1. Has God ever seemed absent from me and my life when I wanted Him present? What have I done to try to get His presence back? Have I ever helped create a "golden calf" so God would seem near? Have I ever borrowed religious practices from others that shouldn't be used? What were they?

2. Do I believe my prayers can lead God to "relent" and respond in new ways to my pleas? What do I really believe prayers have the ability to do? How does what I believe prayer can do affect the nature of my prayers? Have I really interceded in prayer for people like Moses did? What can I learn from Moses about intercession?

3. Does God punish people today like He did Israel? What evidence do I have for my answer? Have I ever been

punished by God? Should we threaten and/or act in punishing others? Why?

4. How much does God's presence mean to me? Israel could
stand to drink burnt golden calf water and suffer destruction and plague, but the people went into deep
mourning when God said His presence could not go with
them. Is God's presence this vital to me? How can I tell
if His presence is with me? Am I so distant from God
that I can't tell whether He is present or not? Do I have
a "tent of meeting" where I can commune with God?

5. Do I really believe God is gracious, compassionate, merciful, forgiving, and slow to anger? Do I sometimes act
toward myself and others as if He weren't? How? Do I
have more trouble forgiving myself or others? Is it easier
to show mercy to myself or to others? Why? If I really
were convinced that God was this kind of God, how
would my actions change? What can convince me of the
goodness of God?

6. What important relationships in my life have been broken or impaired? What has been the result? This
passage talks about the breaking and the restoring of a
relationship. What lessons can I learn about how relationships are broken and restored? What role might a
key person like Moses play in restoration? What attitudes contribute to a renewed relationship?

■ Researching the Word

1. Using a concordance, expand your understanding of
Exodus 34:6, 7. Look up each word that is given here as
a characteristic of God, and read other passages that use
the same words in reference to Yahweh. Begin by looking carefully at the following passages: Numbers 14:8;
Nehemiah 9:17; Psalms 86:15; 103:8; 145:8; Joel 2:13;
Jonah 4:2; Nahum 1:3. What do these verses say about
the Old Testament's view of God, and especially Israel's

view of Him? What can you say to those who say the God of the Old Testament is cruel and vindictive? Why is it important to have a right view of God?

2. Scan through the book of Judges looking for times when Israel rebelled against God after their entrance into Canaan. What similarities do you find between these rebellions and the rebellion at Sinai? What differences do you find? What would constitute rebellion against God by the church as a whole today? What would be God's response, and how would He communicate it to us? How might an individual rebel, and how would you expect God to respond?

■ Further Study of the Word

1. For a general overview of the section, see Ellen G. White, *Patriarchs and Prophets*, 315-330.

2. For more material on prayer and intercession, see Samuel E. Balentine, *Prayer in the Hebrew Bible*; for the specific section on Moses' prayer in Exodus 32:7-14, see 135-139.

3. For more insight on the graciousness of God and Exodus 34:6, 7, see Jon Dybdahl, *Old Testament Grace*, 83-87.

CHAPTER TWELVE

God Manifests His Glory

Exodus 35–40

Even the best of books comes to an end. This last section of Exodus is a fitting climax to the story. Moses has described how a tabernacle for God's presence must be built. The threat to that building, which came about because of the golden calf, has been cared for. All that remains is for construction to take place.

Exodus 35 to 40 is a logical, step-by-step account of the actual building of the tabernacle. When everything has been built, inspected, and set up, the great climax comes. The cloud of the glory and presence of the Lord settles upon the finished sanctuary. The presence is so real and intense that even Moses cannot enter the structure. That divine presence is now in Israel's midst, where all can see it.

When God creates a people, the final step in that creation is a place where He can be present with them. If they are His people, created and made by Him, He desires to be right there with them. The trail has been long and full of struggle, but the basic goal has been reached. God and His people live together. The story may go on, and there remain other tasks to be done. But if God is present with His people, they need not fear, for all is possible, and success is sure if God lives with them.

Take time to savor the conclusion of this story. A tremendous amount of labor goes into this tabernacle that was created for the presence of God. Concern for other things has taken a back seat. But the living presence of God makes all the work worthwhile. Does the presence of God mean as much to our religion as it did to Israel's faith?

■ Getting Into the Word

Exodus 35–40

Read Exodus 35 to 40 at least twice. Some of the construction descriptions may be boring, but persevere to the end. Make sure you read the conclusion carefully. As you read, look for answers to the following questions:

1. Depending on how you look at events, building the sanctuary required five to ten basic steps. Make a list of these major steps in order of their occurrence. What is the logic of this order? Many of the things that are said in this section of Exodus were first stated in chapters 25 to 31, where Moses/God commanded the building of the tabernacle. Review that section of Exodus. How does the order of these two major sections of Exodus differ? How do you explain these differences? Why do you think Exodus has both of these sections? Wouldn't one of them have been enough?

2. The issue of the Sabbath keeps recurring in Exodus. What does chapter 35:1-3 say about the Sabbath that has not yet been said? Why is the Sabbath discussed at the beginning of this section of Exodus? Recall that chapters 25 to 31 have a statement about the Sabbath at the *end* of the section describing the building of the sanctuary. Why does God mention the Sabbath in both of these accounts?

3. Many people and groups had a part in the construction of the tabernacle. Make a list of what each of the following groups of people were to do: (a) all Israel; (b) skilled craftsmen (c) women (d) leaders (e) Bezalel (f) Oholiab (g) Moses. What does this teach us about how God works and how His people are to work on projects?

4. Read and reflect on the conclusion of the book— 40:34-38. Make a list of everything said about the cloud

or glory of the Lord. What does this cloud seem to have looked like? What was the cloud's position? Did it change from time to time? Why is the cloud so crucial to Israel? What did it do for them? Why is this such a fitting close for the book of Exodus? Would you have preferred seeing the book end in a different way? Why?

■ Exploring the Word

The Sequence of Sanctuary Building

Logical steps are followed in the building process as described in this last section of Exodus. Moses opens with a reminder to be faithful to the Sabbath commandment (35:1-3). This passage will receive special attention later in this chapter.

Second, Moses appeals for the offering (vss. 4-29). This offering includes not only metals like gold, silver, and bronze, but yarn, linen, and animal skin and hair. Wood, olive oil, spices, and gems are also part of the gifts requested on a freewill basis.

Next, Moses describes and summons the craftsmen who are to do the building (35:3–36:7). The two leaders are to be Bezalel and Oholiab, but they are assisted by many other skilled craftsmen. The offerings of materials are turned over to them to use. So many materials have been given that word goes out to the people to stop their giving.

Fourth, the actual construction of each part of the sanctuary and its furniture is described (36:8–38:30). The account begins with the tabernacle. Following that, the furniture of the Most Holy Place, Holy Place, and courtyard are constructed, in that order. Last, and probably least in importance, the courtyard building is described. As a postscript, the amount of the metals, gold, silver, and bronze used in all the building is noted!

Fifth, the garments of the priests are made (39:1-31). The order that is followed appears to be from most important to least crucial.

Sixth, Moses inspects the finished work and sets up the tabernacle on God's command (39:32–40:33). Everything is completed exactly as God has commanded.

Seventh and last, the cloud of God's presence and glory comes and fills the completed sanctuary (40:34-38). God's presence and final seal of approval are received.

Several reasons exist for taking the time to look at the organization of this section. The descriptions can seem long and tedious, and the possibility of getting bogged down is great. Seeing the broad sweep and order of the section can make it more understandable and help us see what is happening.

The fact that all this detail is mentioned tells us that Israel reveled in and was very interested in this building. We may not share their feeling, but walking through the process with them can help us begin to appreciate just a little of how passionately they loved their tabernacle.

Looking at the order and sequence also prepares us to compare chapters 35 to 40 with chapters 25 to 31 and begin to answer the question as to why we have two quite similar yet differing descriptions of the sanctuary's construction.

First, I believe good reasons exist for the inclusion of both accounts. The writer and readers of Exodus clearly knew of the similarities between the two sections but constructed the book this way and left it this way for posterity. Why?

There are parallels in other ancient Near Eastern literature for such things, particularly in Ugaritic writings, which come from close proximity to Israel (Durham, *Exodus*, 475). I can remember a long, tedious summer afternoon I spent translating a Ugaritic epic poem. With the afternoon almost gone, I despaired of ever finishing my goal for that day. Then I discovered the entire next section was a virtual repeat of the one I had just translated. The first section contained instructions and the latter detailed their enactment. In a few short minutes, I finished. In other words, this kind of thing was a typical literary device of the period. It would not have seemed strange to the ancient reader.

What purpose does this device have? For one thing, it fixes in the mind certain important details and also points to the importance of the instructions.

It also enables one to look at the same situation from different perspectives. While many of the details of chapters 25 to 31 and 35 to 40 are in the same order, the setting and viewpoint are different. Thus the two accounts are complementary descriptions of a two-part event.

Account/passage one (25–31) is instruction, while account/passage two (35–40) is action or obedience. Passage one is promise, while passage two is fulfillment. Account one describes the sanctuary in order of sanctity, while account two deals with the sequence of construction. Passage one is theoretical, while passage two is practical. Exodus 35 to 40 adds or omits material from Exodus 25 to 31 according to its own theme and purpose. This means that each account must be studied in its own right for the specific perspective it offers. Careful comparison can make the complementary passages' individual perspectives more clear. We know much more because we have both passages rather than one.

The Sabbath

As has been noted earlier, the Sabbath plays an important role in the book of Exodus. Beginning with the account of the manna in chapter 16 and going on to the concluding comment in 35:1-3, the Sabbath is time and again woven into the very fabric of the book of Exodus as a vital component shaping and defining Israel's relationship with God.

We should not be surprised, then, that the Sabbath becomes part of both the account of the plans for the building of the tabernacle and the story of the actual building of the sanctuary. The placing of the reference, however, varies. The Sabbath *concludes* the story of God's plans for the tabernacle (31:12-17) while it *introduces* the account of the actual building.

This placement fits the logic of the accounts perfectly. Since the story of the *plans* means no actual work, the Sabbath can finish the account and simply remind people that in all plans and worth the Sabbath must be "observed" and "celebrated" as a sign and covenant. In the story of the building, since action is to take place immediately, the Israelites need to be told at the very beginning of their work that the Sabbath must be kept.

These instructions about the Sabbath actually form a bridge between the plans and commands to build the sanctuary and the actual construction and obedience. If the story of Israel's disobedience at the golden calf in chapters 33 and 34 were removed, these two passages would come together. Their presence is a direct means of tying these two sanctuary sections together.

As is the case in almost every reference to the Sabbath in Exodus, the passage adds some new aspect to our understanding of the day. The new material here has to do with forbidding the lighting of fires in Israelite dwellings on the Sabbath. This further defines what is meant by work: lighting a fire is a form of forbidden work. This quite possibly had to do with food preparation (16:22-30).

Looking back over the book, one cannot help but conclude that the Sabbath was very important to Israel and is an important theme in the book of Exodus. The Sabbath was a major shaper of Israelite daily life—it molded when they worked and when they gathered and prepared food. More than that, the day was crucial to Israelite *self-understanding* and *identity*. It was a sign of the lasting covenant relationship between Israel and God and pointed to the One who had created the world and Israel as a people. Since Exodus is the story of Israel's salvation and consequent peoplehood, the close tying of the Sabbath to that story ensures it a perpetual, central place in the Israelite mind.

Builders of the Sanctuary

The building of the sanctuary is clearly a community effort. Any Israelite who is willing can help (35:1, 4, 20). The help to be given consists of two types.

Type one is the offering of materials that can be used for construction. This includes the metals—gold, silver, and bronze—as well as linen and yarn. Animal hair and skins can be donated, as can oil, incense, spices, and gems.

The offering is specifically freewill (35:5, 21, 29; 36:3). Universal appeal is made, but there is no required response. People give overwhelmingly. There seems to be no specific time when the offering is taken, for the people bring materials "morning after morning" (36:3). They donate so much that there is more than enough for the work (vs. 5), and the command goes out to tell the people to stop giving more material and to cease making things to bring (vss. 6, 7). This ranks as one of the most successful offering appeals in history!

The second type of help required is of skilled people to *make* or actually construct the sanctuary. *All*, that is, anyone skilled, can have a part (35:10). This work seems, at least in part, to have been classed as a freewill offering as well (vss. 26-29).

Women are specifically mentioned as having a vital role. Not only do they bring offerings—especially gold (vss. 22-29)—but they also spin yarn, linen (vs. 25) and goat hair (vs. 26). Cloth making seems to have been a special skill reserved for women in Israel.

Israelite leaders give onyx stones, gems, oil, and spices (vss. 27, 28). Perhaps the leaders have more possessions and are more able to give such precious gifts to the sanctuary. The clear aim in all of this is to show the universal participation of the community in sanctuary construction.

Two men lead out in the actual work: Bezalel, who seems to have been the chief, and his assistant, Oholiab. Bezalel is filled by the Spirit of God with "skill, ability, and knowledge in all kinds of crafts" (vs. 31). This includes artistic design, stone (gem?) cutting and setting, and woodworking.

In addition, Bezalel and Oholiab are both given "the ability to teach others" (vs. 34). These two abilities—craftsmanship and teaching—are crucial to the building. Some can do skilled work, and some can teach, but it constitutes a special talent/gift to be proficient in both areas. In this way Israelites who want to *learn* craftsmanship can also have a part in making things for the sanctuary.

Clearly the story pictures large numbers of craftsmen at work making the tabernacle (36:8). The only place in the story where the third person plural "they" is not used referring to this group of men and women involved in construction is in the making of the ark (37:1-9). Bezalel makes the ark himself. This special holiest of all furniture is constructed by the master craftsman, but everything else is made by this band of craftsmen. The two leaders are probably mostly involved in the design and oversight of the project.

Bezalel and Oholiab serve as chief contractors, and Moses is the inspector (39:43). Everything that is done has to pass muster with Moses, who had, after all, been the one to receive the original instructions from God. Careful inspection reveals that everything has been done "just as the Lord had commanded" (vs. 43).

Obedience is an important part of the story. In the golden calf experience, which immediately precedes this account, Israel manifested blatant disobedience. This story contrasts sharply, for no less than eighteen times is Moses said to be doing exactly as God commands (see Fretheim, 313, 314). At the onset Moses declares to the Israelite community what God "has commanded" (35:1, 4), and they proceed to follow as ordered (35:29; 36:1; 39:1, 7, etc.).

This obedience, however, is not some forced, wooden, legalistic following. While God commands an offering, the giving itself is *freewill*, yet the wealth itself is a gift of God. While the people are to build, the skill and ability to construct are God-given. The obedience asked, then, is an obedience from the heart, based on a spirit turned toward Yahweh and loyalty to Him. The ability to obey and follow comes from the gifts God Himself has bestowed. This type of obedience is pleasing both to Israel and Yahweh.

One final thing in this account of building that we should notice is that the story contemplates a process rather than a completed object. Exodus communicates the beauty of a harmonious community working in unity and obedience. We are not led to reflect so much on the splendor of a completed project as to rejoice in what has taken place among the people of God. Look at what can happen when God's people follow Him from the heart!

Wonderful things can be accomplished, and in fact, God comes to dwell in their midst. That final fact we consider in the next section.

Yahweh Fills the Sanctuary

We have come to the final dramatic episode in the story of Exodus—the saga of God's creation of His people. The essence of the story is plain and profound at the same time. God fills the completed sanctuary with the cloud of His presence. God comes to live in Israel's midst! That has been the aim of the tabernacle since the beginning (25:8).

When we try to picture exactly what the scene looked like, we are not sure how to do it. "The cloud," clearly the same cloud that has led Israel from Succoth onward (13:20-22; 14:19, 20, 24; 19:9; 24:15-18), covers the tabernacle and settles on it. "The glory of the Lord" *fills* the sanctuary. Are the glory and the cloud synonymous, or are they two manifestations of the presence of Yahweh? The glory seems to have been *in* the tabernacle, while the cloud was *over or above* it. The cloud would seem to be opaque and a shade, while glory is usually connected with lights and brightness. Clearly for Israel, however, fire could be in the cloud as it was at night (40:38). Whatever the case, God clearly came in a visible form that was both cloudlike and glory/firelike depending on the situation and position, and in particular, the need of Israel.

Although God's presence fills and rests above the sanctuary, it is not confined to it. The presence is a *pilgrim* presence, which moves and travels as the people are to travel. The presence guides Israel. They are to follow Yahweh, *not* He follow them.

While the sanctuary is a place, it is a *portable* place. The people whom God has created are on a journey and must keep moving to remain in God's presence. The crucial point is the cloud, not the sanctuary. The sanctuary is a vehicle for God's presence, not the cloud and the glory. Unless the sanctuary follows the presence, it loses meaning and significance.

The cloud and glory of God is Yahweh living with humans.

The presence is so powerful that even Moses, who has been with God in the cloud on the mountain, cannot enter the tabernacle! God has come to be with His people in a way He has never been present before! How thankful and joyful they must be.

This cloud of presence is the stamp of approval on all that has gone before. The building is accepted, and the people are really God's own. The cloud is God's guidance for the future that tells Israel where they need to go. The cloud is God's clock that says when transitions need to be made. The cloud is the constant reminder that God is their God and that they are His people. What more can the people of God ask than for Him to be all of this to them?

It should not surprise us, then, to find that the New Testament picks up this sanctuary story of God's filling and presence and applies it to Jesus (John 1:14-16; Eph. 1:23; Col. 1:19). Certainly God's own Son is the presence of God in our midst, as the tabernacle was the place of God's presence at Sinai. God's people today long for the day when the "dwelling of God is with men, and He will live with them. They will be his people and God himself will be with them and be their God" (Rev. 21:3). That is the day that Exodus and we ourselves look for. That is the day when the final, ultimate creation of God's people takes place, the movable place of presence becomes forever fixed, and God's pilgrim people find their final rest and home.

■ Applying the Word

Exodus 35–40

1. **How do I look at and understand the various skills and technical abilities that people have? Are they gifts, or are they just human abilities? If the Spirit of God gifted Bezalel, how should I view the gifts God has given me? Should all talents be seen as spiritual gifts? Why? How do people usually rank spiritual gifts? What does this story teach us about these issues?**

2. What do I think about obedience to God? Does *obedience* seem like a negative, legalistic word, or does it seem pleasant? Why? What has shaped my views of what obedience is? What would help me understand and practice obedience like Israel's obedience in the building of the sanctuary? How does God help me to obey?

3. Is there any place today (on earth) equivalent to the sanctuary? Where are the cloud and the glory of God's presence for us? Is the church the place for us, or is it a prayer closet or special place in nature? Should we have such a place? How do we know God is there? Should He be visible, like He was in Egypt? Why?

4. Do I have a clear sense of being a part of God's people? Why or why not? Is such a sense needed in my life? Why? What could make such a sense of belonging real to me?

■ Researching the Word

1. Many crafts and skills were used in building the tabernacle. These included woodworking, metal working, gem cutting and setting, weaving, cloth making, and perfume making, among others. Find out all you can about how people in ancient times did this work. A good place to start is with other Bible references to various crafts. Also, you can consult a Bible dictionary and encyclopedias on the various skills. Many books have been written on daily life in Bible times. Such books often have references to the various skills mentioned here in Exodus.

2. Look through Revelation for references and allusions to the furniture in the heavenly sanctuary, including the altar of sacrifice and the laver in the courtyard. Which items of furniture are mentioned most often? Which are not mentioned at all? How does Revelation interpret these items of furniture? What is their spiritual significance to us today? Do you think the Israelites attached the same spiritual significance to these items of furni-

ture? Why or why not?

3. Look up each item of sanctuary furniture in the *SDA Bible Dictionary* or another Bible dictionary (look for *showbread* rather than *table of showbread*). What does it say is the spiritual significance of each one? Your Bible dictionary will probably give references to other places in the Bible that mention these items of furniture. For additional research, look these up and see if you can find additional clues as to their spiritual meaning. Then reflect on how these spiritual lessons apply to us today.

■ Further Study of the Word

1. For a general overview of the topic, see Ellen G. White, *Patriarchs and Prophets*, 343-358.
2. For a discussion of the presence of God as a theme for Israel and Exodus, see R. E. Clements, *Old Testament Theology*, 66-72.

POSTSCRIPT

CHAPTER THIRTEEN

Reflections
on the Journey

In Bible study many people quit just when they are on the brink of the most fruitful phase of their endeavors. I find that I gain the most when I have actually finished a close look at the book. I can then sit down unhampered by ignorance of the actual flow of the story or argument and reflect on the whole experience.

Don't leave Exodus now! You have just invested a major amount of time thinking about the "trees" in the book. Now pause and ponder the "forest." Let the ideas and insights that have been bouncing around in your brain sort themselves out and take expressible shape. Let the message and import of the book grip you and take hold of your being. Let the message sink into your psyche. Take time to feel and experience the book of Exodus. This will really make it a part of your life.

■ Getting Into the Word

Sit in a quiet place when you can uninterruptedly ponder Exodus for twenty or thirty minutes. As you think, answer the following questions:

1. If someone asked me what I got out of the book of Exodus that benefits my life today, what would I say? Why would I tell them they should study the book?
2. What did the book teach me about God? What have I learned about Israel? About human nature? About salvation? About worship and prayer? About my personal

spiritual journey? About mission?

3. **If I had to teach a Sabbath School class or give a sermon on Exodus, what would I preach or teach? Why does this topic stand out in my mind?**

4. **What is my favorite passage in Exodus? Why did I pick this text? What does it mean to me personally?**

■ Exploring the Word

The Ten Teachings of Exodus

It would not be fair for me to ask you to ponder the book and not do so myself! I have thought a lot about the lessons of the book as I have lived close to it during this past year, and the experience has brought me a great deal of joy. I have summarized what have been the most important things for me. There just happen to be ten.

1. *Much value derives from the fact that Exodus is in* story *form.* While laws and rituals are given, the narrative framework is the heart of the book, and this is good. Stories are not only more interesting for most people than philosophy or theory; they are memory aids as well. We can remember the lessons of the book because they come to us as stories.

Stories integrate many factors and help us see the whole picture. Grace, law, worship, ritual, and sanctuary can be seen naturally in their right relationship because a story ties them together. And what a powerful story it is!

I cannot help but think that our Bible studies, sermons, and theology books would all communicate much more clearly if they came in story form, because stories hold people's interest, relate the messages in a practical way, and make the lessons easy to remember. Why is so much of the Bible story, yet so little of our teaching story? Maybe we should try to get back to the Exodus ideal.

Exodus and Romans are the foremost books on salvation in the

Old Testament and New Testament, respectively. I believe most would find the story of Exodus more vivid and easier to follow than the arguments of Romans, and the reason is because it is in narrative form.

2. *The essence of salvation is the presence of God.* When I began to study Exodus, I recognized that many felt that the presence of God was an important theme in the book. However, the power and pervasiveness of the theme really came home to me as I studied the book.

In connection with several classes I teach, I have wrestled with the definition of religion. What is the best and most biblical way to define what religion is? For many people, religion has to do with doctrines and beliefs. For other people, it is a matter of right ethics. Studying Exodus has convinced me that the best definition of religion is the seeking for and experiencing of the presence of God.

This really came home for me in the study of the golden calf incident in chapters 32 to 34. Israel is made to drink the burnt and ground-up golden calf. She suffers the death of three thousand people by the hand of the Levites. Plagues come on her. None of this fazes her or brings her to repentance. Yet when God says He will not go with her into Canaan, she goes into mourning and strips off her ornaments. She can stand everything except the absence of God!

This matter is also crystal clear in the climax of the book. The completed sanctuary is filled with the glory of the presence of God. Yahweh is in the midst of His people. It seems that this is what the whole book has been looking forward to.

How boring, dry, and abstract many of our definitions and understandings of religion seem to be in light of this view! If God is present, everything else can be cared for—everything else is secondary. How do I portray religion to others? Why do they seem uninterested so often? Probably I've missed something of the essence of the real thing!

3. *God must be understood in relationship to people.* While God is God and not just a glorified human being, Exodus does portray

Him as closely related to human beings. He responds to their requests and prayers and hears their cries of desperation. Their sin and wrongdoing upset Him, and their repentance moves Him to reconsider earlier decisions.

Many of the actions of God as portrayed by Exodus greatly distress philosophical theologians. How can a gracious and loving God get angry? Why does an all-knowing God alter His course in response to prayer? How can a forgiving God punish?

The answer in Exodus seems to be that all this happens in the context of God's deliberate choice to forge close relationships to human beings. Their change brings His response. God is a dynamic part of relationships that are in process.

The idea of God as an unmovable power is certainly foreign to the book of Exodus. The good news for sinful humans is that God is searching for meaningful alliances with human beings. He makes covenants or agreements with people, and He lives by them and works to maintain them. He continues to do so today!

4. *Exodus continues to be relevant for evangelism, mission, and church renewal.* I was surprised to see God's interest in sharing the word about Himself with the nations. I knew He cared for those outside of Israel because of what He has said in other places. But I was pleasantly surprised to see how much He and Moses were concerned about how He looked in the eyes of Egypt and the other nations. Even in this book, which is basically about the salvation of Israel, God makes it clear that His ultimate goal is for *all* nations and people to know Him.

I also believe the Exodus paradigm of the four steps that save people and lead them to the status of people of God are universally relevant. God always (1) sees oppression, (2) acts to deliver, (3) makes a covenant, and (4) lives among His people. Any time we hold evangelistic meetings, do missionary work cross-culturally among the unreached, or try to bring renewal in our own churches, we must go back to this paradigm as we call people to become part of the people of God. The Exodus paradigm is always the way God creates His people. The pattern applies to cultures in all times and in all places.

5. *Worship and its accompanying songs, sanctuary celebrations, feasts, and rituals are central to God's community!* Worship is certainly emphasized in Exodus. If we take the twelve chapters dedicated to the sanctuary and its construction and add to it all the passages that deal with song, the feasts of Israel, and then celebration, and simply count the worship responses of people, we are getting close to half of the book of Exodus.

Worship is the forgotten gem in the Protestant church in general, and I believe in the Adventist Church in particular. Worship is the natural response to God's presence and action. Lack of worship can either portray a lack of knowledge about a proper response to God or simply a lack of the divine presence. Either is very dangerous to the life of the people of God. We need a renewed emphasis on worship in the church. Better yet, we need a renewed sense of the presence of God in the church that will lead to worship.

Exodus can teach us much about the centrality of worship as well as the practice of worship. I encourage you to study Exodus from this angle and then implement what you learn in your life and the life of your church.

6. *Dynamic, honest leadership is crucial to the people of God.* Exodus has fascinated me with the life of Moses. After studying the book, I prepared a series of talks about Moses as an illustration of divine principles of leadership. Where would Israel have been without Moses and his brother Aaron?

My generation, which came to maturity in the 1960s, tended to distrust leadership and thus did not aspire to leadership positions, where our help was actually very much needed. I think the church today is hampered by a lack of dynamic, honest leadership. We need committed disciples who heed God's call to the tough task of leading the people to God. In preparation for such a role, the life of Moses should be a constant source of instruction and inspiration.

What appeals to me so much about Moses' leadership is the honesty of Exodus and Moses about his shortcomings. The warts all show. Yet in spite of the warts, Moses is so dedicated to his people that he is willing to be blotted out of the book of life if it means saving them. God grant us such leaders today!

7. *The clear, universal logic of the organization of Exodus continues to guide us.* I spoke briefly earlier of the supracultural nature of the four-step process of becoming the people of God that is found in Exodus. At that time I considered it in the context of mission. I now return to that theme and examine it from a different angle—the theological and psychological.

I am more convinced than ever that the four-step process of (1) recognition of the problem, need, or sin, followed by (2) God's gracious deliverance, leading to (3) the making of an agreement or covenant that contains instruction, finally issuing in (4) worship and actual presence is true in a very universal sense, both theologically and psychologically. This process must be understood and followed for people to have a true relationship with God and/or be mentally healthy.

Step one is necessary because unless people recognize their need or sin, there is no desire for God's deliverance or salvation. The popular twelve-step process first used in Alcoholics Anonymous begins in the same place: recognition of helplessness in the face of the oppression that alcohol addiction brings. Unless there is recognition of some kind of Egyptian slavery, there is no longing for freedom. The disease must be diagnosed before healing can take place.

Step two is where God steps in to deliver. Egyptian slavery is overcome only through the power of God. No Israelites could claim they or anyone else did it. The deliverance took place in such a way that everyone knew exactly where the salvation came from. True theology and true psychology both see help coming from outside. We are delivered by the gracious act of another.

Step three points to the relationship and the obligations that stem from deliverance. A relationship has obligations, and discipline issues from the experience of deliverance. The delivered one must form a relationship with his or her Saviour that is governed by principle. Both can then know what is expected, and growth can take place.

Step four points to the culmination of the process. When the relationship has been formalized and commitments made, the deliverer stays with the delivered. A plan is made for continuing presence and relationship. God lives with humans. New bonds that were formed in the deliverance are perpetuated, and rituals to celebrate the relationship are established.

In this process *order* is crucial. The steps must come in this sequence. No deliverance is desired without need. Calls to covenant and discipline do not make sense before deliverance. The presence is not real without a covenant. If relationships with God are damaged, we must go back to the place in the sequence that is not understood and experienced and begin to repair things at that point. This sequence and order is the same one Jesus and the New Testament use. They got it from Exodus!

Never forget this sequence—its truth, logic, and power. It is God's way of deliverance.

8. *The honesty of Exodus in its portrayal of the story is refreshing and instructive.* Nobody is perfect in Exodus—except Yahweh. Moses is a great leader who is willing to sacrifice for his people, but he also complains, and at times his faith fails. Aaron performs well in Egypt, but his actions at Mt. Sinai with the golden calf are inexcusable.

The people of Israel have problems with faith and faithfulness almost to the end of the book. From all their gripes in Egypt to their fear at the Red Sea to the golden calf at Sinai, one can certainly wonder why God chose them! Yet they end up as His chosen people.

In an age when coverup is epidemic, this honesty about God's people and her leaders is refreshing. The honesty actually helps us identify with the situation and begin to believe that God may want us as His people in spite of our problems. In this honesty the true source of power is more readily pointed out, and successes can result in *God's* glory rather than human exaltation and praise. We can benefit from this teaching of Exodus.

9. *The nearness of God in Exodus is impressive and instructive.* Exodus clearly has God as its chief character. He, Yahweh, the Lord

of Israel and history, is constantly in action. Sometimes He is behind the scenes, changing hearts and blessing people, while at other times He is very public in burning bushes and smoke, fire, and thunder on the mountain.

We could make a long, interesting list of all the ways God reveals Himself in the book Exodus. He seems to be everywhere and into everything in very tangible, real ways. Exodus is the book of a very hands-on God.

I struggle constantly with this issue. Was this true in Exodus just because this was a special time in divine history? Is God portrayed this way because Israel's culture believed very much that He operated in this manner, so Moses simply painted the picture this way? Why do so few people seem to experience Him this way today?

I'm not sure of all the answers, but more and more I'm beginning to believe that a big part of the problem is *us* and *our culture*. I believe God wants to be nearer and more active in our midst, but we have become so accustomed to His absence that we don't know how to seek, experience, or expect His nearness and action. We would do well to ask ourselves how much we believe in, expect, or desire the presence of God.

10. *Exodus has created in me a renewed belief in the power and importance of prayer.* My favorite passage in the book is 33:12-23. Here Moses in dialogue with God (prayer) asks to know God and to have God present with him and his people Israel. In response to Moses' plea, God graciously says, "Yes, I'll go with them." Moses then asks to see God's glory. God answers again and says He will cause *all* of His goodness to pass before him. A powerful display follows.

This, of course, is not the only place such a thing happens. From the initial experience at the burning bush in Exodus to the story of Moses' radiant face at the end of Exodus 34, the book is filled with stories of Moses in dialogue with the divine. Shouldn't these stories teach us something?

Too often, I've sold prayer short and assumed there was no chance of a response. I plan to return often and look at Moses' dialogues with God. They breathe a spirit of real interchange with God that changes lives and situations in powerful ways. I want to learn firsthand that (or is it "if"?) God still operates this way. In short, I'd like to learn to pray and dialogue with God like Moses, or at least see if it can still happen!

Conclusion

I'm sure, as you have made your way through Exodus, that you have seen many things I have *not* seen. One of the greatest joys that can come from Bible study is the discovery of new things the Lord's Spirit has revealed to you. Cherish those things and ponder them often. Share what you have learned with others. The lessons will become even more clear to you.

Above all, don't stop studying and reading Exodus. Now that you understand the book better, *you will get even more* out of it if you return time after time to review and reflect on it.

My prayer for you is that this journey into God's Word has so captured your heart that you will have a constant thirst to hear more and more of what He says. That thirst will lead you to drink more and more of the water of life, and you and your world will change.